ATTRACTING Wildlife TO YOUR Backyard

ATTRACTING
Wildlife
TO YOUR
Backyard

101 Ways to Make Your Property Home
for Creatures Great and Small

JOSH VANBRAKLE

Skyhorse Publishing

Skyhorse Publishing books may be purchased in bulk at special discounts for sales promotion, corporate gifts, fund-raising, or educational purposes. Special editions can also be created to specifications. For details, contact the Special Sales Department, Skyhorse Publishing, 307 West 36th Street, 11th Floor, New York, NY 10018 or info@skyhorsepublishing.com.

Skyhorse® and Skyhorse Publishing® are registered trademarks of Skyhorse Publishing, Inc.®, a Delaware corporation.

Visit our website at www.skyhorsepublishing.com.

10 9 8 7 6 5 4 3 2 1

Library of Congress Cataloging-in-Publication Data is available on file.

Cover design by Tom Lau
Cover Photographs: top, l. to r.: Eileen Hornbaker USFWS; Pixabay; National Park Service

bottom, l. to r.: George Gcentry, USFWS; Steve Maslawski, USFWS; National Audobon Society

Print ISBN: 978-1-5107-2848-6
Ebook ISBN: 978-1-5107-2849-3

Printed in China

CONTENTS

PART THREE: CHALLENGES TO WILDLIFE 157

DISCLAIMER

Always maintain a healthy respect for wild animals. Wildlife can be dangerous if provoked. Do not attempt to approach, touch, or hand-feed any wild animal.

There is inherent risk in any outdoor activity. Be sure you have the necessary skills and safety equipment before engaging in any potentially hazardous outdoor activity. Consult your doctor before engaging in any outdoor exercise.

If you have young children, exercise extreme caution with outdoor water features like streams and ponds. Young children should never be left unsupervised near water of any depth. If children are able to access the water area, fence or gate it off.

All uncredited photos were taken by the author.

Throughout this book, company and product names are included with project ideas. These are for example only and do not imply endorsement from either the author or the publisher.

This book contains links to websites that provide additional resources. Although these links were live at the time of writing, websites change often, and you may encounter dead links.

ACKNOWLEDGMENTS

Writing a book is an enormous undertaking. It involves years of research, drafting, and editing. There are many points along the way where I thought about giving up, wondering if the hard work was really worth it. Fortunately, I have a lot of great people around me who saw the value in me and in this book. Thanks to their dedicated efforts, I'm happy to bring this book to you.

First, I want to thank my coworkers at the Watershed Agricultural Council's Forestry Program. When other people told me this book was impossible, you encouraged me to keep going. Your ideas, feedback, and enthusiasm got me through this project.

I also want to thank Shannon Delany, author of the *13 to Life* series and the *Weather Witch* series. Shannon was the person who first introduced me to writing professionally through an excellent series of workshops in 2011. If I hadn't stumbled upon her classes, this book would never exist. Shannon, thank you for your ongoing advice and friendship.

Other authors have also mentored me along the way: Ginger Strand, John Elder, and Rowan Jacobsen. Thank you all for your advice on improving my craft. I strive everyday to write a little better so that someday I might write as well as you all do.

Many thanks go to my agent, Jennifer Unter, who fought tirelessly on behalf of this book. Jennifer, thank you for your guidance in navigating the world of publishing.

Thanks also go out to the team at Skyhorse Publishing, including my editors Jay Cassell and Ronnie Alvarado. Your feedback improved this book a lot. Thank you both for believing in this book and helping property owners everywhere aid wildlife on their land.

Finally, I want to thank my father, who inspired my love of nature and wildlife through countless childhood camping trips. Dad, I dedicate this book to you. I love you and miss you more every day.

PART ONE

BEFORE YOU BEGIN

1

PRIVATE LANDOWNERS AND WILDLIFE: A VITAL CONNECTION

"I am only one, but I am one. I cannot do everything, but I can do something. And because I cannot do everything, I will not refuse to do the something that I can do."
—Edward Everett Hale

As a forester, you know you're in for an adventure when the first thing a landowner says to you is, "So have you heard about my psychotic deer behavior?"

That was Dan's question to me on the cold March morning I drove to his family's land in the Catskill Mountains of upstate New York. I had gone there to write an article about wildlife food plots, a subject the retired New Jersey police officer is a master of. Dan has them scattered all around his property, especially in former hayfields. In total he has thirty-six acres of them, all planted with nutritious deer foods like clover, turnips, and brassica. He adds a new food plot almost every year, usually about an acre in size.

Dan's latest project is located on a ridgetop that lost its trees to a forest tent caterpillar outbreak. On the day of my visit, Dan was removing the dead trees. Over the next few months he would disk the soil, mix in several tons of lime and hundreds of pounds of fertilizer, and plant a mix of clover and brassica.

Landowners like you can make a difference for wildlife because together you own most of the places where wildlife make their homes. This father and son duo are helping wildlife by planting California coffeeberry, a native shrub in the US Southwest. Its fruit and leaves provide food for mule deer, black bears, and many species of birds. Photo credit: National Park Service

On two visits later that year, I saw the results of that work. A new crop of wildlife food had turned this once-barren hilltop a vibrant green.

Dan's justifiably proud of his work—and protective of it. He asked me not to identify where his property is, and to use only his first name. He doesn't want poachers to find out about his land.

I understand his concern. On my two-hour March tour alone we saw a dozen deer, more than I'd seen the whole previous winter. They weren't scrawny, either. They were the largest, healthiest whitetails I've seen in the Catskills, and my visit occurred during a month when most deer are thin and hungry after scraping through the winter.

Even with all those deer, Dan's woods are in better shape than many I've visited. It's easy for deer to eat themselves out of house and home, damaging native plants and harming other wildlife in the process. On Dan's property, though, tree seedlings and waist-high blackberry bushes are abundant.

As Dan showed me his property, I realized his self-described psychotic behavior isn't just about deer. At one point we drove past an area of dense spruce trees. Dan planted them twenty-five years ago, intending to sell them as Christmas trees. But he abandoned that plan when he realized the trees could shelter snowshoe hare.

Other projects abound. Dan's property has few oaks, but on those

Dan's latest food plot. On my first visit in March (top), he was cutting down the dead ridgetop trees to open up space on the ground. By early June he had cleared, fertilized, and planted the site (middle). By October he had a healthy crop of delicious plants for wildlife (bottom).

he does have, he's removed the trees right around them to give them more space to grow. That added room will let the oaks develop bigger canopies and make more acorns.

Giving an oak tree more room to grow by cutting down smaller trees next to it will let it develop a bigger canopy. That bigger canopy will gather more sunlight and give the oak more energy to make acorns.

A few of the wild apple trees on Dan's property. Keeping them pruned helps them grow more apples, an important fall food for deer and bears.

Then there are the wild apple trees. Dan's pruned more than three hundred of them on his land. Pruning apple trees helps them develop more fruit, which feeds deer, bears, and turkeys. Dan always prunes in the winter, because then deer can eat the buds on the removed limbs.

And what does Dan do with the downed wood created from all that pruning, oak tree releasing, and food plot constructing? "I used to burn it," Dan admitted, but then he discovered that grouse, fishers, and rabbits loved the interlocking brush. Now he builds up the brush in piles to help out these critters. He calls the result "rabbitat."

Back at Dan's house, I saw still more evidence of his wildlife work. Just as he's psychotic about deer, he also admits to being "psychotic about bluebirds." He has thirty bluebird boxes scattered around his property. He also has two hummingbird feeders, and he energetically recounted the day he saw a pair of male hummingbirds fight over them, even though there was room for both.

Why does Dan do all this work? Not for the hunting. He does hunt deer and turkey, but many of the other species like rabbits he lets go. Even when he's hunting, it's more about the joy of being in nature than shooting an animal. "Ninety-five percent of the time I'm hunting, I'm observing," he told me. "Just watching or taking pictures."

If his goal isn't trophy bucks, what is it? Dan sums it up in a single sentence: "I want to maximize the health of my land."

The Role of Private Landowners

Dan's efforts to support wildlife are inspiring, and they illustrate the value private lands and landowners have to US wildlife. You see, the US isn't like most other countries with large amounts of open space. Most other countries have their open lands—especially their wooded lands—in government ownership. But here in the US, about two-thirds of our land is owned by private citizens—folks like you, me, and Dan. That includes 56 percent of US forests. We're the only country with large wooded acreages to have most of our woods in private ownership.[1]

It's on this private land that many wildlife make their homes. One estimate from Colorado State University biologists says private land provides 85 percent

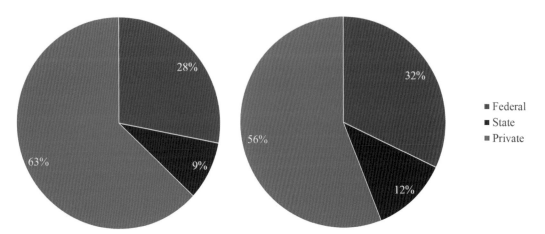

Private landowners control 1.5 billion acres of US land, about two-thirds of the total.[2] They also own the majority of US forests—more than four hundred million acres.[3]

of US wildlife habitat.[4] Private lands tend to be wetter, flatter, and more fertile than public lands, all traits that favor a greater variety of wildlife.[5]

To see the importance of private lands firsthand, visit the Prairie Pothole Region in the northern Plains States. This region of innumerable lakes, marshes, and native grasslands is our nation's most productive waterfowl breeding ground. The nesting of mallards, pintails, shovelers, and other birds is so prolific that the Prairie Pothole Region has earned the nickname "the Duck Factory." Ninety percent of the US part of this waterfowl heaven is privately owned.[6]

The Prairie Pothole Region is just one example of the value private lands bring to wildlife. Nationwide, more than 90 percent of the distributions of brown thrashers, indigo buntings, brown-headed nuthatches, yellow-billed cuckoos, and eastern bluebirds are on private lands.[7] According to the Fish and Wildlife Service, half of all US threatened and endangered species rely on private lands for 80 percent or more of their habitat.[8] And according to the US Forest Service, privately owned woodlands alone support 60 percent of the lower forty-eight states' at-risk species. That's more than 1,900 kinds of animals.[9]

Even in the public-land-dominated West, certain land types and their wildlife still rely on private property. While private woods only make up about 30

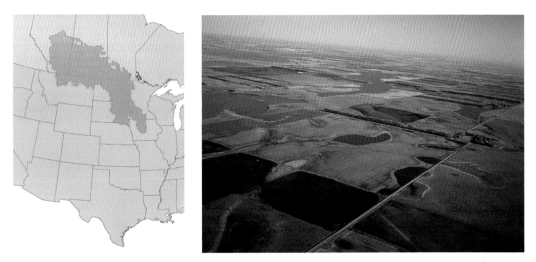

The Prairie Pothole Region (as designated in the orange part of the map) is known as "the Duck Factory" for its many lakes, ponds, and marshes. Ninety percent of its US range is privately owned. Map credit: USFWS; photo credit: Don Poggensee, USDA NRCS

The state amphibian of Alabama, the threatened Red Hills salamander, lives only in that state. It has just sixty thousand acres of suitable habitat remaining, and 98 percent of those acres are on private land.[10] Photo credit: Emmett Blankenship, USFWS

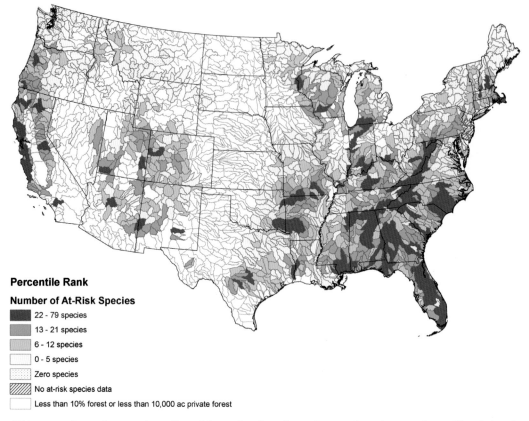

Percentile Rank

Number of At-Risk Species

- 22 - 79 species
- 13 - 21 species
- 6 - 12 species
- 0 - 5 species
- Zero species
- No at-risk species data
- Less than 10% forest or less than 10,000 ac private forest

This map shows the number of at-risk species that depend on privately owned woodlands in the continental US. Private woodlands in the Southeast and Southwest, and on the Pacific Coast in particular provide homes for large numbers of rare, threatened, and endangered species. Map credit: Susan Stein and others, US Forest Service[11]

percent of western forests, for instance, they make up a majority of California and Oregon's oak woodlands. The endangered golden-cheeked warbler, which depends on oak woodlands, in turn is found almost exclusively on private land. 91 percent of its distribution is in private ownership.[12]

From coast to coast, from Appalachian hardwoods to western junipers, private lands provide homes for countless wildlife. Wherever you own land in this great country, there are creatures counting on you and your property for survival.

Even though most western forests are publicly owned, certain land types remain primarily in private ownership. Ninety-one percent of endangered golden-cheeked warbler distribution is on private lands, which have more oak woodland than public lands in the West. Photo credit: Steve Maslowski, USFWS

What Are You Going to Do About It?

But so what? Aside from feeling confident that our yards, fields, and woods help wildlife, why does it matter where animals live? Nature is what it is, right?

Not necessarily. That's why I began this book by talking about Dan. His property didn't start out as a wildlife nirvana. It's, at its core, hardscrabble, thin-soiled land high in the mountains and needed decades of work by Dan's family to get it to where it is today. Dan's father added the property's first pond in 1962. Dan himself has been making food plots for thirty years. Even though Dan lives in New Jersey and can only visit his land occasionally, over the years he's achieved amazing results. And not just for deer, but also for turkeys, rabbits, fishers, bluebirds, hummingbirds, fish, amphibians, reptiles, and the innumerable other wildlife who call his property home.

Dan is quick to point out that you don't need a huge property to benefit wildlife. This area below his house is only a few acres, yet it sports two built ponds that support fish, reptiles, amphibians, and ducks. If you look closely, you might also spy a bluebird box on the tree on the far left. And at the same time that it's providing all this wildlife value, the area also supplies an amazing view of the valley below.

In my day job as a forester, I help landowners care for their woods in ways that protect land, water, and wildlife. Too often in that work, I hear a sense of hopelessness about the planet. There seems to be this view out there that all humans can do to nature is destroy it, and thus the best course of action is to stand out of nature's way and let whatever happens happen.

I reject this pessimistic idea. What Dan's land makes clear is that with knowledge, caring, and deliberate action, we can improve the lives of the creatures we share this world with.

You don't need a ton of land to make a difference either. "Even something the size of this kitchen can be useful," Dan told me during a lunch of venison chili, naturally (for reference, Dan's kitchen was about 100 square feet). Whether you have a suburban backyard, a big rural property, or anything in between, there are projects you can do to make your land better for wildlife. It's not about having endless acreage. It's about making the most of the land you have.

That's what this book is about. Over the next thirteen chapters, I'll lay out 101 projects you can do to make your property more valuable to wildlife. Most of these projects are DIY, though a few call for professional help. Some require more land than others, but many are achievable even if you only own a backyard. It's my hope that these projects will inspire you on your journey to benefit wildlife.

To take you further on that journey, I've included two lists in the back of this book: Beyond the Book and State Resources. Beyond the Book features websites to supplement certain projects, including how-to videos, stores to purchase materials, and professional contact lists. In State Resources, I've linked to local organizations that can help you like landowner groups and wildlife agencies.

The task of protecting North America's wildlife can seem overwhelming. It's easy to tune out and pretend wild animals are all far away in some park or national forest. But if you're a landowner—no matter how small the acreage— you're part of the exciting mystery that is the natural world. Don't run from it. Embrace it.

2

What Do Wildlife Need, Anyway?

"Game cannot live in quarters provided only with beds, or only with dining rooms, or with neither. All animals, including ourselves, need both."

—Aldo Leopold

It's great to say we want to help wildlife, but what does that really mean? What makes a property better or worse for animals?

To answer these questions, let's use an analogy. Suppose you wanted to throw a party. What would you need to provide so people showed up and had a good time?

If it's a party like any where I'm from, the first item on your shopping list would be snacks. You'd likely have some foods that just about anyone would eat, but for the more adventurous, you might make a few specialty dishes. Not everyone would eat them, but those who did would love them. You'd also need plenty of drinks. All that

Wildlife like this American goldfinch need food, water, cover, and nesting spots. The space where an animal gets all these life needs is called its habitat.

conversation dries out my throat, so at parties you'll often spot me with a cup or bottle in my hand.

Also on your list would be a large enough venue to hold your party. It's hard for guests to mingle if the venue is so packed they can't move. If you're just inviting a few friends, your home would probably be big enough. But if you wanted fifty people to come, you might need to book somewhere with more room. And for the introverts in your circle, it would be helpful to have a quiet place they could go to escape the noise and recharge.

If you have kids, you know there'd need to be a place where they could go off on their own and play. Growing up, my family always had a kiddie table at holiday meals. That way the kids weren't bored, and the adults could talk about adult stuff.

There are some extras you could throw in—music and games come to mind—but that covers the basics. To summarize, you'd need stuff to eat and drink, space to talk or escape the crowd, and a place for the kids. Get all that together, and your friends will be tripping over themselves to come over.

The same is true for wildlife. To attract wildlife to your property, the list of things you'll need is pretty much the same as what you'd need for a party. I'm not sure what that says about us humans, but it makes sense—we are animals after all.

So if you want to host a wildlife party, what should be on your shopping list? We'll review the basics in this chapter, and then the rest of this book will focus on specific projects that will help you meet these needs.

Food

Nobody comes to a party that doesn't have food, at least nobody I know. To bring in wildlife, there are few more reliable ways than food. Food works because, for many animals, it's the top worry in their lives. Often their other life needs are met without much concern, but they have a hard time finding enough of the right kinds of food.

That said, understand that feeding wildlife isn't as simple as putting out a birdfeeder or a bucket of corn. In fact, putting out the wrong kind of food—or sometimes any food at all—can be downright harmful to wildlife.

In the coming chapters we'll talk a little about artificial feeding, but in general, when I refer to feeding wildlife, I mean growing the native plants animals would eat if humans weren't around. That's harder than just putting out corn, but as we'll discover, it's healthier for both animals and your property.

The two biggest tricks to providing wildlife food are 1) ensuring all the necessary foods are available for the most diverse group of animals possible; and 2) making sure that variety is available all year long. Just like at your human party, different animals eat different things. Some critters will devour anything you put out, but most are picky. They may only eat a few species of plants or other animals. Some are so picky they will only eat one thing. If you don't provide that food, that animal won't be on your land, period.

Plant-eaters in particular tend to be fussy, and for good reason. Plants don't want to be eaten any more than you or I do, but unlike us, plants can't run away from predators. Their solution is to develop their own chemical mixes that are poisonous to whatever gnaws on them.

To counter those defenses, plant-eaters have developed ways to break down the plants' poisons—often in the form of chemicals or friendly bacteria in their guts. The catch is that only certain chemicals will block certain poisons, and every plant's mix is different. If you're an animal whose species has spent the long millennia developing resistance to one plant's poison, eating anything else will kill you.

This specialization is especially common in insect plant-eaters like caterpillars. Insect researcher Douglas Tallamy writes in his book *Bringing Nature Home* that as many as 90 percent of plant-eating insects are specialists.[1] They can only eat one or at most a few types of plant. If your property doesn't provide the specific plants these insects need, you'll be denying your land 90 percent of the wildlife it could potentially have.

But who cares about a bunch of creepy-crawlies, right? Well, birds care. Nearly all land birds—96 percent of them—raise their young on insects and other invertebrates.[2] It doesn't matter if you're setting out shovelfuls of birdseed. The adults might like it, but they can't feed it to their kids. If you aren't providing the food they need—insects—then you aren't helping them as well as you could be.

Insects and other invertebrates might seem like critters you wouldn't want to encourage on your property, but their high protein content makes them an important food source for many animals, including this common yellowthroat.

Water

It's said a person can go several weeks without eating but only a few days without water. I have no desire to test those limits, but what's clear is that water is essential to human life.

The same is true of wildlife. Without water, animals won't last long. You can put out all the food you want, but if local critters don't have a clean, reliable water source, your effort will be wasted.

Fortunately, as important as water is, its access is rarely an issue for wildlife. In eastern states rain and snowfall are plentiful, and there are lots of streams, ponds, and lakes with year-round water. In the arid West, wildlife concentrate around water, and many species have adapted to use less water. Some get almost all the water they need from the food they eat, so they rarely need to drink water directly.

When it comes to water on your property, the issue isn't usually one of quantity, but quality. Sure, wildlife may have access to a nearby pond or stream,

Adequate water is rarely an issue for wildlife, but access to clean water can be.

but is that water clean enough for them to use? Even though the federal Clean Water Act was passed more than forty years ago, many US waterways are still polluted. Out of more than one million miles of streams and rivers surveyed by the US Environmental Protection Agency, more than half are considered "impaired."[3] That means they're too polluted for their intended uses like fishing, swimming, and drinking.

Most of this pollution comes not from single, massive factories, but instead from spread-out sources like farm and yard runoff. Each of these spread-out sources contributes small amounts of water pollution that together add up to big impacts. Because this pollution happens over a large area, it's tough to reduce through traditional regulation. Instead, it's up to each of us to care for our properties in ways that keep the water clean. Taking simple actions like reducing your use of lawn fertilizers and pesticides can add up to big benefits for the quality of your local rivers and streams.

Cover

Animals big and small need places to hide. They need places to escape the weather, be they desert squirrels burrowing to avoid the noon sun or bears denning up to survive winter's chill. Others need places to escape predators; for example many songbirds love hawthorn because its two-inch thorns deter hawks.

The long, sharp spines of hawthorn shrubs protect smaller animals like this house wren from predators.

Even predators need cover if they want to sneak up on prey. There are few wildcat images more recognizable than the cat's face emerging from tall grass as it creeps toward its unsuspecting victim.

The image of a cat emerging from leaves or brush is iconic for a reason. Wildcats like this bobcat rely on stealth and ambush to catch fast-moving prey. Photo credit: Steve Hillebrand, USFWS

Often you can meet animals' needs for cover if you meet their needs for food. Since wildlife and native plants have lived together a long time, wildlife have adjusted their seasonal activities around what the plants are doing. This is great news because it means that if you focus on providing a variety of native plants for wildlife to eat, you'll also provide them with places to escape predators or hide from prey.

A Place to Raise Young

Cover provides temporary refuge while animals forage. As they eat, it gives them somewhere to hide if a threat appears. But animals also need places they can stay for longer periods, places they feel safe enough to raise the next generation.

Many of the same conditions that make good cover also make good nesting areas. These need to be places with protection from the weather and predators, and they need to be close enough to food so both young and adults can eat.

Meeting wildlife's need for nesting places calls for variety in your landscaping. Each animal has its own preferred place to raise a

Look out below! I almost stepped on this bird's nest several years ago while hiking. The dense ground plants growing around it hid it from predators and people alike.

family. To help as many critters as possible, you'll need potential nesting spots at multiple heights from below the ground to the tops of trees.

Space and Habitat

Food to eat. Water to drink. Havens to escape predators and raise children. Wildlife need a lot to survive, so it should come as no surprise that another wildlife need is enough space to find all of the other life needs.

The space that an animal operates in is called its "habitat." You'll hear me use that word a lot in this book, so it's important to remember. A habitat is an area that provides an animal with all the food, water, cover, and nesting spots it needs to survive. When we talk about improving conditions for wildlife, we're talking about increasing the amount or quality of their various habitats.

The space animals need for their habitats varies a lot by species. In general, the larger the animal, the more space it needs. Many caterpillars spend their

Large wildlife like these moose often range over huge areas to meet their needs. That's why it's important not only to help wildlife on your own property, but also to support the protection of remaining large blocks of open space. Photo credit: Ryan Hagerty, USFWS

entire pre-butterfly lives on a single branch of a single tree. Chestnut-sided warblers need a couple acres. Barred owls hunt over several hundred.[4]

Then there are the big mammals, creatures like elk, moose, and bear. These animals wander over thousands of acres in search of food, cover, and mates.

It's important to realize the ranges wild animals, particularly large mammals, need to survive. You can do a lot to meet the needs of birds and butterflies, but even if you provide useful food and homes for larger creatures, those animals will never be permanent residents of your property. That's okay though. As you provide more, and as your neighbors provide more, you can benefit these bigger wildlife along with the smaller critters.

Doesn't Nature Provide This Stuff?

Before we leave this chapter and get into projects to help wildlife, it's worth pausing a moment for an ethics question: should we bother? By making changes to our properties, especially our woods, aren't we just playing God? After all, wildlife got by without our help for a long time.

Who are we to improve on nature?

Unfortunately, wildlife today face threats their ancestors never had to deal with, and most of them are our fault. Homes, roads, and lawns break up their habitats. Outdoor cats decimate their numbers. Inedible invasive plants replace the species they depend on for food.

Wildlife aren't prepared for these challenges. That's why wildlife nonprofits like the World Wide Fund for Nature and the National Wildlife Federation agree that habitat loss is the greatest threat wildlife face.[5]

Even in a place that seems wild, habitat loss can be a problem. Many of our forests today started out as farmland abandoned at some point in the twentieth century. The trees that have grown up are all about the same age and height, with little food or cover near the ground. These woods are a far cry from the diverse, old-growth forests wildlife used to live in. So while your woodland might feel like wildlife heaven, there's still a lot of room for improvement to bring it back to what nature used to provide.

Improving wildlife habitat on your land isn't about "one-upping" nature. It's about working alongside nature to counteract the negative pressures humans have put on animals. That's a job we can all get excited about, so let's get to work.

Even places that feel wild can be terrible for wildlife. This woodland seems like a great spot, but it provides little for animals. The dominant tree is Norway spruce, a widely planted European tree that few North American animals can eat. The ground cover is sparse and dominated by hay-scented fern. While native to North America, this fern also has low wildlife food value. More problematic, the dense shade from the spruce and ferns prevent other, more wildlife-friendly native plants from growing.

3

GETTING STARTED

*"The vast possibilities of our great future will become realities only
if we make ourselves, in a sense, responsible for that future."*
—Gifford Pinchot

The US has thousands of wildlife species, each with its own requirements for food, water, cover, nesting spots, and space. Even with an
unlimited budget and boundless enthusiasm, it would be impossible
for you to provide all things for
all wildlife on your property. You
would run out of room.

Don't worry; you can still
benefit wildlife. To do that, you
should plan your projects by
choosing ones that will fit your
available time, money, energy, and
land while benefiting the greatest
diversity of animals.

How do you know which
projects those are? In this chapter,
we'll discuss seven activities that
will help you figure out what you
have and then use that information to narrow down the limitless
possibilities.

*Nature is a complicated place. How do you decide
which wildlife projects to pursue on your property?
Getting a better understanding of what you have is
a good place to start.*

Project 1. Make a Property Map

Everything on your land has a place, and every project you do will too. Creating your own property map will help you think about your property as a whole and figure out where you want to focus your efforts. More important, it's crucial to know what you have before you jump into projects to build upon it.

To make a property map, first get an aerial photo. These are easy to view and print for free thanks to Google Earth. You download the free software (I've included a URL in "Beyond the Book"), then zoom in to your property. From there you can print the map on whatever size paper you have. I recommend using the largest size you can so you have the most room to work with.

Once you've printed your aerial photo, grab some thin, brightly-colored markers and a white pencil to mark it up. A good place to start is to draw

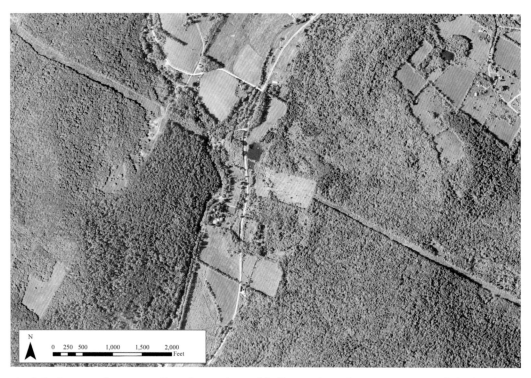

Aerial photographs are excellent for getting a bird's-eye view of your property and the landscape around it. They're also easy to access through free online software like Google Earth. Photo credit: National Agriculture Imagery Program, USDA

in your property lines as best you can. This will give you an idea of how much space you have to work with, as well as reveal a bird's-eye view of what you own.

With your boundary lines marked, next draw lines where your property changes plant types. For instance, separate areas of lawn from those with woods. Be as specific as you can. If you can designate between lawn and unmowed field, go for it. The same is true for separating conifer-dominated woods from those with a lot of broad-leafed trees. Different wildlife use these places in different ways. Being specific will help you know which projects make the most sense for your unique land arrangement.

If writing on your aerial photo is too hard to see, an alternative is to draw the map yourself on a blank piece of paper. This isn't as hard as it sounds, especially if you keep the original, clean aerial photo next to you while you do

it. Start by drawing your property's border so it fills the page. Then sketch out the same divisions you would have marked on the aerial photo on your map. Don't worry if it looks like something a first-grader hung on the fridge. You aren't making an atlas. This map is just for you.

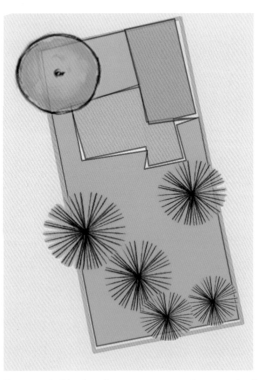

Another way to develop your property map is to use YardMap, a free website from the Nature Conservancy and the Cornell Lab of Ornithology. On YardMap, you set your property boundaries and mark spots on your land over an aerial photo just like you would on a paper map. The advantage to YardMap is that you can easily add, delete, and change parts of your map as you make changes to your land. You can save your map to a free profile, so it's easy to return to it

I created this simple property map for a typical suburban lot in less than ten minutes on YardMap. The free website is a great way both to plan out projects and keep track of your efforts.

later. The site even has recommended projects to support particular wildlife groups like birds, pollinators, and dragonflies. I've included a link to YardMap in "Beyond the Book."

Your property map is never done. It can and should be a living document that is constantly updated as you and your land change. Found a new wetland? Mark it on your map. Installed a bluebird box? Show its location. Keeping your map updated will help you see the effects of your work.

Project 2. Complete the Property Checklist

Once you have your property map, the next step in planning is to gain a better sense of your land's traits. Start by writing answers to these questions about your land:

- What's the climate like where you are? Are the summers hot or cool? Wet or dry? Do you reliably get snow in the winter?
- What's the lay of your land like? Is it flat? Steep? If you own a larger property, you may have a mix of both. Pairing a topographic map, which shows elevation, with your property map will help you answer these questions. I've included a link in Beyond the Book that explains how to add topographic maps to Google Earth.
- What's growing on your land? What kinds of plants do you have? Is there plant growth at many heights, or only one? Are the plants on your land native, or do you have problems with invasive species?

There are scientific methods to answer these questions precisely, but you don't need to be that detailed. At this point you're just taking stock of what you have. It's important not to let yourself get overwhelmed before you ever pick up a shovel or put a plant in the ground.

To help you take these questions further, I've included a "Property Check-list" appendix in the back of this book. It doesn't require firm measurements, just that aerial photo of your property and an observant walk through your land. By filling out the Property Checklist and then comparing it with the paired "Recommended Percentages" guide, you'll get a better sense of what your property has and, more important, what it's missing.

Project 3. Figure Out What's Missing

A core concept in wildlife biology is the "limiting factor." The idea is that the life need in shortest supply sets the limit on the number of animals that can live somewhere. As an example, an animal can have all the food it wants, but if it has no place safe enough from predators to eat that food, it won't stay in the area.

If you can figure out which life need is hardest to find on your property, you'll shorten the number of potential projects you should start with. If your land has few nesting sites, for instance, putting out a birdfeeder won't do much good because you aren't addressing your land's limiting factor.

Figuring out your property's limiting factor can be tough. Just looking at your land, it may be hard to tell what's missing. Moreover, "what's missing" is relative. Again, different species have different needs. What's in short supply for amphibians could be plentiful for birds.

Even within animal groups, limiting factors can differ. Consider two apparently similar songbirds: the golden-winged warbler and the black-throated green warbler. Both spend summers in the northeastern US before migrating to Central and South America for the winter. They have similar sizes (four to five inches long), weights (0.3 ounces), and diets (insects). Yet they're rarely

Even similar-seeming animals can have different needs. Golden-winged warblers (left) prefer short shrubs, while black-throated green warblers (right) need deep, older woods. Providing a diversity of plant types and structures can help you attract more wildlife to your land. Photo credits: (left) Alan Schmierer, USFWS; (right) Steve Maslowski, USFWS

seen together. Their limiting factor is cover. Golden-winged warblers prefer short, dense shrubs in young woodlands. Black-throated greens want older, interior forests of spruce and pine.

How do you deal with all this complexity? The Property Checklist and Recommended Percentages guides from the last project can help. If you find in filling them out that your property is below the recommended amount of young woods, that's a signal that you should focus your efforts there. Similarly, if there are specific habitat elements missing from your property like den trees, creating some makes sense.

These guides aren't perfect. First, they don't take into account your desires for your own property. A pond often isn't the best project to bring in more wildlife, since water is rarely a limiting factor. Yet many people really want a pond. That's fine. It may not have the same wildlife impact as addressing the limiting factor, but it will still do something. Remember, your property belongs to you. It's all right to focus on projects that make you happy, not just those that science says you should do first.

The other reason not to get too obsessed with the recommended percentages is that they're meant to apply at the landscape level. If you own a small property with only a backyard to work with, it may not be possible for you to have everything wildlife biologists recommend. Again, that's all right. It's better to focus on enhancing what you have rather than making wholesale changes to force your land into a strict percentage.

Project 4. Look Beyond Your Borders

Animals don't respect property lines. They couldn't care less whether they're on your land or the Johnson's next door. For all but the largest properties, your land will usually just be one small part of an animal's life. Even for the chestnut-sided warbler, which only needs an acre or two, your property is a temporary stop. It will still migrate south for the winter.

Animals' need for space is both a blessing and a curse. It's a curse because often attracting wildlife to your property depends on your neighbors' actions. If their land isn't providing what animals need, then all your efforts may amount to creating an island that critters can't reach. But a need for space is also a blessing, because it means you don't have to provide all things for all creatures. It's okay if you don't have a stream. Odds are there's one close by.

When planning projects, consider not only your property but also your neighbors' properties and their neighbors' properties. A good place to start is to repeat Projects 2 and 3, this time looking at the area around your land. Use a wider aerial photograph and complete the Property Checklist for an area of about 2,500 acres with your property at

The chestnut-sided warbler only needs an acre or two of habitat during the summer breeding season. But even if your property offers that much space, this warbler still needs room in the Caribbean and South America when it travels there for the winter.

the center. What's missing from this landscape? The answer to that question can become the cornerstone for your wildlife projects.

To see how that can work, let's use an example. Suppose you look at the landscape around your property and discover it's all broad-leafed trees, which lose their leaves in the winter. Planting some conifers, most of which keep their needles all year long, will be a boon to local wildlife. Conifers provide superb winter cover, and certain birds like crossbills depend on conifer seeds almost exclusively for food. In addition, there are more than three hundred species of moths and butterflies in eastern woodlands alone that will eat pine and spruce needles.[1] Many of these plant-eaters can survive on nothing else.

If you can figure out which life need is in shortest supply in the landscape around your land, finding a way to meet that need is perhaps your best chance of attracting more wildlife. Even if they aren't around now, animals have a remarkable ability to seek out favorable conditions. Give them what they need, and they'll walk, fly, slither, and swim their way to your land.

Crossbills spend most of the year in Canadian and Rocky Mountain conifer forests, but they winter throughout the US. Their bizarre overlapping beaks are ideal for breaking into conifer cones so the birds can get the seeds they depend on to survive. Photo credit: Dave Menke, USFWS

Project 5. Find Out If Rare Animals or Plants Use Your Land

In 2015, the northern long-eared bat was listed as "threatened" under the Endangered Species Act (for reasons we'll talk about in the next chapter). We have several caves in upstate New York where I work, so the region is a bat hotspot. Almost immediately after the bat's listing, I started getting questions from landowners asking how it affected them. What were their responsibilities? Did the listing mean their lands would be locked up? The answer to that one is no, by the way.

Rare, threatened, and endangered species are both exciting and challenging for landowners. They're exciting because they're unusual. They're challenging because they may add regulations or permits to certain land uses like farming and timber harvesting.

Northern long-eared bats used to be common, but their numbers have plummeted in recent years. They're now protected under the Endangered Species Act. As a landowner, it's important to know what, if any, protected species use your land so you can stay on the right side of the law. Photo credit: Keith Shannon, USFWS

It's important in your planning process to figure out if you have any protected plants or animals on your land. The easiest way to do that is to get in touch with your state's Natural Heritage Program. I've included links to each state's program in the State Resources Appendix.

Natural Heritage Programs are usually run by a state agency or university. Their job is simple. They monitor the locations of state or federally protected species and provide that information to people who need it, like landowners. They also help with permits or advice related to protected plants and animals.

The quality of these programs varies. If you're lucky, more and more states are putting rare species information online. You may be able to go to your program's website and find your property on a map. If you see a rare species indicated, you'll know to get in touch with the program for more information.

Natural Heritage Programs won't tell just anyone what's living in an area. If everyone knew where some rare orchid grew, then collectors would wander out and pick it. Even on the online maps, there are usually just bubbles that show a rare species is in the area, but there's no information on what it is.

Fortunately, as a landowner, you can request species-specific information about your property. I recommend you make that request, because each protected species has its own requirements. With northern long-eared bat, for instance, the regulations focus on protecting the caves where it hibernates and the trees where it raises its young in the summer. You need a permit from the US Fish and Wildlife Service before cutting trees within certain distances of these locations. Depending on your state, you may also need a permit from your state's Department of Natural Resources or similar agency.

I realize protected species can raise concerns for landowners. There's always the fear that the presence of some rare bug or bird will cause you to lose control of your land. Fortunately, that's almost never the case. When it comes to rare species and private landowners, often you simply need a permit and professional help before doing certain activities, especially commercial practices like farming, logging, and mining.

Regulations aside, there may be voluntary actions you can take that can improve conditions for rare critters on your land. Your Natural Heritage Program may be able to help you identify what those are. These practices can often make good starting projects to help wildlife on your land.

Even though protected species can be a pain from a legal perspective, I encourage you to see their presence as a blessing. Yes, they may mean some extra work, but they also mean your land is something special. It's providing a home for a plant or animal that might not otherwise be around in the future. Part of your role as a steward of the land is doing your part to ensure these amazing creatures are still here for your kids, grandkids, and the generations after them.

Project 6. Focus on Your Favorite Animals

Up to this point, the projects in this chapter have focused on figuring out which projects will get you the most wildlife bang for your buck. But there's another consideration when planning wildlife projects: what you want.

When deciding which project to tackle first, consider choosing one that benefits a favorite creature. It will give you that extra motivation to get the work done. If you like chickadees, hang a suet feeder (Project 16). If you'd prefer to see more and larger deer, build a food plot (Project 24). If fish are more exciting to you, check out Chapter 7, which is all about streams.

Now to be clear, I don't encourage you to pick all your projects this way. Because wildlife meet their needs in different ways, if you focus your entire property on helping one species, you'll exclude many other animals that could potentially use your land. It's better to aim for a diverse property that can provide for a variety of critters.

I once worked with a landowner whose favorite animal was the American woodcock (also called timberdoodle). She was new to making changes to improve her land, so we talked about projects that could create the young woods habitat woodcock need. The project she went with was creating some brushy areas with crabapple and hawthorn thickets. Photo credit: National Park Service

That said, there's nothing wrong with starting out with a project that favors an animal you love. Once you've finished that project, you'll have more experience to tackle other activities, including those that benefit species you're less fond of.

Project 7. Think Small

A lot of people get so excited at the idea that they can make their properties better for animals that they jump into a huge project like restoring a stream. I admire their enthusiasm, but they're almost certainly setting themselves up for disappointment. Odds are their enormous project will fail. Even if it succeeds, the work and frustration will devour their enthusiasm and discourage future effort.

A better approach in the beginning is to gain experience and satisfaction with projects that are fast, cheap, and easy. The projects in the next chapter on backyards are a good place for novices to start. The first time you see a bat flit out of your bat box or a hummingbird stop by your trumpet vine trellis, you'll get that instant joy of knowing your efforts made a difference. That feeling will help inspire you to take on the next project, perhaps one slightly larger. Over time you'll build up the knowledge and confidence to tackle the larger projects that would otherwise have defeated you. But you won't get there unless you practice on some smaller activities first.

If you're just starting out doing wildlife projects, try something small first. Planting a native tree like this white oak is a good first project that even kids can help with. Photo credit: National Park Service

Project 8. Make a Future Property Map

Having just advised you to think small, for the last project in this chapter I want you to dream big. Pull out that property map you drew earlier. That's how your land looks today. Now take out a second piece of paper and draw your property boundaries on it. Think about how you want your property to look in the future, say ten years from now. What kinds of plants will be growing? What projects will you have in place? Sketch your answers on this second map. It will become your dream for the future of your land.

It's all right if you can't draw this map now. In fact, I wouldn't expect you to. For the moment, just hang on to that blank paper with your property lines on it. As you read this book, feel free to return to your future map whenever an idea strikes you. By the time you turn the final page in this book, it's my hope that you'll have filled that blank sheet with all your wild, crazy, wonderful plans.

PART TWO

FOCUS ON HABITAT

4

BACKYARDS

"I don't like formal gardens. I like wild nature.
It's just the wilderness instinct in me, I guess."
—Walt Disney

Now that you know what you have on your land, we can start getting our hands dirty. We'll begin with backyards for two reasons. First, because we'll be dealing with a smaller space, the projects in this chapter are easier and cheaper than those in later chapters. If you're looking for "start small" options, your backyard is a great place to begin. And because the change is near your house, you'll get the added benefit of seeing more of the wildlife you've created homes for.

The second reason for starting with backyards is that not all of us own a lot of land. If you own a small plot in the suburbs, many of the larger-scale projects in later chapters won't work for you.

You don't need a lot of land to benefit wildlife. The owners of this Wisconsin nature center converted their lawn into a small prairie restoration. Their yard is now a stopping location for migrating birds.

Even so, there are smaller changes you can make that, especially if multiple neighbors get together with you, can add up to big wildlife benefits.

Project 9. Replace Non-Native Ornamentals with Native Plants

If you want to attract more wildlife to your backyard, one of your primary tasks should be to replace the non-native plants growing there with native varieties. Why? It all comes down to the first wildlife need: food.

In the modern backyard, food is the life need that's usually in shortest supply. Most animals, particularly insects, can't eat the non-native ornamental plants many of us grow. Recall from Chapter 2 that each type of plant has developed its own chemical mix to discourage plant-eaters from chewing on it. Native plant-eaters have adapted to certain chemicals from certain plants, and as a result they can only eat those plants. Put something that originated in Europe or Asia in front of them, and they can't eat it, even if they're starving. In turn, the animals that eat those plant-eaters, like songbirds, won't stick around your property.

Native plants also matter for another crucial and disappearing wildlife category: pollinators. These are creatures like butterflies, bees, and humming-birds that eat nectar from flowers. When they feed on nectar, pollinators transfer pollen from flower to flower, allowing plants to reproduce.

We depend on pollinators for more than the mere enjoyment of seeing wildlife. An astonishing 87 percent of flowering plant species rely on polli-nators to help them reproduce.[1] Lose the pollinators, and you lose those plants.

And pollinators are in trouble. There's a real danger that in the not too distant future, we could lose many of these amazing creatures. The popula-tion of our most important pollinators, bees, have declined sharply in recent decades. They've been the victims of habitat loss, overuse of pesticides, and Colony Collapse Disorder, a still poorly understood situation in which entire colonies of bees die.

Bees aren't the only pollinators at risk. Butterfly numbers have also dropped. The monarch butterfly, for instance, has lost 90 percent of its population in just the last twenty years.[2]

Monarch butterfly (top left) numbers have dropped 90 percent in recent decades. The monarch caterpillars (left bottom) can only eat milkweed plants, many of which have been killed by pesticide spraying and development. You can help monarchs by planting milkweed (right) in your yard. There's a native variety of it available almost everywhere in the continental US. Photo credits: Eileen Hornbaker, USFWS (butterfly); USFWS (caterpillar); author photo (milkweed)

But even though planting native plants can help pollinators, getting started can be intimidating. The US has thousands of native plant species, and many more non-native ornamentals on top of that. It can be hard to know what's native, and sometimes even experts disagree.

The most common question folks ask when starting out with native plants is, "What should I plant?" Unfortunately, I can't give you a specific answer in a general book like this one. The native plants that are right for you will vary based on where you live, the kinds of soils you have, and how much light your yard gets.

What I can give you, though, are some resources to get you started. In Beyond the Book, I've included a link to a searchable native plant database from the Audubon Society. Enter your zip code, and it recommends native plants. You can narrow your selection by the kind of plant you want (like a tree, shrub, or annual) and even by the types of wildlife you hope to attract.

Once you know your planting options, your next step is to visit a local native plant nursery to narrow your choices further and eventually purchase the plants you want. Beyond the Book has a national database of these nurseries courtesy of the Lady Bird Johnson Wildflower Center.

All that said, my experience has been that what matters more than the species you choose is how you structure them. Don't panic too much over whether to plant native A or native B. Yes, different animals will use different natives, but by using a native, you'll ensure that some wildlife will make use of whatever you plant.

We'll talk more about structuring your native plants later in this chapter, so I won't dive into that here. One tip I do have for you now, though, is that whatever you plant, plant it in clumps rather than in single plants. Larger clumps will be more likely to attract the wildlife that depend on that plant. Even if it means having fewer kinds of plants in your garden, go ahead and group your plantings.

Of course, there's more to backyard gardening than what's good for wildlife. This is your yard after all, so it's okay to think about aesthetics. One reason some gardeners don't use native plants is the belief that natives aren't as showy as non-native ornamentals.

Some homeowners don't want to switch to native plants because they think those plants will be boring compared with non-native ornamentals. But as this native planting in San Francisco shows, native plants can hold their own with a variety of shapes, sizes, and colors. Photo credit: National Park Service

Fortunately, that belief isn't true. Native plants can be just as beautiful as introduced ones, and more and more nurseries are developing showier native cultivars.

You also don't have to rip up and replace all your ornamentals at once to benefit wildlife. One strategy for transitioning your garden to natives is to wait until a non-native plant dies and then plant a native one in its spot. That way you're only changing one or a few plants at a time, so your garden appearance remains close to what it was before.

You can go further with this strategy by seeking out native plants that have similar flower colors and growth forms to the non-native ornamentals you're replacing. For pretty much any non-native in your garden, there's a native option that will come close to matching its appearance.

Finding native plants has also become a lot easier in recent years. As the popularity of native gardening has risen, so too have the number of native plant nurseries. Wherever you live, odds are there's a native plant nursery near you that can help you find the right plants for your yard.

One note of caution on native plant nurseries. When buying plants from any nursery, confirm that the plants are in fact native species and that they were cultivated at the nursery, not collected from the wild. There have been instances of nurseries harvesting wild plants and raising them for sale. These plants are often marketed as "nursery grown," which is technically true, but can harm natural areas, as we'll talk about in the next project.

Project 10. Rescue Native Plants from Construction Sites

One day I was talking with a friend in his garden. He told me about his mother, a woman who loved plants. Several of the bushes in this man's yard were cuttings from his mom's garden. It was a passing down of plants.

The story about this gardening guru that interested me most was how she would go hiking in parks and look for plants she thought were interesting. If she found one, she would dig it up, bring it home, and plant it in her garden.

It's hard to tell anyone, especially a friend, anything negative about their mom. But in this case, I had to. Transplanting wild growing plants is something you shouldn't do. It may seem harmless, especially if there are a bunch of plants and you're only taking one. The problem lies in that you aren't the only person visiting that park. It's easy for too many plants to be removed, and for the park and its wildlife to suffer as a result.

The transplanting process itself is also rough on wild-grown plants, and the survival rate of moved plants is poor. It takes a lot of gardening know-how to move a wild-grown plant. Even then, there's a good chance the plant won't make it. In that case, not only have you harmed the park's plant and animal life, but you haven't improved your yard either.

Fortunately my friend took this information in stride. He'd actually come to the same conclusions about his mom's behavior, though he had no plans to try and change her. It cheered him, then, when I told him about an alternate way his mom could enhance her garden without damaging local parks. She could go on a plant rescue mission, and you can too.

Here's how it works. Sometimes when a new home or business goes in, the construction will bulldoze and destroy native plants. In these cases, with permission from the landowner, you may be able to go in and recover those plants that would have been killed anyway. Even if only a few of them survive, that's still a win over the complete destruction that would have happened.

You can do these rescues on your own, but I recommend connecting with a local garden or native plant club. These groups often do construction transplants as volunteer events, and their credibility may make it easier for them to get landowner permission. These outings are also opportunities for you to meet fellow homeowners who are excited about native plants. Finally, the members of the gardening club may be able to help you with the transplanting process to give your rescued plants the best chance of surviving.

Before we leave this project, let me stress again: a construction site is the only place you should attempt native plant transplants. Never remove native, wild-growing plants from a natural area and attempt to bring them to your property.

If you see a wild-growing plant you like and there isn't a handy construction project going on, there is a workaround. First, take some pictures of the plant. Then show those photos to local native plant nurseries to see if they stock it. A nursery-cultivated plant will have a better chance of surviving in your yard, and you'll leave your local parks and preserves intact for both people and wildlife to enjoy.

You shouldn't transplant native plants from the wild, but if those plants are going to be destroyed by development anyway, then transplanting can be acceptable. Make sure you get landowner permission before transplanting from a construction site. Photo credit: Pixabay

Project 11. Decrease Your Lawn with Lawn Feathering

I mentioned earlier in the chapter that the structure of your yard's plants matters more than the particular species you choose (as long as you're planting natives). Perhaps the most glaring structural issue yards have when it comes to wildlife is an overabundance of lawn.

The US has more than twenty-four million acres of lawn, and all that neat, trim grass is largely useless for wildlife.[3] The thick turf most of us have is made up of non-native grasses that animals can't eat. In addition, its short length provides no cover for animals or places to raise their young.

Expansive lawns like this one are wastes of space for wildlife. Ask yourself: Where is there wildlife food in this picture? How about cover or a place to raise young? Spread across the millions of developed acres in this country, lawns have denied many wildlife what they need to live. While it's fine to keep some lawn near your house, save yourself the effort of mowing and let other areas grow up into meadows, shrublands, or woodlots. Photo credit: Pixabay

Along with replacing non-native ornamentals with native plants, another way to attract more wildlife to your yard is to decrease the amount of lawn you maintain. One method to do that is called "lawn feathering." In lawn feathering, you divide your property into five zones that radiate out from your home:

- Zone 1: Lawn—This is the zone closest to your home. Mow these areas as you normally would.
- Zone 2: Meadow—This zone will have taller grasses and wildflowers that benefit pollinators and ground-nesting birds. If you want to help monarchs, this is a good zone to include some milkweed. You can still mow in this area, but do it less, perhaps once a year. Wait until after August 1st to avoid disturbing bird nests.

- Zone 3: Shrubs—This zone will have short, dense, woody plants. High-bush blueberry and native roses are two options here. These shrubs offer ideal cover for many birds like the indigo bunting as they forage for insects and seeds. You won't mow in this zone, but every three to five years you should brush hog it to keep it from growing up into taller trees. Again, save your brush hogging until after August 1.
- Zone 4: Small Trees—As the name suggests, this zone will have woody plants that are taller than shrubs but not as massive as typical woodland trees. Dogwood, apple, and hawthorn are good choices here.
- Zone 5: Tall Trees—This will be the zone farthest from your home. Full-sized trees like cherry, oak, and pine will grow here.

An example of lawn feathering on a larger property of about 10 acres. Note the gradual transition from mowed lawn in the foreground to taller shrubs and trees in the background. This transition is more like the natural change between forests and meadows than the hard breaks that typically result from lawns. As a result, a feathered lawn will support a richer assortment of wildlife than one that's left neat and closely cropped.

The wider each of the three transition zones (2, 3, and 4) can be, the better. Aim for at least thirty feet for each of these zones if possible. Even better, give them undulating edges rather than hard breaks.

On smaller lots, you won't have ninety feet of transition to work with. Just use the space you have. The point is to have plants at every height from close-cropped lawn to tall trees.

If you already have trees on the edges of your land, lawn feathering is a project you can achieve in a couple growing seasons. Simply not mowing for a year or two in the areas you want to feather will do the trick. If your property is all lawn now, feathering will likely involve tree planting and many years or even decades to develop the tiered structure.

Indigo buntings benefit from lawn feathering because they depend on transition areas between grassy meadows and woodlands. They feed on insects and seeds in meadow and shrub areas, then climb to higher tree perches to sing. Photo credit: Steve Maslowski, USFWS

Despite that time commitment, don't dismiss lawn feathering. Ditching lawn where you can is one of the most powerful ways to bring wildlife, especially birds, onto your property.

Critical to lawn feathering, particularly in suburban areas, is that you don't need to get rid of all your lawn. There are advantages to keeping certain areas of your property well-trimmed, especially walking paths and around your home. We'll talk more about the value of these maintained lawn spaces next.

Project 12. Account for Lawn-Mowing Regulations

Wildlife may love meadows and woody shrubs, but people are another matter. Viewed as ugly and unkempt, these habitats are often forbidden in many towns. Lawn ordinances may require that grass be shorter than a certain height, and violating property owners can face fines and charges of being a public nuisance.

Lawn-mowing regulations are well-intentioned. Their purpose is usually to discourage property neglect. How do we balance meeting these laws with providing meadows and shrubs for wildlife?

The two methods that seem to work best are deliberate action and education. First, show that what you're doing isn't negligence, but part of an active project. This is why keeping some mowed lawn is valuable, as it can help make your case to concerned neighbors. By mowing the area right around your house, you show that you are in fact maintaining your property. You can also mow paths through your meadows and shrubs. Keeping these areas clean and well-edged may go far in convincing neighbors and town officials that your design is a deliberate garden choice and not the result of neglect.

Even taking these deliberate steps, you probably will at some point have to explain what you're doing to someone. Lawn ordinances aside, a neighbor is sure to ask why you're letting the grass get so high. Rather than get upset, use the opportunity to talk about your love for wildlife and how you're helping to provide homes for native animals. Talk about the importance of private lands for protecting wildlife; some of the figures from Chapter 1 might be good talking points. Check out the next chapter on young woodlands for more ideas to share with them.

One way to show that your backyard meadow is done on purpose for wildlife is to leave mowed paths through it, as was done here. An added benefit is the ability to walk through your created meadow and see the wildlife you're attracting.

Ideally, your neighbor will be so excited by what you've shared that she'll go out and start improving her yard for wildlife too. In the long run, it's that neighbor-to-neighbor communication that will make the difference in protecting wildlife, not what I or anyone else says in some book.

Of course, even if you do everything possible to explain what you're doing, not everyone will approve. In stricter towns and counties, you may have to forgo lawn feathering and meadows. In others, you may be able to provide limited meadow or shrub areas, but only in areas obscured from public view like a backyard sheltered with edge plantings.

If lawn feathering won't work for you because of regulation, there are other ways to benefit wildlife in your backyard. Focus your efforts on what you can do, like replacing non-native ornamentals with native plants.

Project 13. Go Vertical with Layered Plants

The biggest limitation for improving wildlife conditions in your backyard is space. If you live in the suburbs, you may not have enough room for lawn feathering. A single large, open-grown tree might take up your whole backyard.

To make the most of limited space, go vertical by adding plants that can stack on one another. Instead of lawn feathering, now you'll have all the layers on top of each other.

To create this layered look, start with an existing single large native tree, or plant a larger sapling if you don't have one. The species choice matters little as long as it's native, but local varieties of oak, cherry, birch, maple, and hickory are all great picks. Beneath those trees can go a few shorter trees or shrubs like hawthorn, winterberry, or dogwood. Beneath those can go taller wildflowers like milkweed and Joe-Pye weed, and still under those can go a native ground cover like mayapple.

Going vertical with your plantings will let you attract more native wildlife species to the same patch of ground. You'll bring not only the animals that enjoy black cherries, but also those that like to hide in the hawthorn, eat the late-fall fruits of the dogwood, and draw nectar from the wildflowers. In one tight area, you'll have provided everything wildlife need to get food and protection for both themselves and their babies.

Another way to go vertical is to use a trellis. These structures are ideal for the smallest yards where even a single tree is out of the question, though they work equally well in larger yards. Trellises can be either standalone structures or frames that lean up against the house.

Trumpet vines are an excellent way to attract humming-birds. By training the plants to grow on a trellis, you can have them even on the smallest lots. For best results, choose a trumpet vine with red flowers. Hummingbirds are drawn to the color red. Photo credit: National Park Service

You can use trellises to grow native climbing vines like trumpet vines, which will attract hummingbirds. These vines are also good alternatives to English ivy, which is invasive.

Project 14. Install a Bat Box

Planting native plants in various arrangements like feathered lawns and vertical stacks can provide wildlife with food and cover. But while native plants are the most natural way to draw wildlife to your yard, there are many backyard wildlife projects that don't require a green thumb. For the rest of this chapter, we'll pivot away from plants and discuss other ways to make your yard more wildlife-friendly. First up is a way to help a kind of creature we haven't talked about yet: bats.

A lot of people are spooked by bats, but I love them. They're simply fascinating creatures. Apart from being the world's only flying mammal, bats play an enormous role in controlling insects like mosquitoes. A single little brown bat will eat half its body weight in insects every night, and it can live for thirty years.[4] So while it might sound crazy to want bats in your backyard, if you don't like mosquito bites, having bats around is handy.

Another common misconception about bats is that they roost in caves. Yes, some bats do that, but others seek shelter in tree cavities or under loose bark. Even those that do use caves rely on them mostly to hibernate during winter. In the summer they seek out warm, sunny spots in trees to raise their babies.

Bats are in trouble these days because of a non-native fungus called White-Nose Syndrome. Like Colony Collapse Disorder in bees, we still don't understand

You might think bats are creepy, but they're superb insect catchers. Unfortunately, many bats, including the little brown bat pictured here, are now infected with the fatal disease White Nose Syndrome. You can help bats in your yard by setting up a bat box. Photo credit: Marvin Moriarty, USFWS

much about this disease. What is known, though, is that it has caused the deaths of millions of bats, up to 99 percent of them in New York, New Brunswick, and many other US states and Canadian provinces.[5] The fungus is the reason the northern long-eared bat I talked about in the last chapter is now on the Endangered Species List.

You can help local bats by setting up a bat box for them to roost and raise their babies in. You can purchase bat boxes online through major retailers, or you can build your own. In Beyond the Book, I've included a link to a free guide that has bat box plans. There's also a link where you can buy pre-made boxes if you'd rather do that.

The key to a good bat box is what lies inside. A good bat box has several layers of vertical slices of wood separated by empty space. The bottom of the box is left open, and bats enter and leave through the bottom, not the front like on a birdhouse. The back piece of the bat box hangs down lower than the other sections to provide a landing area for incoming bats.

A view up into a bat box from the bottom. Bat boxes contain layers of wood that the bats cling to. Photo credit: National Park Service

Take care when buying bat boxes online to ensure they have this multi-layered design. Bigger boxes with tighter spaces between the interior slats are most desirable. Small boxes with larger spaces may go unused.

Temperature also matters with bat boxes. Contrary to the cooler temperatures of caves, many bats prefer warmer temperatures, up to 100 degrees Fahrenheit, so install your bat box in a sunny area.

You should stain the outside of the box to help it warm up. Staining the box will also repel moisture and keep the box in good shape for longer use. When staining a bat box, choose an exterior-quality, water-based stain or a flat, water-based paint. Coat only the outside. Painting or staining the inside can release fumes that can harm the bats.

The color stain or paint to use depends on your location. In general, the farther north you are, the darker stain you should use. In most of the

Bat boxes can be mounted on the side of a building or on a pole like the one pictured here. A dark stain or paint will help keep the box warm and more suitable for bats.

continental US, a dark brown stain or paint is ideal. In the desert Southwest, go with white paint or a light stain to keep the box a little cooler.

If you can, mount your bat box where it won't get rained on, but don't jeopardize sunlight exposure in the process. Hang the box at least fifteen feet off the ground. You need that height because bats don't "take off" the way birds do. Rather, they drop and then spread their wings. If they don't have enough drop distance, they won't be able to fly out of the box.

Project 15. Build a Bee Nesting House

Next on the list of "why would I want that in my yard?" are bees. I already mentioned how bees are our most important pollinators, and that they're taking a huge hit from Colony Collapse Disorder. Still, I can understand if the idea of creating a home for them makes you nervous. What you should know, though, is that North America alone has more than four thousand bee species, and most of them rarely, if ever, sting.[6]

You also don't have to worry about a bee nesting house turning into a gargantuan hive. Most native bees don't form hives at all. Instead, they're solitary. The females lay eggs in tunnels in sand or rotting wood. A bee nesting house simulates those natural nesting conditions.

Like a lot of wildlife options for your yard, you can now buy bee houses online. Constructing your own bee house is so cheap and simple, though, that there's no reason to waste your money on the purchased options.

All you need to build a bee house is a little bamboo, some rope, and a small section of chicken wire. To start, cut a bamboo stalk into eight five-inch pieces. Tie the bamboo in a bundle with the rope so all the ends point in the same direction. Use a cordless drill to remove the central walls of the bamboo on one end, enough to hollow out about three inches.

With your bamboo bundled, hang it in a spot that catches the morning sun. If you have some chicken wire, wrap it around the bee house to deter woodpeckers from attacking and eating the bees.

Replace your bee house every two years. If you leave it up longer than that, fungi can invade and kill the bees.

This bee nesting house is more complex than the basic one I've described, but it gives you an idea of what these structures look like when finished. The hollowed-out bamboo tubes protect native bees, many of which do not form hives and rarely sting. Photo credits: Pixabay

Project 16. Set Up Birdfeeders

Birdfeeders are a curious topic among ornithologists (people who study birds). Some birds, like the popular northern cardinal, have expanded their ranges thanks to feeding by humans. Cardinals can live farther north and endure harsher winters because they can count on feeders.[7]

Based on that example, some ornithologists contend that feeders are now an essential part of many avian diets, and that maintaining bird numbers warrants continued feeding. But Dr. Stephen Kress has a different perspective. The ornithologist and author of *The Audubon Society Guide to Attracting Birds* points out that birds are highly skilled at finding food within their environments. Only rarely do feeders provide the bulk of nutrition in a bird's diet. Kress contends in his book that if all artificial birdfeeders disappeared today, there would be no extinctions or even major declines in any US bird species because of it.[8]

Northern cardinals have expanded their range north in part due to birdfeeders that make food more available in the winter. Photo credit: Pixabay

Whatever the biological necessity of birdfeeders, overall they seem to be beneficial. While some studies have linked birdfeeders to increased rates of disease, that risk was more than offset by the extra nutrition the feeder provided.[9] Fed birds are healthier, have better winter survival, and are more likely to successfully raise young.[10] And because birds base their migration largely on day length, putting out a feeder won't prevent or delay birds from migrating.[11] If you want to put out a birdfeeder, do it and don't feel guilty about it.

In fact, I encourage you to do it. Why? Two reasons, and neither has anything to do with the birds themselves. First, without feeders, it's hard to catch a glimpse of most wild birds. Sure you'll see a robin strut in your yard or hear a blue jay cackle in the distance, but many other songbirds keep a low profile. Without a feeder, you'll have few opportunities to see the remarkable diversity of bird life North America offers.

Second, feeders are a great way to connect nature and kids. Because feeders let you observe birds up close, they give you and your family a chance to build a love for birds that can translate into greater care for your land.

There are lots of feeders to choose from, with different designs and foods suited for different birds. To prevent overcrowding, limit yourself to one feeder for each type of food you plan to put out. That said, it's fine to put out multiple feeders as long as they have different foods. This diverse feeding method will also help you attract the greatest variety of birds.

We can divide feeders into rough categories based on food type. Seed feeders are the best known and most common types, but take care with commercial seed mixes, as not all seeds are equally liked by birds.

When it comes to seed, black oil sunflower seeds are in a class by themselves. If you only put out one kind of feeder, a seed feeder with just black oil sunflower seeds is a solid choice. Other good options include white proso millet, nyjer (also called thistle), and unsalted, in-the-shell peanuts.

Unfortunately, most commercial mixes don't focus on these desired seeds. Often they add cereal grains as filler, but birds don't like these seeds. Avoid seed mixes that contain buckwheat, oats, wheat, and especially milo, also called sorghum. Birds will usually toss these seeds on the ground rather than eat them.

Also, as weird as it sounds, avoid mixes with sunflower seeds. Birds enjoy sunflower seeds so much that they'll poke through the mix to get them, tossing

Black oil sunflower seeds attract many kinds of birds including these tufted titmice.

the other parts of the mix on the ground in the process. That leads not only to waste but also attracts squirrels and can cause mold. A better option is to have two feeders, one for sunflower seeds only and another for a non-sunflower mix.

Besides seed, there are a host of other foods you can put out that will attract different kinds of birds. One easy option is a suet feeder, which is a thin, square cage that you put a suet block in. Suet is rendered beef fat, and it's adored by insect-eating birds like woodpeckers, chickadees,

Suet feeders are one of the best ways to attract woodpeckers like this male downy woodpecker.

and wrens. The high-fat suet especially helps birds that don't migrate, as the fat provides extra calories to get through long, cold winter nights.

You can make your own suet, but this is one instance where I recommend going with the commercial option. Unlike suet you make yourself, many commercial suet cakes don't need refrigeration and produce a lot less mess (and smell).

When choosing a commercial cake, choose one without a lot of seeds. Otherwise, seed-eating birds will come to your suet feeder and toss aside the suet to get at the seeds. You should also avoid those that have corn, cornmeal, or peanuts, as these additions are largely filler and can be a breeding ground for harmful bacteria.

Both seed and suet feeders are most beneficial to birds from fall through early spring. In the fall they help migrating birds build up fat reserves before they head to the tropics. In the winter they help non-migratory birds when food is scarce. And in the spring they're a welcome sight to returning migrants looking to refuel after the journey north.

There's no need to leave feeders up year-round. Suet will turn rancid in the summer, so put away that feeder at least during warm months. As for seeds, during the summer most birds are looking for insects to feed their young, so seed feeders are of less importance. It's fine to bring these feeders inside for the summer. Birds will remember them in the fall.

In place of seed or suet, two summer feeding options are fruit and sugar water. Fruit stations are excellent for attracting migratory birds like scarlet and western tanagers that avoid traditional seed feeders.

Fruit feeders are easy to set up. Simply cut an orange or grapefruit in half, spear it on a stick, and let the birds have at it. Migratory birds can tell these fruits are similar to what they eat in the tropics, and they'll eagerly eat from them.

As for sugar-water stations, these are good for attracting hummingbirds and other nectar eaters like orioles. The two keys for sugar water stations are cleanliness and concentration. Boil your sugar-water solution briefly before adding it to the feeder. Boiling will kill bacteria as well as remove chlorine from the water. Even with boiling, replace the sugar-water and clean the feeder every three days to avoid mold that will harm the birds.

Fruit feeders can attract cedar waxwings, especially if you put out smaller fruits. You can also attract waxwings by planting shrubs that produce small fruits. Dogwood, serviceberry, winterberry, and cedar are good waxwing attractors. Photo credit: Pixabay

The sugar-water should also be an appropriate concentration. Use one part sugar to four parts water for hummingbirds, and one part sugar to six parts water for orioles. These concentrations provide birds with food without risking liver damage that can occur if they ingest too much sugar.

When preparing your sugar-water solution, use only white cane sugar. Never use honey, raw sugar, corn syrup, brown sugar, or artificial sweeteners. All these sugar alternatives can harm hummingbirds.

Cleanliness matters with all types of feeders, not just sugar-water stations. Clean seed feeders several times a year. Discard any old seed, then scrub the feeder with a 10 percent bleach-and-water solution. While feeding, sweep up fallen seeds twice a week to avoid mold, and use a feeder with a secure roof to keep rain and snow off seeds. Moisture on seeds leads to mold, and mold leads to sick and dead birds.

Finally, keep in mind that although birdfeeders provide fun experiences for birds and people alike, they aren't a substitute for the broader landscaping

Watch out! Some people add red food coloring to their sugar-water mixture, but it isn't necessary. The red color of the feeder itself is enough of an attractant. Food coloring can harm humming-birds. Your sugar-water solution should be just that: white-cane sugar and water, nothing else. Photo credit: Pixabay

changes discussed in this chapter and throughout the book. Even if you put out the best bird-attracting foods, you'll see fewer birds if your property is unsuited for them in other ways, particularly cover. Moreover, those birds that do visit won't stick around. They'll grab a quick snack and then be off to somewhere that better fits their needs. If you want more birds to use your property and not just fly in for the occasional sunflower seed, it's worth taking the extra effort to make your property more diverse.

Project 17. Recycle an Old Christmas Tree

When the holidays are over, don't just pitch that old Christmas tree. Use it to help backyard wildlife! There are a bunch of ways to do this. Perhaps the easiest is to prop it up near your birdfeeders. The tree will give birds waiting for your feeders a spot to rest, and it will give birds on the feeders cover to fly to if danger approaches. If you put the old Christmas tree upwind of the feeder, it can also provide feeding birds some shelter from cold winter winds.

Another option is to turn the tree itself into a birdfeeder. String popcorn, whole peanuts, and small fresh or dried berries and grapes together, then hang these edible ornaments from your tree. Squirrels and larger birds like blue jays will make heavy use of this food. You or your kids can even make ornaments out of pine cones by coating them in peanut butter and then rolling them in bird seed. When using popcorn, make sure it's the plain, unbuttered and unsalted kind. Peanuts should also be raw and unsalted.

When the tree starts to break down, its usefulness to wildlife can continue. Composting the tree can provide nutrients to help your native plant garden grow better. It can also

After the holidays, prop up your old Christmas tree by your birdfeeder to give birds a place to rest while waiting their turn. An easy way to keep it standing is simply to leave it in the same stand you used while the tree was in your house. Photo credit: Heather Hilson

form part of a brush pile (Project 37), providing small animals with a place to hide.

Finally, if you have a decently-sized pond, you can sink the tree in it. All those nooks and crannies that once held ornaments will now supply cover for fish instead.

Project 18. Add a Birdbath

Birds need water not only for drinking, but also for cleaning their feathers. If clean, reliable water sources are difficult to find in your area, adding a birdbath to your yard can be a simple yet effective way to help local wildlife.

When placed properly and maintained well, a birdbath can attract birds that rarely visit feeders.

A good birdbath has gentle slopes leading down from the edge of the bath. These slopes are important so birds can get in and out of the bath. Too-steep bath bottoms are a big reason many commercial birdbaths fail to attract birds.

Rather than spend a lot of money on a commercial birdbath, a cheap yet effective option is to make your own using an upturned metal garbage can lid. These lids tend to be flatter than most commercial baths, and they're a good, shallow depth for birds. Set the lid on the ground, preferably in a shaded, out-of-the-way spot. This is the ideal placement for a birdbath as long as outdoor cats aren't a problem. If your neighborhood has outdoor cats, then keep the bath away from shrubs and raise it at least three feet off the ground to offer birds some protection from ambushing felines.

When filling your birdbath, keep the water less than three inches deep. Replace that water every other day to discourage mosquitoes. Mosquitoes are more than annoying; they can carry diseases like West Nile Virus, which can kill birds as well as sicken humans.

Keeping your birdbath stocked with water is key if you want birds to use it. Birds want reliable water sources. If your birdbath is empty half the time, birds will skip it in favor of a bath someplace else.

Where outdoor cats aren't a problem, a birdbath on the ground will attract birds better than a pedestal version. The on-the-ground kind is more like a natural puddle birds would encounter. Photo credit: Pixabay

Moving water is also more attractive to birds than still water, so consider incorporating a small pump into your birdbath design. Commercial, solar-powered birdbath pumps exist and can provide a slow drip, a misting fountain or something in between.

Birdbaths don't have to go away when it gets cold. In the winter, you can maintain your birdbath with a birdbath heater, some of which are also solar-powered. These heaters keep the water above freezing so birds have a drinking and bathing source throughout the year.

Project 19. Protect Your Avian Visitors

The last several projects have all focused on bringing more songbirds to your yard. That's a noble goal, but take care that you aren't drawing birds to their doom.

A suburban yard is a dangerous place for birds. Many of their biggest threats are right there waiting for them.

One of those threats isn't even something that moves. Every year, window collisions kill as many as one billion (yep, with a "b") birds in the US alone.[12] Even if they're just stunned, birds that hit a window are more vulnerable to predators like outdoor cats.

If bird strikes on your windows are a problem, there are several methods for reducing them. First, reposition your feeder. Collision risk is highest when feeders are between three and thirty feet of a window. Closer than three feet, and birds can't work up the speed needed to hit the window and get hurt. Farther than thirty feet, and birds have plenty of space to maneuver around the window if they get startled.[13]

That's usually what happens in a feeder-to-window crash. Something scares the birds at the feeder, and they panic, diving for cover. Glass is invisible to them, so they smack right into it.

This reflex leads to the next two strategies for reducing bird strikes. First, hang objects on the outsides of your windows like stained glass, decals, and wind chimes. Bizarrely, these same objects on the insides of windows typically aren't as effective. Don't ask me why. Second, provide cover in the form of native shrubs near (but not up against) your feeder. A distance of fifteen to twenty feet is ideal to give birds a close enough spot to fly to without it being so close that predators could ambush the feeder.

Providing this cover will also reduce the instances of hawks claiming birds at your feeder. It's common for feeders to draw in hawks and owls looking for an easy meal. Birds at your feeder will be able to evade these raptors as long as they have a dense shrub nearby to escape to.

Finally, perhaps the simplest yet most important thing you can do to protect birds in your yard is to keep your cat indoors. In the suburban backyard, cats are the single greatest threat that birds face. A study in the journal *Nature Communications* estimated that outdoor cats kill between one and four billion birds every year in the lower forty-eight states alone.[14]

Outdoor cats devastate not only birds but many other kinds of wildlife as well. The same *Nature Communications* study estimated that US outdoor cats kill as many as 871 million reptiles, 320 million amphibians, and an astounding twenty-two billion mammals every year. If you want to protect wildlife in your yard, no step is more important than keeping Mr. Whiskers inside.

Bringing your cats indoors isn't just good for wildlife. It's good for the cats too. Outdoor cats face huge risks from diseases to parasites to car strikes. As a result, life spans for indoor cats are two to four times greater than those of outdoor cats. It's no wonder why both businesses like Petco and nonprofits like the SPCA and the Humane Society all encourage indoor-only cat ownership.[15]

Thank you for keeping me inside! I'm much happier in here, and the birds and other wildlife are a lot safer this way.

5

GRASSLANDS, SHRUBLANDS, AND YOUNG WOODS

"The bluebird carries the sky on his back."
—Henry David Thoreau

Even in a space as small as a back-yard, there's a lot you can do to make your property better for wildlife. If you own more acreage, though, your options open up to the spectacular. Now you can think beyond individual plants and consider whole habitats like fields, woods, and streams.

The first set of these habitats we'll tackle are collectively called "young woods." These areas include open, brushy places like old fields, shrublands, and woodlands dominated by seedling- or sapling-sized trees.

Whatever their form, young woods are defined by having few, if any, tall trees.

Meadows, shrublands, and seedling and sapling woods support many wildlife species, like this eastern bluebird, that are rarely found deeper in the forest. Photo credit: Michelle Smith, USFWS

Grass and shrublands (left) and young woodlands (right) aren't as breathtaking as old forests, but many plants and animals can only live in these areas. To attract the most species to your property, you need some of these younger, shorter habitats.

This structure means they're sunnier at ground level than the typical woods you might walk through on your property or in a local park.

But why would animals prefer short, scrubby woods over the grand and majestic old ones? Two reasons. First, food is abundant. All that sun near the ground makes young woods warmer and drier than older woods. Those conditions are perfect for invertebrates like insects that larger animals like to eat. A study in New Hampshire found young woods had 1.5 times the variety and three times the abundance of invertebrates as older forests.[1]

Second, young woods provide superb cover. You might struggle to pick your way through the brush, but then, so do predators. That's why many songbirds nest in young woods. A study by the New York Audubon Society found that young woods had both more and a greater variety of birds than older forests. The same study also found that birds that needed young forests were the species most in decline in the state.[2]

Indiana is in the same situation. That state has lost 65 percent of its shrubland birds and an astonishing 85 percent of its grassland ones.[3] The cause? Loss of young woods habitat.

It's not just New York and Indiana. Young forest birds are the most at risk across much of the US, according to the US Fish and Wildlife Service's Breeding Bird Survey. Performed annually since 1966, the survey has documented steady declines in fifteen of nineteen native grassland bird species. By contrast, only two of forty eastern forest birds have faced similar drops.[4]

Young woods support a lot of wildlife thanks in part to their dense cover. This mass of herbs, shrubs, and sapling trees growing in a six-year-old former clearcut is typical of young woods.

Young woods matter even to birds that prefer older woods for nesting. In a four-year study, wildlife biologist Scott Stoleson found that after nesting, many "old forest" birds seek out young woods for food. Without access to young woods, the birds were in poorer health when they began their southern migrations.[5]

It doesn't take a lot of young woodlands on the landscape to make a difference for wildlife. A typical healthy forest will have 5 to 15 percent of its area in young woods, according to wildlife biologists.[6] That amount provides space for

Found only in Florida, the threatened Florida scrub jay can only survive in short, dense vegetation that can shelter it from hawks. Scrub jay survival plummets when a tall tree is as close as eight hundred yards away. Photo credit: Robert Owens, USFWS

wildlife that need these younger conditions, and it helps ensure the forest has a future as older trees die.

As low as that number is, many properties fall short of that mark. Young woods face several challenges that make them just as at risk as the birds that rely on them. For example, young woods are easier to convert into farmland or housing sites than older woods because they lack large trees. And even if young woods don't get paved or plowed, they face another enemy: time. Young woods don't stay young. Absent human action to keep them young, they lose the traits that make them special places for wildlife within about twenty years. Because of our efforts to suppress wildfire—a historical way nature created young woods—not enough new young woods are being created naturally to replace the ones that are getting older. The net result over time has been the loss of these crucial wildlife habitats.

You can see this problematic trend in the forests near my property in the Catskill Mountains of upstate New York. New York City owns about 100,000

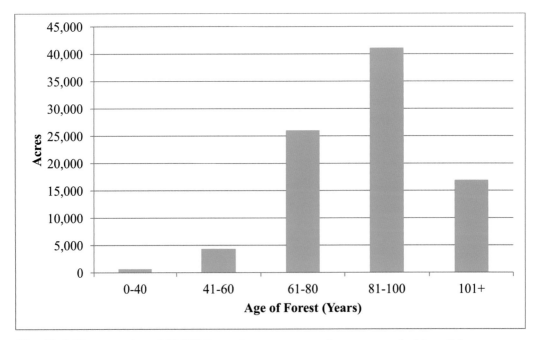

New York City owns about 100,000 forested acres to protect its water supply. Most of those acres are about the same age: sixty to one hundred years old. There's little old forest and even less young forest that would both provide more wildlife habitat.

forested acres in this region to protect its drinking water supply. Only 1 percent of those acres are in woods less than forty years old.[7]

Fortunately, it's relatively easy to create young woods on your property. While maintaining them is more difficult, there are techniques for doing that too. In this chapter, we'll discuss first how to establish new grasslands, shrublands, and young woods. We'll then transition to projects that can make these areas more attractive to the species that love them.

Project 20. Site Your Young Woods

Size matters with open habitats, particularly grasslands. A minimum size of twenty-five acres is preferred for grasslands, while shrublands and sapling woods can be as small as three acres.

The arrangement of young woods matters too. A key condition for these areas is the near or total absence of tall trees, so the best young woods have a

This prairie restoration in Wisconsin is set up in a square. You can see one of the corners on the right side of the photo. The shape maximizes interior space to allow more habitat for grassland birds.

lot of interior space away from edge trees. Most grassland birds, for instance, won't use grasslands less than six hundred feet wide. The closeness of taller trees makes them too vulnerable to predators.[8]

When creating young woods, then, aim for circular or square-shaped blocks rather than thin strips. These designs will maximize interior space and reduce edge, so you'll get more wildlife attraction for the same amount of open area.

If possible, it's better to site new grass, shrub, or sapling woods next to areas that are already in a similar state. If your land has an existing old field, consider expanding it rather than making several small open patches. Scattered patches won't serve grassland animals in particular, and they can break up valuable interior forest space, something we'll talk about in the next chapter.

Powerline corridors are an easy choice for siting young woods, because power companies don't want tall trees under their lines. While these corridors are too narrow to provide interior space for grassland birds, they can make excellent shrub habitat. Get permission from the utility that owns the lines before doing habitat work in a powerline corridor on your land.

Project 21. Combine Adjoining Meadows

Depending on your property's layout, your options for creating more young woods vary. Often creating more natural grass, shrub, and sapling habitat is as easy as not mowing a field or mowing it less often. This approach is similar to the lawn feathering I discussed in the last chapter, but on a larger scale.

Another easy option for creating young woods habitat is to combine two meadows by removing obstructions between them. Old fencerows of trees are common in many parts of the country. These straight lines historically marked a difference in property between neighboring farmers. As land changed hands over time, though, these lines now often pass through a single ownership.

Fencerows of trees turn one large field into two smaller ones that are less useful for grassland species. Removing these fencerows by cutting down the trees will benefit wildlife by creating more interior meadow.

Even though these barriers are narrow, they block grassland animal movement. Getting rid of them will create one large field with more interior space than two smaller fields. As a result, your meadows will attract more grassland species even though your total meadow acreage hasn't changed.

Project 22. Create Young Woods through Timber Harvesting

What if you don't have a fencerow to remove? Or what if you don't have a massive lawn that you could shrink? Many landowners' properties are almost all woods. To create young woods on these properties, you'll need more drastic measures. You'll need to cut trees.

This might sound like an extreme step, but in many places it's warranted and in keeping with a natural distribution of woodland ages. Remember New York City's woods? Only 1 percent of its woods are younger than forty years old, but they have a lot of woods in the sixty- to eighty-year range. The city could benefit wildlife by converting some of that sixty- to eighty-year-old forest to young woods using careful timber harvests.

You don't need to log your whole property to create young woods. Keep in mind that a healthy forest only needs 5 to 15 percent of its area in woods less than twenty years old to provide habitat for young woods wildlife. You don't have to sacrifice your property's scenic beauty or deep, old woods to provide what these animals need.

There are several timber harvesting methods that can create young woods. One, called a shelterwood, involves two cuts spaced about ten years apart. The first cut removes about half the trees, focusing on the smaller trees to give the bigger remaining ones space to grow and produce more seeds. This first cut also opens up light to the forest floor to help those seeds sprout and survive. Once that new generation of trees gets started, the large trees that weren't cut the first time are removed in a second harvest to create a young woods.

Timber harvesting is a big step for any landowner, and getting the result you want doesn't happen by accident. I don't have space in this book to go into the topic in detail, so if you're planning a harvest, I encourage you to check out my other book, *Backyard Woodland*. In it, I lay out a six-step process for harvesting to help you get the best job possible.

In a shelterwood harvest, loggers first remove most of the smaller trees, leaving the largest and healthiest trees to serve as a seed source (left). The extra sunlight on the ground encourages rapid growth of seedlings and shrubs. In the six-year-old shelterwood on the right, you can see the extensive regrowth of young birch, cherry, and maple trees along with wildlife-friendly undergrowth like blackberries.

Project 23. Do a Clearcut (*Gasp!*)

A shelterwood is a good way to get a seedling or sapling woods started, but if you're going for more grass or shrubland, a faster method is to clearcut next to existing old fields. The grasses and shrubs will expand into the clearcut area and create younger, open habitat for wildlife.

Now I can see a few raised eyebrows in the audience. A shelterwood is a drastic enough step, but clearcutting? Yet as bad a reputation as clearcutting has, it does have a place in improving wildlife habitat.

Clearcuts offer two advantages when it comes to creating young woods. First, because they remove all the taller trees, you get the genuine short, brushy condition many animals need. Leaving even a few scattered trees can lead to these animals avoiding the area, or at least decreasing their use of it.

Second, clearcuts for wildlife let you concentrate your impacts in the woods. By focusing your young woods efforts on a few small, intensely harvested areas, you can provide young woods while leaving more of your land as intact, older woods.

Now before we get carried away, let me clarify. I'm not talking about logging whole hillsides or wiping out trees on your property. The watchword here is "small." Patches as small as three acres work well for shrub and sapling habitat. Remember, you only need 5 to 15 percent of your woods in a young

Clearcuts, even small ones, can look like devastation incarnate right after they happen (left). But give them a few years to green up again with young shrubs and trees (right), and they become fantastic habitat.

condition at any given time to provide for young woods wildlife. That still leaves you with 85 to 95 percent of your woods in a traditional older state.

I can understand if you're skeptical, so let's look at two examples where limited clearcuts have been used to help wildlife. First up, the northern bobwhite quail has declined by 82 percent since 1966.[9] That's one of the biggest bird declines in the US. In New Jersey the bird has essentially gone extinct. Only a few quail are thought to exist in the southern part of the state.[10] Bobwhite quail need young, open lands to survive. The small, chicken-like bird with a sharply whistled call hides its nests in tall grass.

At one time New Jersey had a lot of this open land, but as the state developed and its woodlands aged, areas suitable for bobwhite quail disappeared. As went the open grasslands, so went the bobwhite.

Then the New Jersey Audubon Society got involved. They wanted to reintroduce bobwhite quail to New Jersey's Pinelands region, but they couldn't just toss in some birds and expect them to do well. Instead, they worked with a cranberry farmer who had a history of timber harvests on his property, including clearcuts. It was in those areas—places where full sun could reach the ground and grow the tall grasses the quail needs—that New Jersey Audubon reintroduced eighty quail trucked north from Georgia in 2015.[11]

The birds haven't been in their new home long, but they've done well so far. In late 2015, Audubon teams visiting the cranberry farm found the first New Jersey-born quail since the 1980s. As of 2016, all indications are

The northern bobwhite quail is a ground-nesting bird that depends on tall grass to hide its eggs and young from predators. It's best known for the emphatic way it whistles its name: "Bob-WHITE!" Photo credit: Steve Maslowski, USFWS

that this reintroduction could be the start of a comeback for bobwhite quail in the state.[12] That comeback would not have been possible without timber harvesting, clearcuts included.

Similar work is happening in Maine to help the threatened Canada lynx. These wild cats can weigh more than thirty pounds. Taking the cat stereotype of being fussy eaters to the extreme, lynx hunt only one species: the snowshoe hare. In Maine, those hares love dense groves of young spruce and fir trees.

As recently as the 1980s, Maine had plenty of these groves thanks to an outbreak of spruce budworm, an insect that feeds on spruce and fir. Concern about the budworm killing trees led many industrial forest owners to clearcut their lands to capture the lumber value. Young spruce and fir sprouted in the clearcuts, providing lots of habitat for snowshoe hare and by extension Canada lynx.

Since the 1980s, though, those young woods have grown up. They no longer provide the dense cover that snowshoe hare prefer. With clearcutting understandably more regulated now, new young woods aren't replacing the ones that get older. As a result, the state is predicted to lose up to 60 percent of its snowshoe hare habitat and 60 percent of its lynx within fourteen years. According to the state's lynx biologist, natural disturbances like wildfires won't create enough young woods to halt the loss.[13]

But Maine isn't taking that predicted loss as a given. The state is working with large landowners to develop plans that will help lynx and snowshoe hare— through clearcuts. The effort has contributed to more than 500,000 acres of woods getting forest management plans based around promoting lynx specifically and wildlife generally.[14]

To be sure, clearcutting can and has caused environmental harm. When practiced irresponsibly it leads to soil erosion, damage to streams, and reduced wildlife habitat. But when planned and executed well on a small scale with

Forest ecologists in Maine are using clearcuts to stimulate young spruce habitat. That habitat will support populations of snowshoe hare and its specialist predator, the Canada lynx. Photo credit: Erwin and Peggy Bauer, USFWS

professional guidance, it can benefit a host of rare and declining wildlife species. The key is to approach clearcutting with the knowledge that you're using it not as an end unto itself, but as a means to create wildlife food and cover by applying it in a specific way in a specific place.

Project 24. Make a Food Plot

Once you have some young, open habitats to work with, you can start on projects to make those lands better for wildlife. One way to do that is to create a food plot.

Food plots originated with hunters. Hunters would clear small areas of land—typically less than half an acre—and plant them with nutritious ground plants. The idea was that if they planted the right foods, they could grow bigger bucks with bigger antlers.

But food plots don't have to be just for hunters. They can be good all-around sources of wildlife food.

A food plot like this one consists of nutritious ground plants to draw in wildlife, especially deer.

Because food plots focus on ground plants, they need at least 50 percent sun. You could make a small clearcut like the one Dan used for his latest food plot back in Chapter 1, but that usually isn't necessary. Old farm fields, power-line corridors, and past insect infestation or ice storm sites are all good food plot sites that don't require logging.

Once you've chosen your food plot location, take some soil samples and have them tested by your local Soil and Water Conservation District. You are planting a crop, after all. You need to know whether your soil can grow that crop all on its own. Dan's thin, high-mountain soils demanded hundreds of pounds of fertilizer and lime to create food plots. Your property may not need that much, which is why a soil test is useful. It can help you identify what nutrients your soil has and what it needs so your food plot can succeed. Beyond the Book contains a link to a national map of conservation districts along with their contact information.

Clover is a good choice for food plots because, apart from its nutrition value, it can grow back year after year. Many other food plot plants need to be reseeded annually.

As far as what to plant, common choices among hunters are clover, rape, cereal rye, wheat, brassica, and turnips. You can check with a local cooperative extension office or hunting club for ideas specific to your area. I've included a link to a cooperative extension locator in the Beyond the Book section. Also visit local garden centers and nurseries. They often carry seed mixes designed for food plots.

Once you have your seeds, you'll need to till your food plot's soil. A rototiller or cultivator pulled behind a four-wheeler will make this job easier, so locate your food plot close to a trail to provide vehicle access. Use a hand-spreader to distribute the seeds. Make sure to follow the directions on the seed package for how much to plant. Planting too much can be as bad as not planting enough.

You don't need to do much to maintain a food plot. Occasional watering can help if it's been really dry, but even that is optional.

Project 25. Install a Bluebird Box

One grassland animal that took a heavy beating early in the twentieth century was the eastern bluebird. These charming songbirds faced stiff declines from the introduction of the invasive house sparrow and European starling, which competed with it for nest sites.

Beginning in the 1970s, though, bluebird numbers started to turn around. Why? It's thanks to people. People realized that with careful construction and placement, artificial nesting boxes could attract bluebirds while excluding sparrows and starlings. Thanks to these efforts, bluebird populations have increased through recent decades.[15]

One consequence of this change is that eastern bluebirds have become dependent on humans for nesting sites. More than half of all bluebirds now build their nests in

Eastern bluebirds depend on human-provided nesting boxes. Installing a bluebird box is an easy project to help protect this beautiful species.

human-made boxes.[16] With house sparrows and starlings here to stay, that situation isn't going to change.

If you want to attract bluebirds to your property, one of these boxes is the ideal way to do it. In Beyond the Book, I've included links to both a set of free plans and an online store where you can buy finished boxes. Of the many box designs available, I prefer the Peterson bluebird box design, which has a smaller floor and distinctive sloped front. The smaller floor means adults spend less time building a nest, and the sloped front swings open for easy cleaning.

Look for a box with a single front opening 1.5 inches in diameter. This size is large enough for bluebirds but will exclude invasive starlings that would otherwise take over the nest. Adding a predator guard (a second 1.5-inch block of wood on the front door) will help keep raccoons and cats from reaching in and grabbing eggs or nestlings.

Proper bluebird box placement is key to its success. Bluebirds like low, open countryside with a scattering of trees. Old fields, pastures, and even some lawns can all be good spots for them. To reduce nest takeovers by invasive house sparrows, locate boxes as far from buildings as possible.

Install your bluebird box three to six feet off the ground and within fifty feet of a tree. The tree gives a spot for baby birds to perch after they emerge from the nest.

If possible, mount the bluebird box on a pole or post rather than nailing it to a tree. Setting up the box this way allows you to attach a downward-facing metal cone that will further deter raccoons and cats.

Bluebirds are territorial. If you install more than one box, separate them by at least three hundred feet. The exception to this rule occurs when swallows are in your area. Swallows are also territorial and will use bluebird boxes, but they'll only chase away other swallows. If you put two bluebird boxes a few feet apart, swallows can use one and bluebirds can use the other. Even though the birds won't tolerate others of the same species, they will tolerate each other. Weird? Yes. But it works.

To keep bluebirds using your boxes year after year, it's important to clean the boxes annually. Clean nest boxes early in the year before bluebirds arrive—no later than mid-March.

To clean your bluebird box, open it and sweep out the old nest with an ice scraper. You should also remove any dead nestlings or unhatched eggs from the previous year. To reduce nest parasites, wipe down the inside of the box with a 10 percent solution of bleach in water.

Bluebirds aren't the only birds that benefit from nest boxes. There are lots of bird box designs depending on which birds you want to attract and what kind of habitat you have. To help with this complexity, there's a link in Beyond the Book to the website NestWatch, created by the Cornell Lab of Ornithology. On NestWatch, you select your region (ex. Northeast, Southwest) and habitat type (ex. forest, grassland, mountain), and the website recommends birds you could install nests for. You can then download free nesting box plans for each bird right off that page.

Project 26. Build a Grouse Drumming Log

Ruffed grouse are gamebirds that live in woodlands from Appalachia to Alaska. About a pound in weight, ruffed grouse have exact habitat needs. They prefer seedling- and sapling-dominated woodlands, especially those with a lot of aspen trees.

Perhaps the most interesting aspect of the ruffed grouse is their elaborate courtship. Each spring, male ruffed grouse stand on large, fallen logs and beat their wings against the sides of their body. This wingbeat produces a thumping sound audible from half a mile away, a sound known as "drumming." The drumming alerts females that the male is nearby, and it alerts other males to stay away.

If you've created young woodlands through timber harvest, odds are you have some good drumming logs already in place. If your young woods started as lawn or field, though, they likely lack drumming logs. You could drag a log into the area, but an easier option may be to use the artificial drumming log developed by outdoor writer Bill Marchel.[17] First, roll up a six-foot length of boxwire fence into a tube at least eight inches across. Next, attach outdoor carpet (look for carpet that has an all-weather "marine" backing) to the wire using cable ties. To make the log more natural-appearing, use extra wire to attach sticks and grass to one end. This will give the log a fake, upturned root system.

Ruffed grouse have exact habitat needs, one of which is a fallen log where the male can signal to females that he's ready to mate. Photo credit: National Park Service

Place your artificial log in an area of your woods dominated by younger trees, especially aspens. Higher-elevation sites like ridgetops are ideal. With luck, next spring you'll hear the characteristic drumming of an amorous male grouse.

Project 27. Prune a Wild Apple Tree

Many properties have wild apple trees on them, and they're common in young woods. In almost all cases, these apple trees are non-native. They're usually planted legacies (or their descendants) put in the ground by past farmers. That's why you'll often see wild apple trees in old fields, at field edges, and by former house sites.

But even though most North American wild apples are non-native, they're a rare exception to the "non-natives are bad, natives are good" perspective introduced in the last chapter. Wild apples are related closely enough to the few native North American apple species that our plant-eating creatures do fine with them. More than three hundred species of caterpillars from the Northeast alone will feed on the leaves of these non-native apples.[18] Combine that leaf feast with the apple's well-known fruit, and apples and crabapples become superb wildlife trees.

Just because you have a wild apple tree on your property doesn't mean it will provide apples for wildlife. To get the best-possible fruit production out of that tree, it needs annual pruning.

Wild apple trees like this one prefer full sun, so you'll often find them in old fields and along field edges. A well-pruned apple tree will produce more fruit for deer, bears, and turkeys.

Pruning apple trees isn't hard, but it does require knowledge of which limbs and stems to remove. When done well, pruning will make the tree healthier and increase the number of apples it grows each year.

The best time to prune wild apple trees is in late winter before bud break. The tree is dormant at that time of year, so your pruning will direct growth during the coming warmer months. Start your pruning by removing any dead or diseased branches. Look in particular for signs of fungus or rot, and get those limbs out of there. Once those limbs are gone, sterilize your pruning shears to avoid spreading disease to the rest of the tree or to other trees.

Next, remove any branches that stick either straight up or straight down. The branches that stick straight up, called water sprouts, are especially troublesome and should be removed every year. These branches grow quickly but yield little fruit and get in the way of more productive branches.

From here, your priority is to open up the tree so more sunlight reaches its middle. Focus on cutting branches that scrape against each other, and thin out clumps on the outside of the tree. Sprouts at the tree's base can also be removed. You can prune up to a third of the tree's crown in one year without harming it.

As you prune, you'll notice many limbs have short nubs growing out of them. These nubs are called spurs. Even though they look a little odd, keep them on the tree. Spurs are the spots where the apples form. The more spurs you have, the more apples your tree will grow.

Apple trees grow best in full sun, so if you want the most fruit from your tree, give it the space it needs. Remove any tree seedlings growing beneath it, and cut down nearby taller trees that shade it. For the best growth, apple trees should

The nubs on an apple tree's branches are called spurs. Spurs are where the apples grow; you can see an apple starting on the spur the arrow is pointing to. You want as many spurs as possible, so leave them in place when pruning.

get at least six hours of direct sunlight daily.

The final result of a good apple tree pruning won't look at all like the aesthetic pruning you may be familiar with from gardening. Apple tree pruning isn't about looks; it's about fruit. A well-pruned apple tree frankly looks ugly. There will be a lot of sideways branches and spurs sticking out all over the place. From the perspectives of hungry deer, bears, and turkeys, though, that pruned tree will look gorgeous.

A well-pruned apple tree may look ugly, but the payoff is worth it when you see the tree loaded with these beauties in the fall.

Project 28. Maintain Your Young Woods

With your young woods in place and providing for wildlife, the question turns to maintaining these areas. If you do nothing, they'll grow into older woods. That will benefit some species, but it will kick out animals dependent on open conditions.

Keeping existing grass, shrub, or sapling woodlands in their current state is harder than creating these habitats in the first place. These areas want to grow into older woods, so you're fighting that natural tendency by forcing them to stay young.

If you look at other books and articles that discuss how to maintain young woods, you'll see two methods repeated over and over. The first is using chemical herbicides to kill taller trees before they grow up and shade out the sun-loving grasses and shrubs. The second method is prescribed burning: deliberately setting fire to the grass or shrubland to return the area to a younger state.

Despite their prevalence in other publications, I don't recommend burning or herbicide maintenance as DIY activities. Both are complex projects with the potential to do lasting harm if not handled properly. Fire, in particular, can easily get out of control and spread beyond the prescribed burn's boundary. Proper technique and professional supervision can keep most of these fires contained, but every so often even the experts have one get away from them.

Although these techniques are effective at keeping young woods young, I advise you to pursue other alternatives and consider the above only as last resorts. If you decide to burn or spray, make sure you involve professionals.

If you want to maintain your young woods yourself, the most practical option is periodic mowing or brush hogging. In most meadows, mowing once every other year will be enough to prevent woody plants from taking over. For shrubby areas, brush hogging every five to ten years will keep the area from growing into taller trees.

For those with larger acreages, there's a more natural way to maintain your young woods: don't. Let them grow into older woods, and create new young woods to replace them.

Mowing, haying, and brush hogging are good ways to maintain old fields and shrublands. Photo credit: Pixabay

Adopting this approach takes some scheduling. The Young Forest Project—a multi-organization effort that includes landowners, Native American tribes, government agencies, and environmental groups—advises the "5-5-5" technique to keep yourself organized. In this approach, you create a new five-acre patch of young woods every five years with the goal of always having at least 5 percent of your land in woods less than twenty years old. Granted, this method takes more space than maintaining the same area as grass or shrubland. Over time, though, it will give your property the highest diversity of tree ages from young to old.

Project 29. Protect Ground-Nesting Birds from Mowing and Haying

As effective as mowing can be for maintaining grass and shrublands, it can harm wildlife if poorly timed. Many birds that live in these areas nest on the

You can help ground-nesting birds like this ring-necked pheasant by waiting to mow or brush hog your old fields until after August 1. Photo credit: Pixabay

ground during late spring and early summer. If you mow during those months, you'll wind up chopping the nests and killing the young.

To avoid this wildlife disaster, save your periodic maintenance mowing until after August 1. Waiting until Labor Day is better still. By then most animals have finished nesting, so mowing won't harm them.

If you produce hay in your fields, waiting until August may not be an option. In these cases, there are a couple ways to reduce the damage haying causes to ground-nesting birds. Where possible, one solution is to locate high-productivity hayfields next to low-quality fields. Mow the high-quality field, but leave the other field uncut. The ground-nesting birds that lost their nests in the high-quality field will often try again in the low-quality one.

Changing your haying technique can also reduce damage to wildlife. Setting your blade to six inches or higher will cause it to miss most nests. Mowing during the day is much better than mowing at night, as night-mowing exposes not only nests but also the sleeping adults to blades. Finally, haying from the center of the field out will give animals in the field easier escape options than if you start at the edge and work in.

6

OLD AND
INTERIOR WOODS

"The clearest way into the Universe is through a forest wilderness."
—John Muir

Ispent the last chapter talking about how we're losing young woods, and how replacing some older woods with younger ones can benefit wildlife. So why have a chapter on older woods at all? Aren't these woods in great shape?

To be sure, here in the US we've done a good job helping our woods get older in the past century. As farms were abandoned and people moved to cities during the Industrial Revolution, much of that land returned to forest. Since the 1940s the US cut trees at a slower rate than it grew them, and the net result was that forests got older as time passed. The US has more wood in our forests today than at any time in the past hundred years.[1]

But just because woodlands are getting older doesn't mean they're

Scarlet tanagers need large, unbroken areas of older woods. Your best chance to spot this bird is to listen for its "chick-burr" call, then look up for a flash of red as it dashes off in pursuit of a bee or wasp. Photo credit: National Park Service

providing what wildlife need. Although woodlands have been aging, they've also been broken up by farm fields, lawns, and construction. Our total amount of older woods may be increasing, but we're losing the older woods wildlife need most: the deep, interior woods far from roads, homes, and other openings.

I mentioned in the last chapter that grassland wildlife need at least six hundred feet away from trees to get the most benefit out of the land. As it turns out, many woodland-dwelling species have a similar need. Often they must be hundreds of feet inside the woods' edge to have the best possible nesting success.

As with grasslands, it's useful to create as much interior old woods as possible on your property. Once you have that space, you can either leave it alone to age naturally, or you can help it on its journey toward that Holy Grail of forest habitats: old growth.

Project 30. Connect Isolated Woods with Corridors

In the last chapter, one of the projects was to join adjacent fields by removing the fencerow between them. In that situation, the single, large joined meadow resulted in more interior space than two equally-sized smaller meadows. The same problem and solution occur in reverse with interior woods. If you have two patches of woods separated by a lawn or field, those patches won't support as many interior forest animals as they could if they were a single, joined woods.

To get started joining isolated woods, the simplest method is to plant native trees. As with planting in your backyard, the particular species mix isn't as important as sticking to native trees. Often the best approach is to look at the patches of woods you want to join and use the same kinds of trees if possible. I've included a video url in Beyond the Book that walks you through how to plant a tree.

A good source for trees may be your local Soil and Water Conservation District. These groups often have annual tree sales where you can purchase seedlings of various species at a lower cost than you can through for-profit nurseries.

Planting isn't the only way to create a wooded corridor. You can also get birds to make one for you. In this method, you plant the occasional tree that can handle full sun between the blocks of woods you want to join. Local varieties of hawthorn, dogwood, and cherry are all good options. Birds will spot these new trees and fly to them. As they fly, birds will do what birds do, and their seed-laden droppings will land on the open ground between your woods and the planted trees. Over time, a natural hedgerow will grow between the woods.

But a hedgerow by itself won't create a joined woods. Corridors between wooded patches need to be wide for animals to feel comfortable using them. How wide? One hundred fifty feet is considered the minimum, and the wider, the better. Anything too narrow is too easy for predators like foxes and raccoons to find nests and eat eggs and young.[2] With such a high risk to their children, most forest-interior wildlife will stay away from narrow wooded bands.

If 150 feet sounds absurdly wide, bear in mind that some research suggests even a thousand feet may not be enough to support every interior forest species.[3] These wide distances are particularly important for forest interior birds, which suffer from nest takeovers by the brown-headed cowbird. Rather than build its own nests, the cowbird lays a single egg in the nests of other birds, often destroying the original parents' eggs for good measure. The foster parents then raise the cowbird chick, never realizing they're helping a different species. A single cowbird female can lay eggs in more than twenty different nests in a single breeding season, so you can get a sense for how much damage they can cause to other birds.

Cowbirds are open field birds, but they'll fly a short distance into the woods to lay their eggs. Only if the woods are wide enough can forest birds nest without risk of cowbirds ruining their nests.

The brown-headed cowbird (male pictured here) lays eggs in other birds' nests, often destroying the original eggs in the process. Cowbirds are open-field species and will only venture so far into a forest, so wider woodlands are the best defense against them. Photo credit: National Park Service

I realize a thousand feet is a huge area to talk about, especially if you're planting from scratch. If you can't provide this level of corridor width, don't despair. Although animals need wider corridors for nesting, migratory birds can still use smaller patches as temporary stops. If you can't create interior woods because of your property's size or layout, that's ok. Focus on providing what wooded areas you can and then enhance those areas using the later projects in this chapter.

If you really have your heart set on getting some interior forest, an alternative method to corridors does exist. Rather than join two disconnected woodlands, you can make an existing woods wider. In this case, you would use an aerial photo to figure out where the shortest distances are between the center and edge of your woods. You would then plant trees at the woods' edge in those shorter sections. If you can push that shortest edge distance out to six hundred feet, you can create at least some of the interior forest condition that has become so rare in this country.

Project 31. Learn the Four Types of Wildlife Trees

With your woods in place, your next task is to make those woods as useful for wildlife as possible. That might seem unnecessary at first. I know what you're thinking: it's a forest; isn't it already providing a home for wildlife? But even among older forests, some provide more for wildlife than others. That's because different trees have different wildlife values, and not all trees contribute equally.

Among living trees (we'll talk about dead ones shortly), there are four types of "wildlife" trees. These are trees that, because of the foods they produce or the cover they provide, go above and beyond other trees in your woods. By favoring trees with the following traits, you can make your land more attractive to animals.

By favoring, I mean two things. First, when cutting firewood or selling timber, consider leaving trees that provide the values below rather than cutting them. Second, give these trees more growing space by focusing your cutting on the trees around them. Removing those competing trees will let the ones with more wildlife value expand their crowns and ultimately produce more of the food, cover, or nesting spots that make them so valuable.

Wildlife Tree Type 1: Hard Mast

When many people think about what makes great wildlife food, one image tends to come to mind: acorns. The classic sight of a chipmunk with a pair of acorns shoved in its cheeks is well known, not to mention adorable.

Acorns—along with other tree nuts like walnuts, hickory nuts, and beech nuts—are together known as "hard mast." "Mast" is a broad term for any fruit from a tree, and "hard," as you might guess, means these fruits are, well, hard. Their tough shells may take effort for animals to break into, but the reward is a dense package of nutritious protein and fat.

Hard mast used to be a more reliable food for North American wildlife. For centuries, animals could count on an annual supply of nuts, thanks to the prolific American chestnut. But since the arrival of chestnut blight around 1900, this reliable food source has all but vanished. That's why remaining hard mast trees are so important for animals.

More than just having these species on your land, having a variety of them is important for attracting wildlife. That's because, unlike chestnut, other hard mast providers don't make consistent nut crops every year. Instead they fluctuate, producing bumper crops in one year and then hardly anything for a few years after. Oaks in particular are notorious for this pattern. They drop so many acorns one year that you feel like you're walking on marbles, and then you'll barely see any for the next three to seven years.

Individual species—through mechanisms still not understood—seem to know which years are bumper crops and which aren't. So all the red oaks will produce at the same time, and they'll also hold back at the same time.

During a seed year, acorns like these from a chinkapin oak can cover the forest floor. Because acorn crops are inconsistent from year to year, wildlife need a variety of hard mast trees to make up for lean years. Photo credit: Ryan Hagerty, USFWS

The way to combat these famine years is to have many species of hard mast trees. While the oaks are recovering from their bumper crop, perhaps the hickories will have a good year and make up for it.

Wildlife Tree Type 2: Soft Mast

Not all wildlife have the patience or ability to break into nuts. So while hard mast gets a lot of attention as wildlife food, another group of foods, called soft mast, are just as important.

The difference between hard and soft mast is pretty much what you'd expect. Where hard mast provides tough, shelled fruits, soft mast includes the squishy, fleshy fruits like those on black cherry trees.

As with hard mast, the key to soft mast is diversity. Anyone who's picked wild raspberries or blackberries knows the season for these fruits only lasts a

Staghorn sumac fruit clusters aren't the first food choice of many animals. But because these shrubs keep their clusters throughout the winter, they provide valuable emergency cold-weather food for turkey, ruffed grouse, pheasant, and quail.

week or two. Go too early, and they're all green. Go too late, and they've all been eaten. The same is true for a lot of these softer fruits. If you concentrate on one or two species, you'll only provide food for a short time. Instead, encourage species that fruit at different times of year.

Late fall, winter, and early spring are all great seasons to focus on for soft mast plants. Birds are either leaving to or arriving from their seasonal migration, and they're looking to bulk up. Those birds that tough it out through winter—like wild turkeys—can also benefit from having berries in the cold months. The same is true for mammals that are active through the winter, like deer.

Some reliable soft mast choices to encourage on your property include black cherry, serviceberry, apple, American holly, staghorn sumac, blueberry, persimmon, and winterberry. Note that this mix includes both trees and shrubs. You may not be able to see as far through your woods with more shrubs in them, but your tradeoff is in providing essential nutrition to a wide assortment of birds and mammals.

Wildlife Tree Type 3: Wolf Trees

Wolf trees are the large, oddly shaped trees that pop up now and then in the woods. They have short, wide trunks, branches flung to all corners of the woods, and a huge crown of leaves. Usually they're older than the trees around them, and their weird shapes are the result of having grown in the open before your woods were woods at all. They may once have marked a field boundary or a property line. Often they were simply the one tree that was left in the pasture so the cows would have some shade.

The name "wolf tree" hints at how many landowners and foresters historically viewed them. Like the Big Bad Wolf, these trees were targeted for removal as quickly as possible. Short trunks make wolf trees useless for quality lumber, and their wide-branching shapes take up a lot of space where profitable trees could be growing.

These days, though, wolf trees are enjoying a surge in popularity. The same large size and complex growth that make them worthless for timber make them favorites for wildlife. Black bears, for example, will only den in trees with trunks more than twenty inches wide. In most family-owned woods, there are few trees that size except for wolf trees.

Wolf trees like this white oak are older and bigger (though not necessarily taller) than their wood-land neighbors. These trees were grown in open pastures or field borders, as revealed by their short trunks and enormous crowns. Apart from the trees' visual appeal, wildlife prize them for their many nooks, crannies, and den sites.

Songbirds are drawn to wolf trees too. One biologist in Vermont observed twenty-two kinds of birds foraging in wolf trees, compared with just seven species in regular trees nearby.[4]

Wolf trees provide for many different animals because, apart from their size, their age gives them structural features that younger trees lack. For instance, wolf trees often have some dead limbs. Those limbs attract insects that in turn draw in woodpeckers and small mammals like chipmunks. They may also have loose bark, which bats will roost underneath.

All these smaller animals in turn lure in predators. The Vermont biologist I mentioned set up motion-sensing cameras around wolf trees. He discovered that foxes, bears, raccoons, coyotes, and fishers visited wolf trees nine times more often than regular large trees nearby.[5]

If you have the occasional wolf tree on your property, don't cut it down. In an ideal world, you would have one of these trees for about every two acres of woods. Most woods won't have nearly that many, so it's important to protect the few you have.

To help maintain the wolf trees on your property, remove nearby taller trees to allow the wolf trees to access more light. The large size of the wolf tree demands a lot of solar energy, but because these trees were open-grown, they're usually shorter than forest-grown trees of their species. Cutting the trees that shade them could help these old behemoths keep drawing in wildlife for another hundred years.

Bats love the loose bark common on wolf trees. In the summer, mother bats will raise their children in the relative safety of this bark shelter.

Wildlife Tree 4: Cavity Trees

In forestry, the general advice is to cut down less healthy trees first to give healthier trees room to grow. It's sound guidance for increasing long-term income, improving a woodlot's mast production, and making your trees more resistant to pests and diseases. It's guidance I use when helping landowners decide what to do with their woods.

That said, this guidance can cause problems if followed too closely. Those same unhealthy, diseased trees benefit wildlife too. In some cases they can be more valuable than if they were healthy. Why? Like the dead limbs on wolf trees, the softer, decaying wood of a wounded tree is easier for insects to colonize. In turn, woodpeckers come along and hollow out openings

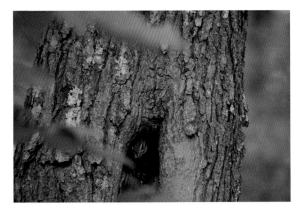

Holes in trees can provide cover and nesting spots for wildlife like this chipmunk.

to get at them. Those openings then provide much-needed cover for cavity-nesting animals like kestrels, barred owls, and red squirrels.

Since diseased trees are more likely than healthy ones to harbor insects, cavities, and dens, these wildlife homes are also the first that traditional forestry advises removing. As a landowner, it's important to balance your desire

Before cutting a diseased tree, check it first for cavities like this one. This cavity is likely some animal's home, so choose another one for your firewood or timber.

for a healthy, productive woodland with the needs of local animals. One way to meet this balance is to check each tree over before you cut it for firewood or commercial harvest. Look for cavities and other signs wildlife make above-average use of a particular tree. If you see them, consider passing up that tree in favor of another one.

Project 32. Identify and Protect Legacy Trees

Individual hard mast, soft mast, wolf, and cavity trees all provide wildlife value. But how those trees are structured in your woods matters even more. Without a healthy woodland structure, your woods could be almost as useless for wildlife as a close-cropped lawn.

To see what I mean, look at the paired photos on the next page. The one on top is a typical woodland where I work in the Catskill Mountains of upstate New York. The one below it comes from the coastal forests of Oregon, one of the few remaining places in the country where you can still see genuine old-growth forest.

At first glance the family woodlot appears to offer a lot for wildlife. It has trees of different species, including American beech, a hard mast producer. It has some cavity trees with soft wood. It even has a little growth on the ground.

Place this woodlot up against an old-growth forest, though, and now it looks bare. Notice how much farther you can see into the Catskills woodland than you can in the old-growth woods. There's far more variation in tree

A typical family woods (top) appears to provide a lot of variety for wildlife. Yet when compared against a true old-growth forest (bottom), it becomes clear that many of our woods are missing key traits that wildlife need. Photo credits: author photo (top); David Patte, USFWS (bottom)

height and width in the old growth, and its variety of plants is greater too. All that variety means more animals with more diverse needs can live in the old-growth woods compared with the younger woods.

Sadly, these days far more woodlands look like the top photo than the old-growth forest in the bottom one. Many of the woods we see and own today got their start when the former farmland they now grow on was abandoned. As a result, the trees are all about the same age. They have similar heights, and their uniform canopy blocks out light to the forest floor. In those conditions, undergrowth struggles to survive. Even though these woods are "natural" in that nobody planted them, they only provide food, cover, and nesting spots in the canopy itself. The rest of the forest is a wildlife wasteland.

To be clear, there's nothing you can do that will turn your woodland from what it is today into true old growth. Only time can do that. That said, there are projects you can do that can give your woods more of the traits—and by extension habitats—that make old-growth forests valuable to wildlife.

So what makes old growth so fantastic for animals anyway? Yes, old growth has variety, but what does that mean? What do old growth forests have that our younger and middle-aged woods lack?

We can break down what makes old growth so important into four key traits: legacy trees, growth at every level, small gaps, and dead trees. By enhancing these traits in your woods, you can make those woods more like the old-growth forests of centuries past. We'll tackle legacy trees in this project, and we'll deal with the other three traits in the next three projects.

The most obvious difference between old-growth forests and the standard woodland is the presence of massive trees. By living for centuries, select trees in old-growth forests have achieved mammoth height and girth.

You can help your woods on their journey to old growth by identifying legacy trees—the biggest, healthiest trees you have. Keeping these trees rather than cutting them down will let them continue growing to someday become giants.

But it isn't just age that makes trees big. In fact, a tree's width in particular is a terrible measure of how old it is, because different trees add different amounts of wood every year. In a good year where a tree gets plenty of light and water, it will grow a lot of wood. In a dry year or if a bigger tree shades it out, it will hardly grow at all.

You can use this varying growth to your advantage. To develop old-growth-sized trees faster, give your legacy trees more of what they need to grow. Cut the smaller trees around them, the ones whose branches touch the legacy trees' branches. This cutting will give your legacy trees room to expand their canopies and absorb more sunlight.

How do you know which trees to keep as legacies? Use the wildlife trees we discussed in the last project. Focus on keeping the best specimens of each type, like a prize oak or a sweeping wolf tree. Cavity trees likely won't be your legacy trees since they're already in decline, but it's still sound advice to leave them in place unless they're interfering with your legacy trees.

Project 33. Thin the Woods to Get Growth at Every Level

The second trait that makes old growth forests so valuable for wildlife is that they have greenery at every level. One of my forestry professors called old-growth forests "green walls," a stark contrast to the desolate forest floors many of us see in our woods.

Those often-missing middle levels can make the difference between a ho-hum woodlot and one that brings in a diverse bunch of creatures. Some birds, for instance, will only nest on the forest floor or in woodland shrubs. The wood thrush is an example. It browses the forest floor looking for insects, and it builds its nest in the lower branches of a sapling or shrub. Take away vibrant undergrowth from your woods, and you're far less likely to hear this thrush's beautiful flute-like song.

All that undergrowth is also perfect for a variety of mammals. Smaller creatures like chipmunks will use it for food and cover, while predators like foxes and bobcats will use it to sneak up on prey.

The wood thrush depends on a healthy, diverse forest floor to locate insects to eat, and it needs short shrubs and saplings to nest in. These traits aren't common in many modern woods. As a result, wood thrush numbers have declined by more than half since the 1960s.[6] Photo credit: Steve Maslowski, USFWS

You can get this multi-level greenery by accomplishing two feats. First, you need to let enough light through the canopy to let herbs and shrubs grow beneath the trees. Second, you need to limit the effects of a key plant eater: white-tailed deer.

We have a whole chapter on deer coming up, so for now, let's stick to getting light on the ground. An easy way to do that is to cut some smaller canopy trees. This is similar to freeing up space for your legacy trees, but instead of clustering your removals, they'll now be scattered throughout the woods. You don't want huge openings. You just want to remove a tree here and there so more light can reach the ground.

The trees you cut for this thinning will be small, probably too small for lumber. Don't worry about it. You can use these trees for firewood or leave them on the ground to provide habitat as rotting logs.

Project 34. Create Small Gaps

Having just encouraged you not to create large openings, I now want to encourage you to create small ones. That's because the third trait of old-growth forests is that they have occasional openings where young trees can get started.

As your woods age, they will lose certain tree species. That's because some trees like black cherry need a lot of sun to grow, while others like sugar maple do all right in the shade. Over time, the trees that need a lot of sun have a hard time replacing themselves. As they die, those that can handle shade take over.

Unfortunately, many of the trees that need a lot of sun are also the ones most beneficial to wildlife. To avoid losing these trees while maintaining forest interior, mimic what happens in old growth forests. Every

Storms brought down two large trees in this two-hundred-year-old pine and hemlock woods. The greater sunlight reaching the ground allowed new seedlings to sprout and grow. Mimicking this multi-layered structure by creating small gaps will provide more food, cover, and nesting options for wildlife.

now and then in an old-growth forest, one of those big legacy trees comes crashing down, usually taking a few smaller trees with it.

You can simulate this event in your woods by creating a tiny clearcut, no more than an acre. That small size is crucial. A gap larger than that will let more sunlight reach the ground, but too big and it will break up the interior forest condition by creating new edge. Keeping your cut smaller than an acre will get you some of the more full-sun trees without disrupting interior-forest wildlife.

Project 35. Leave Dead Trees in Place

You might think dead trees in a forest mean something is wrong, that the woods are sick. But death is part of the forest. Dead trees, both standing and fallen, are important for a host of wildlife.

Standing dead trees, also called snags, provide both food and cover for animals. Like the dead limbs on wolf trees or the decaying wood of diseased trees, snags have softer wood that's easier for insects to feed on and woodpeckers to drill into. That also means that even though they may be dead, snags are important for the wide assortment of cavity-nesting wildlife that inhabits our woodlands.

In fact, dead trees can often be the limiting factor for cavity nesters. As I mentioned earlier, traditional income-focused forestry removes diseased trees. That means the trees most likely to form cavities get cut. If your woods have a history of harvesting—and most private woodlands do—do what you can to protect the dead trees you have so they can support cavity nesters.

The easiest way to protect dead trees is simply to leave

About eighty-five species of North American birds use cavities in dead or dying trees for their nests.[7] These trees are often targeted for removal in traditional forest management, so cavities are frequently the limiting factor for cavity nesters like this mountain bluebird. A combination of hanging nest boxes and leaving dead trees standing can help cavity nesters on your land. Photo credit: National Park Service

Dead trees seem like a bad thing, but they benefit wildlife in many ways. Woodpeckers hollow out openings in search of insects (left), creating homes for other animals like screech owls in the process. Once a tree falls, its upturned roots (right) provide shelter, including potential den sites for bears, wolves, and coyotes.

them alone. A lot of landowners will use these trees for firewood, thinking that's better than taking a live tree, but they're actually harming their woods by removing this rare habitat. As weird as it sounds, your woods will be better for wildlife if you leave the dead tree and use a live one for firewood.

All snags are important, but those with trunks more than twenty inches wide in particular warrant saving. These big snags are rarer than small ones, and they're often the only ones larger animals like bears, barred owls, and fox squirrels will use.

Smaller snags have value too, but they're more common because smaller trees are more likely to be shaded out by bigger trees. In any given acre of your woods, wildlife biologists recommend that you try to maintain at least one snag with a trunk wider than twenty inches, four snags with ten- to twenty-inch

Red efts are the juvenile form of the eastern newt. They do best in the damp forest floor of an older woods, and they will often seek shelter under fallen logs.

trunks, and two snags with six- to ten-inch trunks.[8] This range will help you attract cavity nesters of various sizes.

Even when a snag falls to the ground, its usefulness to wildlife is far from over. As a fallen log, it offers shelter to invertebrates and amphibians like red efts. The upturned root wads can house winter wrens, rabbits, and foxes. And as we talked about in the last chapter, larger logs can serve as drumming sites for ruffed grouse.

Project 36. Girdle a Tree

If your woods are well below the recommended number of snags per acre, particularly among large trees, it can be helpful to kill a few trees to provide that habitat. The best way to create new snags is through girdling.

Girdling a tree involves using a chainsaw to remove two narrow bands of bark and wood about an inch deep all the way around a tree. These cuts leave the tree standing, but they block the flow of nutrients up and down the tree, eventually killing it (it may take a year or two). Making two cuts provides greater assurance that the tree will die, because some trees will survive a single girdle ring.

An advantage to girdling over letting snags form naturally is that you can pick which trees will provide the best snags for wildlife. Here are a few general guidelines for choosing which trees to girdle:

- Bigger is better for snags. Pick a tree that has a trunk at least twelve inches wide, and go for above twenty if you can.
- Bigger trees are also more valuable for lumber, so choose trees that have low financial value. Trees with crooked trunks or of undesirable timber species are better choices than girdling that perfectly straight sugar maple.

Though you'll sometimes see girdled trees with only one cut, the most effective girdling technique is to make two cuts. The cuts should encircle the trunk and penetrate at least an inch into the tree on all sides. Following these techniques is important, otherwise the tree may grow over the wound and recover.

- Similarly, bigger trees also tend to produce more wildlife food like berries or acorns, so pick trees that don't have as much wildlife value.
- Pick shorter-lived species over long ones. They would die sooner anyway.
- After combining all these recommendations, aspen and tulip poplar both emerge as good choices for snag creation. By contrast, avoid girdling oaks, cherries, or hickories. They have greater value both economically and for wildlife while they're alive.

If you want to make your girdled tree even more valuable to wildlife, you can give cavity nesters a helping hand by starting cavities in it. Find a limb you can reach that is at least three inches thick, then cut it off six inches from the trunk. The spot where you made the cut will rot and hollow out, becoming an ideal wildlife home.

One note of caution on girdling: locate girdled trees away from roads, trails, campsites, and any other areas people spend a decent amount of time in. As a girdled tree dies, it can drop branches that can injure or kill someone if they're standing beneath the tree.

Project 37. Build a Brush Pile

Whether you're creating space for legacy trees, thinning to get greenery at lower levels, or creating a tiny clearcut to start some new trees, you're going to wind up with wood on the ground. Most of it will be useless for any human purpose, even firewood. While you can let that wood decay on the ground, with a little work you can make it into a better animal home: a brush pile.

Brush piles aren't anything fancy, just a collection of logs, sticks, and twigs. Their primary purpose is cover. All the interlocking branches create hiding spaces for smaller wildlife. Done well, brush piles make excellent homes for a variety of woodland creatures. Butterflies, chipmunks, foxes, lizards, quail, rabbits, salamanders, skunks, snakes, songbirds, squirrels, toads, and woodpeckers are all known to use brush piles for cover.

A good brush pile combines sturdiness with space. It needs enough room to allow animals to move through it, but it also needs to be sturdy enough that a windstorm or hungry bear won't smash it to oblivion.

They may look unsightly, but brush piles like this one are easy to make and offer superb cover.

To make a brush pile, start out with logs to form the base. The logs don't need to be huge. Four- to six-inch thick logs are plenty big enough. They should be about six to ten feet long. If they're longer than that, use a chainsaw to get them to the appropriate length.

Position the logs so they make a tic-tac-toe-board shape. Put four logs on the ground parallel to each other, then put four more logs on top of them going in the opposite direction. This setup will keep the brush pile off the ground and create space for animals to build dens and tunnels.

Add brush on top of the logs, working from larger branches to smaller ones. You don't need to work at right angles. If the sticks go in lots of different directions, they'll lock together better and make the pile more stable.

When the pile's done, it should be about six feet high, six feet wide, and igloo-shaped. It should last ten to fifteen years, though you may need to add new brush every five years to make up for what decays.

Project 38. Don't Graze Livestock in the Woods

Before we leave the woods, this final project is more of a caution than an actual activity. If you keep livestock, especially cattle, among the worst things you can do for your woods is to let those animals graze in them. Because of the shade from their tree canopies, woods work hard for every plant that appears in the undergrowth. Livestock can deci-mate this growth and leave a simplified woodland that lacks those lower levels so important to wildlife. Animal hooves also churn up soil and damage tree roots, injuring and, in some cases, killing trees.

I've seen this uncontrolled wood-land grazing on too many farms. It just isn't worth it. If you care at all about the wild animals in your woods, keep your domestic ones out of there.

That said, there are select ways live-stock grazing can happen in forests without major damage. The methods require a lot of supervision, clever use of fencing, and moving animals a lot. These techniques, known collectively as silvopasture, aren't covered in this book. For more information, I recommend the USDA's National Agroforestry Center website. I've linked to it in Beyond the Book.

Livestock in the woods, especially cattle, can devastate the land. If you keep animals, fence them out of your woods to protect ground plants and the wildlife that need them. Photo credit: Pixabay

7

STREAMS

"Rivers and the inhabitants of the watery element are made for wise men to contemplate, and for fools to pass by without consideration."
—Izaak Walton

Water is a basic need of life, so it comes as no surprise that North American wildlife use the areas around water more than any other habitat.[1] Not only do upland species come down to drink, but a rich variety of creatures spend most if not all their lives in or near the water. If you want to protect wildlife on your property, or if you want to attract more creatures to your land, you need to pay attention to your water sources. Often the only actions you need to do are preventive, but in situations where your water bodies have become damaged, you may need to take an active role to restore them.

Over the next two chapters, we'll talk about how to protect the water supplies on your land and how to repair them if they've been

Streams and other bodies of water are of course important for fish, but many other wildlife spend their lives near the water too. River otters dig burrows along streambanks and lakeshores, then enter the water to hunt for fish, crayfish, and freshwater clams. Photo credit: Ken Thomas

damaged. We'll start with the most common water source on many properties—streams—and then discuss other water bodies in the next chapter.

The Three Cs of Healthy Streams

Streams come in all shapes and sizes, from tiny trickles to lazy rivers. As far as science defines it, even the mighty Mississippi River is a stream.

You probably don't have anything as big as the Mississippi on your land, but you might have its beginnings, or the beginnings of some other river. Just because your streams are small, doesn't mean they're worthless. Small streams flow into larger streams, so what happens in those first few drops affects everyone and everything down the line. Even if your streams could never support a minnow, they still matter for wildlife.

But what makes a stream better or worse for animals? Generally speaking, if you want to attract creatures to your streams, focus on achieving the 3 Cs: clean, cold, and complex. We'll review these Cs first, and then the projects in this chapter will focus on ways to maintain and enhance them.

C #1: Clean

This might sound like an obvious one, but it's the most important. The best streams for wildlife have clean, clear water. They're free of chemical pollutants like pesticides, low in nutrients, and low in fine soil particles like silt and clay. These pollutants can lead to algae blooms that can kill fish, and the fine soil can smother fish eggs.

There are many ways to keep your streams clean, and most have nothing to do with the streams themselves. Instead, they're all about the land. Because water flows downhill, every inch of your

One of the simplest ways to keep streams clean is to leave a buffer of natural plant life between them and human activities like farming, logging, and development. Performing these practices right by a stream, like in this photo, degrades the stream by adding excess soil, nutrients, and chemicals to the water. Photo credit: Lynn Betts, USDA NRCS

property eventually drains into some body of water somewhere. That means what you do on your land has the potential to impact a local water supply and the animals that use it.

C #2: Cold

Like us land critters, animals that live in water need oxygen to breathe. But while we have plenty of oxygen around us in the air, water-bound creatures aren't so lucky. Yes, water is part oxygen, but the oxygen in water itself isn't available for animals to use. Aquatic creatures rely on oxygen gas that gets mixed into the water and dissolved. Appropriately, this oxygen is called "dissolved oxygen."

Think of dissolved oxygen the way you might sweeten tea by adding sugar. You pour in the sugar, stir, and the sugar dissolves. Dissolved oxygen works the same way. As water flows in a stream, the churning current picks up oxygen from the air and mixes it into the water.

Shade along the streambanks is one of the best ways to maintain a stream's cold temperature. When banks are bare like they are here, a lot of sunlight hits the stream and warms it up, making it less suitable for aquatic life.

The catch is that the concentration of dissolved oxygen in water is really low. There's about 20 percent oxygen in the air we breathe, but water only has about 1 percent dissolved oxygen. That's not a lot for animals to use.

What does all this have to do with temperature? Cold water can hold more dissolved oxygen than warm water. That means as a stream warms, it loses its dissolved oxygen, and animals have a harder time breathing. To have the greatest variety of creatures in your stream, then, colder is better.

C #3: Complex

Just as different land animals need different habitats, aquatic life also needs complexity. Some critters need fast, shallow water with a lot of dissolved oxygen. Others can't hang on in a current and prefer deeper, slower spots. In the same way that having a mix of older and younger woods will increase wildlife use of your land, making your streams more complex will too.

The classic structure for healthy streams is the "riffle-pool-run" trio. Maintaining this structure in your streams—or restoring it if it's been lost—is essential if you want the most wildlife.

Riffles are shallow, rocky-bottomed areas. Because of their uneven beds, riffles have disturbed surfaces and extensive mixing of air and water. As a result, riffles are important for adding dissolved oxygen to the stream. They're also important for fish eggs. The big spaces between larger stones keep the eggs safe from the current while exposing them to large amounts of dissolved oxygen to help the baby fish develop.

The opposite of riffles are pools—the slow-flowing, deeper areas of streams. They're important for animals that can't handle faster flows, in particular young fish.

In between riffles and pools are runs, areas of moderate current and depth. Runs have few obstructions or changes in direction, so water flows smoothly through them.

Less healthy streams consist largely of runs, with straight flow and little variation. By contrast, healthier streams will be more complex. They'll have fewer runs and many deeper pools with corresponding shallow riffles.

Riffles and pools often occur in combination. In this photo, the white shows fast-moving water flowing in a riffle over rocks. By contrast, the deeper, slower-flowing pool in the top-left of the photo shows up as clear.

Project 39. Assess Your Stream's Health

I've described the three Cs in absolute terms, but all of them are shades of gray. Just looking at your stream, you may not be able to tell if it's healthy or not. If you know what to watch for, though, you can get a sense of your stream's condition by walking along its banks. Look for these common symptoms of unhealthy streams:

- Grass, often mowed or grazed, is the only plant growing right up to the stream's edge.
- Livestock move freely in and out of the stream.
- The stream has little variation in width, depth, or current speed.
- The water is brown and cloudy.

In this unhealthy stream (left), grazing has mowed down the plants on both banks. The stream is also forced into a straight, narrow channel with little opportunity to vary in speed or depth. By contrast, the healthy stream (right) has wooded stream banks and a wide bed with lots of variation. Photo credits: Gary Kramer, USDA NRCS (left); author photo (right)

- Fine grains of soil like silt and clay form the streambed. Larger rocks like gravel and cobbles are covered.
- The stream has few if any obstructions such as boulders and fallen logs.
- Few macroinvertebrates live in the stream. Those that do are the ones that can tolerate pollution (see the next project for more information).

If a stream on your land exhibits any of these symptoms, then it isn't as healthy as it could be and it means the 3 Cs aren't being met. As a result, your stream will have fewer animals living both in and around it.

Fortunately, your streams don't have to remain in poor health. Streams have a remarkable ability to recover if conditions around them improve. I've seen many examples of barren streams brought back to supporting a full suite of wildlife through projects like those discussed in this chapter.

Project 40. Look for Stream Macroinvertebrates

The indicators in the last project are obvious if your streams are really degraded, but they may be less clear if your stream is in a middle condition—not decimated but not pristine either. To gain a more nuanced view of how your stream is doing, try looking for stream macroinvertebrates.

What are macroinvertebrates? They're small animals that don't have backbones but that are big enough to be seen with the naked eye. I'd call them "insects" or "bugs" to keep things simple, but macroinvertebrates also include other animals like clams, crayfish, and snails. They're an important link in the stream food chain, and they're a useful indicator of stream health.

Macroinvertebrates are an excellent gauge of your stream's health for two reasons. First, the various kinds all look different, so identification is easy. I've included a link to a simple, printable key in Beyond the Book. Second, and more impor-

Macroinvertebrates are superb for revealing the health of your stream. Some can survive in polluted waters, while others, like this stonefly larva, will only live where water quality is excellent. Photo credit: National Park Service

tantly, macroinvertebrates have varying sensitivities to pollution. As the water quality in your stream drops, the most vulnerable macroinvertebrates disappear first. By the time a stream is severely degraded, only the most pollution-tolerant critters will remain. If you know which macroinvertebrates your stream supports, you'll be able to tell where on that healthy stream continuum you are.

To find macroinvertebrates, you'll need a D-frame net. This is a net with at least one flat edge so you can set it flush with the bottom of a stream. D-frame nets are inexpensive and available to buy online. You'll also need a five-gallon bucket and some clothes you don't mind getting muddy.

Supplies in hand, head out to your stream and walk along the bank. Add a few inches of stream water to your bucket as you go.

Enter the stream and set your D-frame net in the water downstream from you. With your foot, kick at the streambed just upstream of the net. Water will flow through the net, but macroinvertebrates living in the streambed will get caught. Pull up your net and empty it into your bucket.

Repeat this process at least five times, each time from a different spot in the stream. If possible, collect from a variety of stream features like riffles, pools, and runs as well as areas that have a lot of woody obstructions.

Once you have your samples, retreat to a dry spot and sit down. Take a closer look at the creatures you've captured. (Tip: for this step, it may be easier to transfer the critters from the bucket to a disposable cake pan.) The animals you've found are macroinvertebrates.

The critters you're hoping to spot are larvae of three different insects: mayfly, stonefly, and caddisfly. For mayflies and stoneflies, look for multiple long, thin tails coming off their rear ends. As for caddisfly larvae, they're often found attached to logs, and they encase themselves in wood as protection from predators.

The reason you want to see these insects is because they're highly sensitive to pollution. As a result, they're only found in streams with excellent water quality. If you find them, you know your stream is in good shape, which means the stream restoration projects later in this chapter aren't necessary for you. Instead, focus your stream protection on preventive actions, like using Best Management Practices (Projects 42 and 43).

If you aren't seeing mayflies, stoneflies, and caddisflies, that indicates cause for concern about your stream's health. All may not be lost, though. The next level down for macroinvertebrates are those that can handle a little pollution, but not a lot. These moderates include dragonfly larvae, freshwater clams, and crayfish. If you see these critters but not the more sensitive three listed above, your stream is in trouble, but not in catastrophic shape.

If your pickings reveal only worms, leeches, and snails, your stream is in poor health. These are the macroinvertebrates most tolerant of pollution, so they're the last critters left when a stream becomes heavily polluted.

Even if your macroinvertebrate hunt reveals that your stream is in bad shape, don't give up on it. Macroinvertebrates may be small, but they will find their way back into streams if water quality improves.

Project 41. Create Old Woods around Your Streams

Now that you know what makes streams healthy and what shape yours are in, we can talk about how to protect and improve them. The first and best way to do both is to grow trees along your streams.

Trees are natural water filters. Their thick ground layer of fallen leaves and decaying plant material slows water down, allowing it to seep into the earth rather than rush along the surface (carrying away that surface with it). Their roots also remove excess nutrients and anchor soil and streambanks to help hold them in place during floods.

The benefits of having trees along your streams are hard to overstate. A hundred-foot wide wooded area on both sides of a stream can block 85 percent of sediment and half of nitrogen pollution from reaching the water.[2] That same wooded area also provides food for healthy bacteria and invertebrates in the stream that can break down pollutants like pesticides.[3]

Trees are also useful for maintaining the second C: cold. When they grow along streambanks, trees' leafy canopies spread over the stream and keep it shaded. By blocking sunlight from the stream, trees can lower the water temperature by ten degrees or more.[4] For some aquatic creatures, that's enough to mean the difference between life and death.

For all their cleaning and cooling power, trees can't protect streams by themselves. The finer, tighter-packed roots of grasses, herbs, and shrubs work with tree roots to better hold soil in place and take up more polluting nutrients before they hit the water.

The best stream edges, then, are the older woods we talked about in the last chapter. Of the various woodland age groups, they alone combine different plant types at every level to give the greatest protection to stream-side areas.

To keep your streams in good shape, use the projects in the last chapter to make your streamside woods act more like an old-growth forest. If possible, provide this old woods condition for at least one hundred feet on either side of all streams on your land. In steeper areas, it's helpful to make this distance wider, up to 150 or even two hundred feet.

Older woods around streams are better for wildlife for another reason: dead trees. Remember them? They're still important in streamside areas. Cavity-nesting animals often prefer trees near streams for easier access to food

A mix of plant sizes and types near streams will best anchor soil and provide the most effective buffer for both clean water and wildlife habitat.

and water. If you took my advice in the last chapter and created some den trees through girdling, make a few more near your streams.

If you don't have trees along your streams, it could take a century to recreate the complexity of an older forest. Even so, there are techniques you can use to make these exposed streams cleaner in the meantime. Check out the Stream Restoration projects at the end of this chapter for more information.

Though found in many eastern US forests, the red-bellied woodpecker is most associated with areas near water. Suitable cavity trees are a limiting factor for this and many other cavity-nesting species.

Project 42. Install BMPs like Waterbars to Reduce Trail Erosion

No matter how many trees you have in your streamside areas, some soil is going to wash into your streams. This natural process, called erosion, is unavoidable, especially during heavy storms. That said, human activities can increase erosion beyond what would naturally occur. To keep your streams as clean as possible, minimize how much soil enters your streams because of your actions. Having woods around your streams will help, but another important step is to use Best Management Practices, or BMPs, on your trails and woodland roads.

What exactly are BMPs? They're simple, low-cost changes to your trails largely designed to do one thing: get water off the road.

The ground on trails is almost always compacted from logging equipment, ATVs, or even just feet traveling over them. This pressed-down surface keeps water from sinking in. In turn, that allows it to speed up, gain energy, and wear away the trail. By diverting water off the trail into undisturbed soil, BMPs slow water down, limit its erosive power, and give it a chance to seep peacefully into the ground.

BMPs were originally created to protect water quality from logging. Yet even if you never intend to harvest timber, BMPs can still benefit your streams.

The US Environmental Protection Agency reports that up to 90 percent of sediment pollution from forestry comes from trails.[5] With or without logging, your trails could cause water quality problems. They should have BMPs even if you don't plan on logging.

Particular BMPs vary based on the trees and terrain common to different places. For this reason, every state has its own BMPs. I've included a reference in Beyond the Book that will help you find your state's guidelines.

Pretty much wherever you are, the standard trail BMP is the waterbar. Waterbars are raised berms of soil that go all the way across a trail. As water flows down the trail, it hits the waterbar and then drains off the road.

Waterbars can take a multitude of forms depending on a trail's size, steepness, and types of use. On trails that see only foot traffic, the mound may be

The most common trail BMP is the waterbar—a down-sloped earthen berm that redirects water off the trail before that water can build up enough speed to erode the trail surface. The waterbar pictured here was installed on a nature preserve to protect the trail even though the owners have no plans to log the property.

little more than a slight bump, just enough for small amounts of water to flow sideways off the trail. You can build these smaller diversions by hand using a pick or mattock. Cut a ditch into the trail at a 30-degree downslope to allow the water to drain, then pile up the fill below the ditch to create a raised mound.

On wider trails like those used by logging equipment—typically about ten feet wide—waterbar berms need to be taller to handle more water. New waterbar berms on these trails should be at least two feet above the trail level so they can withstand storms.

Two-foot berms in your trails might sound excessive, but those heights are only temporary. After two or three months the soil will settle, and the waterbar height will get smaller. At that point it should accommodate most traffic, including ATVs.

Waterbars can take many forms to accommodate different needs. This waterbar was reinforced with a log to help it withstand the frequent vehicle traffic on this farm road.

If your property sees heavy vehicle use, you can reinforce your waterbars. One method is to add a fallen log to the top of the berm. The log should be at least twelve inches in diameter, and it should be almost submerged by the berm itself.

If you have a lot of trails, and especially if they're wider logging roads, installing waterbars by hand is impractical. It takes many waterbars spaced out along a trail to protect against erosion, and the steeper your trails are, the closer together the waterbars need to be. On typical woodlots here in the mountainous Catskills, it's common to need dozens or even hundreds of waterbars on a property to keep trails stable.

For these larger trail systems, it's best to install waterbars mechanically, most often with a dozer or excavator. Unless you're experienced running these machines, bring in a professional for this work. You can do more harm than good to your trails if you don't know what you're doing.

That said, it's my experience that it's hard to find contractors who will come to your property just to install BMPs. Your best shot for getting BMPs is during a timber harvest, because professionals and equipment are already on site. If you harvest timber on your property, it's critical that you have BMPs installed before the loggers leave at the end of the job. You may not be able to find someone to come back and fix problems later.

If you aren't going to harvest timber but still want to protect your

Seeding trails with a ground cover is another way to help keep them stable. Seeding may be more practical for you than installing waterbars if you don't plan on harvesting timber. This landowner seeded his trails himself using a spreader attached to an ATV. His seed mix combines creeping red fescue (a grass that can handle shade) and white clover, which he chose for its wildlife food value.

trails, another option is to seed them. A ground cover like a shade-tolerant grass or clover works well. These plants' roots will help hold the trail's soil in place during storms.

Seeding your trails may be easier than installing waterbars yourself, especially if you have an ATV. You can attach a seed spreader to the ATV, then drive your trails to lay seed on them. Follow your chosen seed mix's instructions on when and how much to plant.

Project 43. Choose a Water- and Wildlife-Friendly Stream Crossing

If your trails are washing away, your stream crossings are where all that loose soil will enter the water. To protect your streams, pay attention to your stream crossings.

I'm not a fan of fording (driving through) streams, because of the high potential for damage to the streambed and banks. But if you have a wide stream like this one, a ford may be your only practical option for a permanent crossing. If you do ford a stream, choose a spot where the streambed and banks are stable. Ideally the streambed will be bedrock or large cobbles that will be unlikely to shift when you drive over them. Photo credit: Gary Kramer, USDA NRCS

The best BMP for stream crossings is not to have any. Plan logging and recreational trails to avoid streams if possible.

Of course, sometimes you have no choice but to cross a stream. When that happens, do what you can to minimize damage to the streambed itself. Even healthy streams often have a layer of fine silt and clay below the larger cobbles of the streambed. Normally that sediment is held in place by the rocks above it. But if those larger stones are disturbed, the smaller pieces can wash away and pollute downstream areas.

For this reason, I recommend against fords or culverts as stream crossings. Both of these crossing methods permanently alter the streambed. They also have a high potential of harming water quality downstream, especially if installed incorrectly or in the wrong location.

The best stream crossing structure—at least for timber harvesting—is the temporary bridge. Loggers usually only have to enter the stream once to set the bridge, and then equipment stays outside the stream for the duration of the harvest.

For all their wildlife and water quality benefits, temporary bridges have one major drawback: they're temporary. When the loggers leave, the bridge leaves with them, and the crossing isn't available to you for recreational use.

If you need a permanent crossing, one option for smaller streams is an arch culvert. Think of these as regular culverts sliced in half. The advantage

Culverts are popular choices for permanent stream crossings, but I don't recommend them. They need a lot of maintenance, and they're prone to plugging and washing out if they're too small. They also disrupt the stream bed and can block fish movement. The falling water coming out of this culvert reveals that it was poorly installed and will prevent fish from traveling upstream. It is also undersized. In a flood, the road above this culvert is at high risk of blowing out.

If you need a permanent stream crossing, an arch culvert like this one in Washington State will allow for continued access without disrupting the streambed or preventing fish movement. Photo credit: Ron Nichols, USDA NRCS

to arch culverts is that their open bottom leaves the streambed intact. Loggers place the arch culvert in the stream and then pile fill on top of it to create a permanent crossing.

Whenever you put in a permanent crossing, it helps to get professional advice. Work with a forester to locate the best crossing spot and to choose an appropriate-sized bridge or culvert that will last through floods.

Project 44: Let Your Streams Flood

I realize this project sounds crazy. I live in a town that was flooded by Hurricane Irene in 2011, so I understand the desire to avoid floods at any cost. But while wooded streamsides and BMPs will help with the first two Cs, to get the last C, complex, you'll need to become comfortable with the idea that your stream can't and shouldn't be confined to one place.

Recall that complex streams have a mix of depths, current speeds, and bed materials. How do they gain this complexity? Given time and space to flow, they'll adopt it all on their own.

As a stream meanders back and forth, the areas on the outside edges of curves start to erode. Water flows faster in these areas, so it wears away the streambed and banks, making the outside edges deeper. Eventually these edges become too deep for water to move quickly, and they transform into pools. Meanwhile, on the inside edges of streams, current is slower. The streambed gradually builds up as heavy gravel and cobble fall out of the current. Over time, riffles form in these shallow areas.

Key to this natural complexity is the fact that streambanks move with time. Banks on the outside edges of curves will tend to erode, while those on the inside edges will tend to build up. This wandering, changing structure is the nature of streams. Wildlife like fish depend on it. And as scary as it sounds, the only way to get it is to allow your streams to flood.

Wildlife benefits aside, letting your streams flood can be better in the long run than trying to hold them back. I know that sounds backwards, so let me explain. Historically, to reduce flood risk, people simplified streams. They would straighten the channel, remove obstructions, and reinforce streambanks with rock. The idea was to get streams flowing as quickly as possible so they didn't have time to rise. Unfortunately, these strategies destroyed the complex stream structure that aquatic life needs. More important, though, these flood-control methods often made floods worse, not better. Faster water may not back up as much as slower water, but it has more energy and therefore more destructive power. That causes more erosion and ultimately more damaging floods.

In the long run, you'll lose more soil and land trying to straighten your streams than if you let them flood naturally. By slowing water down, yes it may back up and spread out. But in the process, it will also lose much of its ability to wash away soil. Instead, it will tend to drop new soil onto the streambanks and floodplains around it, enriching them and allowing them to grow plants bigger and faster.

As scary as all that sounds, the final result is a stream that's more stable and less prone to damaging floods. As plants and especially trees grow up along the streambanks, they help keep those banks intact. In one study of 748 river

Artificial structures like the stone gabions on the right side of this stream are common tools to reduce flooding. Unfortunately these structures can make floods worse by speeding up water and increasing its destructive power. They also simplify the stream and eliminate a lot of wildlife habitat. Photo credit: Bob Nichols, USDA NRCS

bends in British Columbia, major bank erosion was thirty times more prevalent on unforested bends than on forested ones.[6] In another project from California, deforested farm floodplains were 80 to 150 percent more likely to erode than floodplains with streamside forests.[7] These results are consistent with other studies from elsewhere in the country finding that streams bordered by woods migrate roughly half as fast as those without trees.[8]

Letting your streams flood may involve some sacrifices on your part. You won't be able to have your home right along the stream. If you grow crops, you may need to leave a wider buffer of trees between them and the water. But if you can handle these losses, the gains for your stream and its wildlife will be immense.

Giving your stream room to flood and providing a buffer of trees around it can actually make floods less damaging. In the top stream, the straight channel and lack of trees have led to severe erosion that has carved the stream six feet below the fields around it. When a flood comes through, water rushes through this tube and carves away more and more soil. By contrast, the wooded stream on the bottom has room to flood. When it sees high water, there is space for that water to spread out and slow down. The result is both better habitat for animals and less erosion of the streambanks.

Project 45. Add Wood to Your Streams

Letting your streams flood isn't the only way to make them more complex. Another common way pools and riffles form is as a result of obstructions in the water. Water speeds up around the blockage, creating a riffle. Below the obstruction the current slackens, resulting in a calm pool.

Fallen logs are an excellent way to create this complexity, and streams benefit from them for more reasons than changes in current. Fallen logs provide two key life needs for aquatic animals: food and cover. Clean, cold streams don't have a lot of nutrients, so stream animals depend on decaying leaves and wood to provide the base of their food chain. As for cover, logs provide spots where invertebrates can latch on so they aren't swept away in the current.

If you already have trees near your streams, it's easy to introduce one to the water. Just cut a tree so it falls into the stream. Alternately, girdling some

Obstructions in water like this boulder create complex streamflows and more habitat for aquatic wildlife. In this photo, the water speeds up on either side of the boulder, while downstream of it there is a low-flow area that creates a pool.

streambank trees will let them serve as nest and den sites, and then serve in the future when they fall into the water.

Many landowners see wood in their stream and remove it right away. They worry it poses a flooding hazard. Yet in almost all cases, it's better to leave in place any limbs or trees that fall into your streams. This woody material almost never forms a complete dam to block water, so it rarely poses a flood risk.[9]

How much wood should be in your stream? Biologically, there is no upper limit. Some pristine streams have woody pileups that extend for miles.[10] The only limitation is how much you're willing to tolerate.

If you don't have trees near your stream, you can still introduce a log to the water. The easiest method is with an ATV. Some ATVs have attachments that will let you drag a log to the water.

Fallen leaves, limbs, and even whole trees are all good for streams. Unless they pose a flood risk, which is rare, leave them in place rather than remove them. You'll help aquatic animals, and you won't risk damaging the streambed or banks by hauling trees through them.

Before you add anything to your stream, pause and do some research on permits first. Streams in the US are usually considered public resources, so you'll typically need a permit to make any changes to a stream or its banks.

What permits you'll need and which government agencies you'll need to get them from vary from stream to stream and place to place. Your best bet to avoid trouble is to reach out to your local Soil and Water Conservation District before starting any stream work. These districts are organized by county, so they'll usually know any local as well as state or federal requirements. And because they're usually non-regulatory, they tend to be more approachable than state or federal agencies. Often they can help with technical advice specific to your project. In some cases they may even be able to point you toward funding to help get the work done.

Project 46. Stream Restoration, Part 1: Stop Harmful Practices

Up to this point, this chapter's projects have focused on protecting streams. But what if you already have a degraded stream? In that case, protection isn't enough. You'll need to take an active role in your stream if you want it to return to a more natural state that will attract wildlife. You'll need stream restoration.

Stream restoration is a profession unto itself. Large-scale restoration projects involve complex science, massive engineering, and big budgets. Fortunately, there are some basic restoration projects you can use without spending millions of dollars.

In fact, you may not have to spend money at all. One of the best stream restoration techniques is simply to stop the practices, if any, that you do that are making the situation worse. Often this step is enough for the stream to restore itself without any further involvement from you.

One of the worst practices for stream health is letting livestock enter the stream and graze on the streambanks. If you have livestock, installing a fence to keep them away from the stream will let new plants grow and anchor the soil. The streambed and banks will also become more stable without the constant smashing from heavy hooves.

The benefits of fencing streamside areas are impressive. In one California study, researchers looked at streams with barren streambanks that were then fenced off from grazing. Within ten years, the regrowth was enough to lower the stream temperature to a level suitable for trout. After twenty years, the regrowth had started contributing large pieces of wood to the streams.[11] These benefits happened without the landowners making any changes to the streams. Fencing alone was enough for nature to restore the stream all by itself.

Aside from grazing, other common practices to avoid near streams include driving vehicles, growing crops, diverting water for irrigation, using pesticides, and dredging that straightens or deepens the channel. On farms, there are often lower-impact ways to achieve the same goals as these practices. In New York, for instance, many farms now use solar-powered water pumps that draw water from streams into troughs for livestock. The animals get needed water, and they don't have to go near the stream itself.

On farms, fencing off your streamside areas from livestock is a vital first step in stream restoration. Photo credit: Gary Kramer, USDA NRCS

Project 47. Stream Restoration, Part 2: Plant Trees

Stopping the practices that have damaged the stream isn't always enough to bring the stream back. Even when it is, you may want to give nature a helping hand so your stream returns to health faster than it would if left to its own devices.

A good way to speed up stream restoration is to plant trees. Planting isn't hard, especially if you have a few people to help. It's also cheaper than you might think. You can usually buy seedlings from local nurseries and Soil and Water Conservation Districts at low cost.

Plant trees either in fall after they lose their leaves or in spring before new leaves emerge. Planting during these seasons will give trees time to establish their roots before the freezing cold of winter or the dry heat of summer.

As for what to plant, local varieties of willow, alder, cottonwood, oak, elderberry, and serviceberry are reliable choices for streamside areas. All these species

To improve your stream's health and habitat for wildlife, plant trees along it. Photo credit: Jeff Vanuga, USDA NRCS

can handle occasionally wet soil. Oak, elderberry, and serviceberry offer the extra advantage of providing wildlife food in the form of acorns and berries. In addition, oak and willow are the top two woody plants for supporting moths and butterflies.[12]

Where streambank stability is a primary concern, I recommend willows and cottonwoods. You can plant live cuttings from existing plants in muddy streambanks. The cuttings grow quickly and provide faster protection against erosion than traditional tree seedlings.

If possible, aim for at least a hundred-foot tree buffer on both sides of the stream. For full canopy closure as your trees grow, plant at least two hundred trees per acre. For a hundred-foot wide buffer, that's roughly one hundred trees on each side for every two hundred feet of stream.

I know that sounds like a lot, but research shows one hundred feet of tree cover is the minimum needed for proper stream health.[13] You need that distance to provide shade to the stream while filtering out pollutants like fine soil and nitrogen.

If you can't follow the recommended planting levels, that's ok. It's still worth planting some trees along your streams. It won't be as effective as a real buffer, but a few trees are better than none.

Project 48. Stream Restoration, Part 3: Stabilize Stream Banks

If your streambanks are steep and exposed, they may erode too quickly for trees to establish. For these streams, you should first stabilize the site by laying down erosion control blankets. These blankets are basically interwoven straw mats that hold the ground in place until grasses and other small plants can grow in. After that the straw breaks down, and the ground plants stabilize the soil.

To use erosion control blankets, first spread some grass seed on the exposed bank. You can often find a "conservation mix" at local nurseries and garden supply stores that is well-suited for this job. Then lay down the mats and secure them to the ground with metal wire staples.

In some situations, you can substitute loose straw for erosion blankets. Straw is more vulnerable to blowing or washing away during storms, but it can be easier to buy and spread than blankets. It's also a good choice if you intend

Erosion control blankets are useful for more than just streambanks. Highway crews on Interstate 81 in Pennsylvania installed these erosion control blankets to protect an exposed section of median until grasses could grow.

Combining multiple stream restoration methods is sometimes the fastest way to restore an eroding streambank. This project used loose straw, erosion control blankets, grass seed, willow cuttings, and tree seedlings all on the same site to get both immediate and long-term protection. Photo credit: Gary Wilson, USDA NRCS

to plant trees, because you can plant the trees at the same time that you spread the straw and grass seed. To reduce the chance of invasive plants taking over your streambanks, choose only certified "weed-free" straw.

Project 49. Stream Restoration, Part 4: Willow Weaving

The worst-case scenario for stream restoration is a stream that has become completely separated from the land around it. In these cases, you'll see a sharp, vertical drop of exposed soil from the land above the stream to the water itself. Bringing these streams back is challenging but not impossible. One technique for repairing them is willow weaving, also called brush mattressing.

In this unprotected farm stream, soil washes away from the streambank and the farmer's field with every rain. When stream erosion gets this bad, just planting trees may not be enough to address the problem. Willow weaving could be a technique on this stream to limit future damage. To address the problem in the long term, the farmer should supplement that willow weaving with tree planting for one hundred feet from the edge of the streambank. Photo credit: Lynn Betts, USDA NRCS

In willow weaving, you and your friends—don't expect to do this project on your own—take live, untrimmed willow poles and insert one end into the streambank so they lay horizontally, parallel with the direction the stream runs. Next, you'll insert vertical poles into the base of the streambank or streambed. Finally, you'll weave the horizontal willows around the vertical ones and then insert the other ends of the horizontal willows into the streambank.

When you're finished, you'll have what looks like a woven mat of willow stalks lying against the streambank. These interlaced willow cuttings hold each other in place long enough for them to take root and secure themselves.

Willow weaving isn't a task to undertake lightly. Even for small sections of stream, you'll need hundreds of willow poles to make a clump that won't wash away. Work with a local nursery to see about getting the supplies you need.

Willow weaving is an involved process, but as a natural tool for healing the most damaged streambanks, it's hard to beat. Planted correctly, woven willows will root and grow quickly. Within three or four years, your once barren streambanks will be lush and green.

The advantage to willow weaving is that willow cuttings root and grow rapidly. That growth helps stabilize the streambank faster than traditional tree planting. This willow project is only two years old, and the growth is already taller than a person. Photo credit: USDA NRCS

An alternate approach to willow weaving is to plant the willow cuttings only vertically, then secure them with stakes and twine, as shown here. Photo credits: USDA NRCS

8

WETLANDS

"My temple is the swamp."
—Henry David Thoreau

Admittedly, wetlands aren't the most glamorous parts of the outdoors. Even their names are forbidding: bog, marsh, swamp, fen. They conjure images of mosquitoes, snakes, and boot-stealing muck—hardly the kinds of places most of us would think worthy of attention, let alone protection.

But what wetlands lack in beauty, they make up for in their incredible diversity. Precisely because they're so unusual, they support many plant and animal species that can survive almost nowhere else. Most well-known are water birds like herons, egrets, ducks, and geese. Less seen but no less important are a wide assortment of reptiles, amphibians, fish, and invertebrates that together provide food for larger animals.

Even if the wetlands on your property are tiny, don't dismiss their value. In fact, the smaller, more easily-missed wetlands can be the most useful for certain animals.

Wooded wetlands like this swamp in Onondaga County, New York may not be the prettiest spots on your land, but few areas are more important to wildlife or more vulnerable to damage by people.

Wading birds like this green heron depend on wetlands, in particular wetlands near woods. Green herons commonly nest in trees and shrubs along wetland edges to provide shelter for their eggs and young. Though herons are known as fish hunters, green herons will also eat a variety of wetland critters including insects, snails, amphibians, and reptiles. Photo credit: Lee Karney, USFWS

Unfortunately, because many wetlands are small, they're often overlooked. Worse, wetlands are some of the most sensitive parts of your property to human disturbance. With a single careless act, it's easy to damage or even destroy these unique wildlife homes. That's why before we get into ways to make these areas better for wildlife, the first projects in this chapter are about simply finding your property's wetlands and keeping them safe.

Project 50. Find and Mark Your Wetlands

To protect your wetlands, first you need to know where they are. Often that knowledge will be easy to come by. If you have areas with a lot of year-round open water like ponds, lakes, and marshes, you're probably aware of them already.

Other wetland types, though, are more difficult to spot. They may only have water part of the year, and if they're small enough, they won't show up on an aerial photo. You can easily miss them while hiking too, especially if you limit your walks to the summer.

Perhaps the trickiest wetland to track down is the vernal pool. Vernal pools are small, seasonal ponds that dry out at certain times of the year. Often they form in the spring when melting snow or a rising water table collects in a depression on your land. Then as summer comes on and the water table falls, the pool vanishes.

This cyclic wetting and drying makes vernal pools especially important for amphibians. Fish are major amphibian predators, but since vernal pools don't

Many amphibians like this California tiger salamander lay their eggs in vernal pools. The fish-free pools let young salamanders grow up with fewer predators. According to the National Wildlife Federation, loss of vernal pools to construction is the greatest threat facing tiger salamanders.[1] Photo credit: John Cleckler, USFWS

have water for several months of the year, they can't support fish. As a result, baby frogs and salamanders in a vernal pool have a better chance to survive than they would in a permanent pond or stream.

The drawback to vernal pools' drying is that many landowners never realize they have one. That's fine as long as you aren't making changes to your land, but it can become a problem if you build a new road, site a cabin, or convert some woods to farming. If you choose where to locate these changes in the summer, you may inadvertently locate them right through a vernal pool without realizing you're destroying a rare wetland habitat.

To find vernal pools, walk your land in early spring. Go on a day after snowmelt but before the dry heat of summer. In many climates, April is a good month to look for vernal pools. If you find one, mark off the area using wire flags that you stick in the ground or with plastic flagging that you tie to tree branches. This way, you'll know even in the hottest, driest months that that small hollow is actually an important amphibian nursery.

This on-the-ground marking is important for vernal pools, but it's a good idea to find and mark all the wetlands on your land—even the obvious ones. As familiar as you may be with your property, a contractor coming to build a road or harvest timber may not notice (or, sadly, not care) that a wetland is on your property. By marking your wetlands, you'll give both yourself and anyone working on your land a signal that you consider these areas worthy of protection.

If you can't mark your wetlands outside, at least make sure they're indicated on a property map. That way, when you go to plan projects on your land, you'll remember those wetlands are there and that they matter for wildlife.

Project 51. Buffer Wetlands from Equipment and Development

The same mucky soils that steal your boots are the reason wetlands are so vulnerable to damage from people. Wetlands' poorly-drained soils can't support the weight of machines like ATVs and logging equipment. When vehicles travel through a wetland, they compress the soil and create deep ruts that channel water. At best, that channeling leads to erosion on your trails and makes them harder to use. In the worst case, ruts can destroy the wetland by draining its water. If that happens, the unique plant and animal life that needs that wetland will disappear.

To protect these sensitive areas, locate trails or development away from them. If you have existing trails that lead through wetlands, mark them off as closed. Don't let vehicles use them, whether for recreation or timber harvesting. To preserve your access, work with a professional forester to design and install new trails that go around the wetland. Locate these new trails at least three hundred feet from the wetland's edge on firmer, better-drained soils. These soils will handle vehicle traffic better with less rutting.

Construction is the other major threat to wetlands on your property. If you're siting a cabin, house, driveway, or other structure, locate it at least a thousand feet from any wetlands.

Why are these buffer distances for trails and structures so large? Many amphibians that reproduce in wetlands spend most of their lives on land far from the water itself. Salamanders in particular are known for this wide-ranging movement. They return to the water to breed, often the same pool where they hatched. Putting trails and buildings too close to the wetland—even if they aren't in the wetland itself—could make it difficult or even impossible for these animals to reach the water to start the next generation.

Project 52. Improve Winter Food and Water Supplies by Thinning Seeps

Based on what I've written in this chapter so far, you may be thinking the best thing you can do for wetlands is leave them alone. To be sure, wetlands are great for wildlife all on their own. Given the high risk of damaging these areas if you aren't careful, wetlands are places where it's okay to do nothing.

That said, there are a few cases where some limited action by you can make these already valuable areas even more useful to wildlife. One such case occurs with small wetlands called seeps.

Seeps are places where groundwater flows to the surface. They may be self-contained, or they may be the beginnings of a larger stream. Often they're formed by mountain springs, so you may see them referred to as "spring seeps."

Like vernal pools, seeps can be difficult to spot on your property. They may not have water flow throughout the year, especially during the summer, and they will rarely show up on aerial photos.

The best time to find seeps is during the winter. Because seeps are formed by groundwater, their temperature isn't determined by weather. Even in bitter winters, the water stays a constant temperature—between 50 and 60 degrees depending on where your land is. Thanks to that warmth, seeps almost never freeze, and snow melts off them quickly. A winter hike or snowshoe trek will quickly reveal your property's seeps, which will stand out in stark green against the otherwise white or brown background.

Seeps' never-freezing trait makes them excellent winter food and water sources. In cold months, seeps' warmer water means animals can drink without lowering their body temperature as much as they would if they ate snow or drank surface water. Seeps' warmer ground temperature also allows plants to grow and otherwise dormant insects to remain active through the winter. In turn, these plants and insects provide food for larger animals.

Seeps are especially important during snowy winters, since most other food sources will be buried. When snowpack depth reaches four inches, for instance, about 85 percent of winter wild turkey feeding occurs in seeps and the small streams they flow into.[2]

Formed by groundwater coming up to the surface, seeps stay the same temperature all year long. This warmer temperature means seeps don't freeze, providing wildlife with a warmer water source and green growth even in winter when most plants and insects are dormant. Photo credit: USDA NRCS

Even as winter ends, seeps keep on showing their wildlife value. Since they're already warm, seeps start growing spring plants like wildflowers sooner than other areas. This early growth makes seeps preferred dining spots for animals recovering from winter. Finally, because of their abundant water, seeps are important breeding areas for frogs, salamanders, crayfish, and aquatic invertebrates.

What does all this have to do with you? To provide winter food for wildlife, seeps need enough sunlight at ground level so shorter plants like sedges can grow. In woods dominated by trees that lose their leaves, that sunlight usually isn't a problem. In areas with more evergreens, though, the low winter sun can be blocked and reduce plant growth in the seep.

That's where you come in. Cutting or girdling a few evergreens around your seeps will open up the canopy and encourage ground plants.

You don't need to cut a lot of trees to benefit seeps. As a general rule, aim for 60 percent tree cover. Focus on keeping larger trees that lose their leaves as well as shorter mast-bearing trees like hornbeam and serviceberry. Remove trees like spruce that keep their needles year-round.

When cutting trees in seeps, remember that you don't want to bring equipment anywhere near the seep itself. That three-hundred-foot buffer from the last project still holds true. Because of seeps' sensitive nature, it's better to leave the cut trees on the ground rather than drag them out. Most of these trees will be too small for lumber anyway, and since they're evergreens, they'll have little value for firewood. Wildlife will get better use out of them as fallen logs or snags.

Before you head out with a chainsaw and get to work, a note of caution. Depending on where you live, your state or town may have rules limiting tree cutting in and around wetlands. Often seeps are so small they aren't covered by these laws, but it's better to do your research ahead of time rather than risk a fine. Consider contacting a local forester for advice prior to cutting trees in a seep.

Project 53. Install a Wood Duck Nesting Box

Thinning seeps is one way to make your wetlands better for wildlife, but you don't need a chainsaw to attract animals to these areas. For a smaller-scale project to do in your wetlands, try adding a wood duck nesting box.

Many ducks nest on the ground. They trust in tall, dense wetland plants to hide their eggs and young from predators. Wood ducks take a different approach. They're cavity nesters. Their natural nesting areas are hollows in trees near open water.

One of North America's most beautiful ducks, wood ducks nest throughout much of the US. A lack of good nesting sites is an issue for these water birds, so if you want to draw a few to your property, an artificial nesting box is a good way to do it.

You can buy wood duck boxes online, but it's easy to build one yourself. All the pieces are rectangles, and you can make an entire box out of a single twelve-foot long, 1" × 10" board. I've included a link to some free box plans in Beyond the Book.

The wood of choice for duck boxes is cedar. It will last a long time outside without any finishing. It's a good idea not to finish or paint bird boxes of any kind. The fumes can suffocate birds.

Wood ducks are some of North America's most attractive waterfowl. One way to encourage them to visit your pond or marsh is to install and maintain a nesting box for them. Photo credit: George Gentry, USFWS

Wood duck boxes are easy to build and a good project to help these cavity-nesting birds. Photo credit: Steve Hillebrand, USFWS

Once you've built your duck box, add four inches of fresh wood shavings or wood chips to the inside. Since wood ducks are used to nesting in tree cavities, these small wood pieces will help the box better simulate a natural nest. Be aware that shavings and chips break down over time, so replace them annually.

You can mount your wood duck box on a dead tree near open water, but a better strategy is to attach it to a steel pole that can be inserted into the bottom of a pond or marsh. The top of the pole should be about six feet above the water's surface. This pole method offers better protection from predators like raccoons not only because of its location, but also because it lets you install a predator guard such as a galvanized steel cone between the water's surface and the box.

Another advantage to the pole method is that you can put multiple boxes near each other. Unlike the territorial bluebirds from Chapter 5, wood duck females are colonial. They will nest in boxes placed even a few inches apart.

You can use this knowledge in your favor, because it means you can mount more than one wood duck box on each support pole.

Female wood ducks usually nest near the place where they themselves hatched, and they'll often reuse the same nest. If you maintain your wood duck box annually, you stand a good chance of seeing these beautiful ducks and their babies year after year.

Project 54. Help a Muskrat

I've mentioned several bird nesting projects in this book, so let's switch it up. Here's an idea for you furry animal lovers. Muskrats are rodents (though not truly rats) that weigh between one and four pounds. They live almost exclusively in wetlands, where they dine on water plants like cattails, sedges, and water lilies.

Looking a bit like miniature beavers, muskrats are sometimes considered pests. But for those who like seeing waterfowl, muskrats are a natural way to maintain open water and keep cattails from taking over a marsh or pond. Photo credit: R. Town, USFWS

A lot of articles on muskrats consider them pests and focus on how to get rid of them. But while muskrats have become invasive in Europe, here in the US they can play a positive role in wetlands. In particular, they're useful if you like seeing ducks, herons, geese, and other waterbirds. Muskrats help keep down plants like cattails that would otherwise take over the open water these birds need.

You can encourage muskrats in your marsh by providing them with nesting material. Muskrat families will construct a den along the banks of a marsh or pond using leaves, sticks, roots, and mud. Like beavers, they'll also build lodges in areas with open water two to four feet deep. You can help them establish these homes by leaving a few hay bales scattered around the edges of your pond or marsh. The muskrats will use the bales as starting points for den construction.

Project 55. Build a Pond, Step 1: Purpose

I mentioned in Chapter 2 that water typically isn't a limiting factor for wildlife. Generally speaking, you'll attract more wildlife by focusing on food or cover projects than you will building a new water feature. That said, a pond is a classic structure many property owners want. If designed well, a pond can help a variety of animals like amphibians, turtles, and water birds.

Artificial ponds don't need to be big to make a difference for wildlife. A half-acre pond is plenty large enough to have open water that will draw in ducks and the occasional heron. Even at a quarter-acre, a pond can attract land animals for a drink and support both amphibians and small fish.

Before you get too excited, bear in mind that a pond is a major project. A successful pond installation demands a lot of upfront work to figure out where it should go, what it should look like, and what permits you'll need to get it built. Once the pond is in place, more work is required to create the conditions that will make it suitable for wildlife requires ongoing maintenance to keep up water quality and retain native plants.

The first step in building an artificial pond involves no tools except your brain. Long before you call in the contractors, spend some time thinking about your pond and what you want to get out of it.

This step matters because artificial ponds fall into three rough categories: fishing, boating, and wildlife. Although some ponds can have a balance of these

A well-designed artificial pond can be a boon to wildlife, especially if your land doesn't have natural wetlands. Photo credit: National Park Service

three, ponds designed for fishing and boating are less useful for wildlife than ponds designed for animals. Why? Two reasons. First, fishing and boating ponds usually have too basic a structure to support many animals. In particular, they have too much open water and lack the complex edges and the numerous wetland plants wildlife prefer. Second, a pond stocked with sport fish is a death sentence for pond wildlife. The added nutrients from feeding these large fish can lead to algae blooms that will kill wild pond species. Even absent these blooms, sport fish themselves harm wildlife by eating amphibians and baby birds.

All this isn't to say you can't have a pond for canoeing or catching bass. It's fine to have a recreational pond on your land. Just don't fool yourself into thinking that pond is helping wildlife.

Since this book is about attracting wildlife, I'm going to assume your purpose in building a pond is to help animals. That's the pond design and construction I'll describe in this chapter's remaining projects.

Project 56. Build a Pond, Step 2: Site

Once you've decided what you want to use your pond for, the next step is to figure out where you want that pond to go. Not just any place on your land will support a pond. Broadly speaking, you want your pond in a spot where your land's contours will hold the most amount of water with the least amount of excavation. For most ponds, the preferred location is a moderately sloped area that has a low point at one end. By damming off that low point, you'll create a block that will prevent water from escaping. Surface water will then flow downhill and become trapped, forming your pond.

In addition to slope, take soil type into account when siting your pond. The underlying soil needs to be clay-based so it will hold water. Coarser soils with a lot of sand or silt will wind up with the pond water draining right through them.

If you don't know the soil types on your property, reach out to your county's Soil and Water Conservation District. They can usually provide you with a soils map and help you interpret what it means. Some districts will also test your soil to figure out what it contains and whether it can support pond construction. There may be a fee for these services, but they're worth the cost. You don't want to put in all the work of building a pond only to find that it leaks.

Beyond these soil services, it's worth involving your Soil and Water Conservation District at this point for two other reasons. First, ponds often require permits from local and state agencies. As I mentioned in the last chapter, your conservation district is a good resource for figuring out which permits you need and how to get them. Second, conservation districts can provide crucial site-specific expertise for your pond. It's fine to gain general advice and ideas from a book like this one, but for a project this complex, there's no beating an expert visiting your land and checking your pond's site and design.

If your work with the conservation district reveals that your land has no clay-based soils, don't despair. Commercial pond liners do exist, though they're typically designed for small backyard water features. For larger ponds, a better option may be bentonite, a heavy clay usually pressed between layers of plastic. Both bentonite and pond liners will add significantly to construction costs, but if you want a pond in a spot with otherwise unsuitable soil, they're your best bet.

Project 57. Build a Pond, Step 3: Design

Now that you know where you want your pond, you can think about how it will look when it's done. If you live in a colder climate where the pond will freeze in the winter, design your pond so at least part of it is more than ten feet deep. Otherwise the whole pond could freeze, killing any aquatic animals.

Within the limits of your pond site's contours, aim for a shallow-sloping design. Wading birds like herons and egrets prefer gentle slopes no steeper than one foot in drop for every six feet from shore.

Like other habitats on your property, a complex pond will provide more for wildlife than a simple one. Ideally your pond will have areas with different depths, including some shallow parts near shore as well as deeper areas farther out. It will also have a small island where animals can rest and birds can build nests.

A pond with a wavy edge like this one provides many secluded coves where different birds can nest that would otherwise be territorial with one another.

Your pond should have as much shoreline as possible. A complex, wavy pond edge with many points and coves will maximize the number of secluded areas where birds can nest and where frogs, turtles, and invertebrates can feed.

The ability to drain your pond in an emergency or for maintenance is important, so factor a drainage system into your design. Two good options are a spillway to divert water during floods and an underground drainpipe that goes from the bottom of the pond to another area of your property. The drainpipe gives you the ability to remove all the water in your pond if necessary, and some states require that you install one.

Aside from helping you meet state laws, a drainpipe can benefit wildlife too. If you took my advice and used a shallow slope for your pond, draining a few inches of water now and then will turn your pond edges into mud flats, which are prime waterfowl feeding and resting areas.

Project 58. Build a Pond, Step 4: Install

Assuming you've done your homework up to this point, the actual installation of your pond will be anticlimactic. The contractor will set up the dam, drainpipe, and any other structures according to the plan you developed with professional help. Costs vary, but budget at least $2,000 for construction assuming a small, basic pond with no bentonite or liner.

Once your pond is built, your task will be to stock it with appropriate pond plants and animals. Fish are the easiest place to start. Although sport fish will harm wildlife, minnows can be useful. They'll keep mosquitoes down, and they're preferred food for herons, kingfishers, and mergansers.

To stock minnows, first talk to your local cooperative extension office to learn which native species they recommend. Then take those species recommendations to a local licensed fish hatchery to buy the fish you want. While you're there, get advice on how to introduce the minnows to your pond. Following the hatchery staff's directions will give your minnows the best chance of surviving.

If your cooperative extension doesn't have a recommended minnow species, fathead minnows are a reliable choice. They can survive in small ponds, have a distribution across North America, and are readily available from commercial hatcheries.

As for the other animals that will make up your pond's life—amphibians, turtles, crayfish, and insects—don't worry about introducing them. These animals can travel a surprising distance over land to find new water sources, and commonly do so.

Plants are trickier. You'll need some aquatic plants to provide food for animals and produce the oxygen your water-bound critters will breathe. But if you have too many plants, you'll reduce open water habitat and make viewing the pond harder.

Like other aspects of landscaping, stick to native species when planting in or around your pond. While cattails are a common choice, I recommend avoiding them. They provide little wildlife value, and they can take over the pond. Arrowheads, bulrushes, and sedges are good general choices that have local species throughout much of North America.

That said, in most cases you won't have to plant aquatic plants. Often seeds from nearby ponds or wetlands will travel by wind, water, or birds to your pond. If you've provided a good pond site, plants will grow all on their own. Before you run out to a nursery, give your pond a growing season and see what springs up.

If you had to use a liner or bentonite for the base of your pond, you may have trouble getting wild aquatic plants growing. In this case, you can sink potted aquatic plants into your pond as a substitute for wild ones.

Finally, you can add non-living elements in and around your pond to make it more useful for wildlife. A partially submerged log or boulder will provide a sunning spot for turtles. On land, girdling a tree near the pond will create a snag that can house cavity-nesting, water-loving birds like hooded mergansers and protho-notary warblers.

Adding a partially submerged rock or log to your pond will attract turtles like these red-eared sliders by providing a sunning spot.

Project 59. Build a Pond, Step 5: Maintain

Because it's an artificial structure, your pond will need ongoing effort to maintain its usefulness to wildlife. There are three main parts to pond maintenance: soil quality, water quality, and halting plant transitions.

Soil quality might sound like something you wouldn't have to worry about in a pond, but in most artificial ponds, soil fertility falls off sharply after four years. To deal with this issue, a drainpipe that can empty your pond is crucial. Every four years, drain your pond in late winter or early spring. Mix the pond soil with all the decomposed plant material that's built up over the years. You can then let the pond refill in spring and summer.

Between drainings, keep on the lookout for algae blooms. They're a sign you have too many nutrients in your pond—a dangerous situation that can lead to fish kills. To avoid them, keep excess nutrients out of the pond. Keep livestock away from the pond, maintain a buffer between the pond and any fertilized crops, and don't mow right up to the pond's edge. Within the land that drains into the pond, maintain tree cover if possible and use BMPs on any trails.

Finally, one of your toughest tasks will be keeping the aquatic plants around your pond as aquatic plants. Over time, these plants will naturally die out and be replaced by field species and invasives like purple loosestrife. It's best not to use chemicals to control these invaders, because certain herbicides can harm water quality. Rather, rely on hand pulling to keep these plants at bay while retaining the native water-loving plants that first colonized the pond edge. You can then plant native wetland species in the gaps if necessary to replace the ones that have died.

PART THREE

CHALLENGES
TO WILDLIFE

9

INVASIVE PLANTS

"One of the penalties of an ecological education
is that one lives alone in a world of wounds."
—Aldo Leopold

I mentioned earlier how wildlife benefit from plant growth at every height in a woodland. By that measure, the woodland in this chapter's introductory photo is ideal. Look at all that green! It seems like this property would be a smorgasbord for animals, not to mention all that thick cover.

But this photo is why I chose the Aldo Leopold quote to start this chapter. As green and luscious as this photo appears, this woodland is no better for wildlife than a woods with no plants on the ground at all. It is a "world of wounds," even though it appears healthy.

This woodland in upstate New York may look like excellent wildlife habitat, but it's actually a wildlife desert thanks to a takeover by bush honeysuckle, an invasive plant.

What's going on here? The trees in the photo are native, but all that plant growth in the shrub layer comes from a single species: bush honeysuckle. This non-native, invasive plant has taken over the undergrowth. It's crowded out all the space where native plants could be growing.

Bush honeysuckle isn't the only invasive plant that can take over your property. There are hundreds of these non-native pests spread across the US, taking over areas where native plants once grew. No property is safe. Every US county has at least three invasive forest pests, and many counties—particularly in states in the Northeast and on the West Coast—have far more than that.[1]

All those invasives create a huge problem for wildlife. Despite invasive plants' prolific growth, nearly all native wildlife can't eat them. Not won't, *can't*. Recall our discussion from Chapter 2 about plant chemicals. Non-natives have chemical mixes that native plant-eaters aren't adapted to and can't digest without becoming sick or dying.

Invasive plants create another concern for both the woods and wildlife: they prevent new trees from growing. Notice in the photo above that as dense as the honeysuckle is, there's a fair bit of light hitting these woods. New trees should be growing up beneath the adult ones, but they aren't. The honeysuckle shades them out.

Many of the projects I discussed in previous chapters will fall apart in the presence of invasive plants. Japanese knotweed can take over stream restoration sites, providing little streambank protection thanks to its shallow roots. Purple loosestrife can dominate wetlands, reducing habitat for rare animals like bog turtles. And a variety of invasives from bush honeysuckle to Japanese barberry to multiflora rose can spring up in clearcuts and other tree-cutting operations, smothering the native plants you're trying to encourage.

As important as dealing with invasive plants is, controlling them isn't as simple as having at them with pruning shears. Invasives are invasive for a reason. They're tenacious survivors. Beating them back takes persistent effort over multiple growing seasons. Even then, you're unlikely ever to wipe them out. Ones you controlled may return, and many more are waiting nearby for a chance to come in.

When it comes to invasives, my approach is pragmatic. I don't aim for total annihilation. Rather, my goal is to reduce invasive plants' impacts on your property. That's about the best you can hope for.

There's a lot more to invasives than one chapter can explain, so I'm going to skip details such as species-specific identification and control. There are whole books filled with that information. I have provided the link to one I've found useful in Beyond the Book. For this chapter, I've focused on laying out a four-step system that, if followed, will give you the best chance of keeping invasives from harming the native plants and wildlife on your property. This process works regardless of the invasive plant or plants you're dealing with, though the specifics will vary depending on your local invasive mix and how big a foothold they have on your land. The general process looks like this:

1. Prevent—Keeping invasive plants off your property in the first place is the best way to deal with them.
2. Locate—Finding invasives while they're still small makes control easier and more effective.
3. Control—Dealing with invasives takes persistence and a combination of methods.
4. Restore—Ensuring native plants come back after control is vital. Otherwise you're in for a never-ending fight.

Project 60. Prevent: Use Native Landscaping

Have you heard the saying "an ounce of prevention is worth a pound of cure?" When it comes to invasive plants, truer words have never been spoken. It can be almost impossible to get rid of an invasive plant once it arrives. The best way to protect your land from invasives is to ensure they don't cross your property line in the first place.

Our first prevention method is a project from the chapter on backyards, but it's so important that it is worth repeating: use native plants in your landscaping. While some of the worst invasive plants are now illegal to sell in the US, many can still be bought at nurseries. Often there is no warning that a potential plant could take over your property.

To be fair, not every non-native ornamental will become invasive. Many are well-behaved and stay right where you plant them. Unfortunately, it's often hard to know which ornamentals will become invasive and which won't. The simplest solution is to stick to native plants.

Even if you're only planting natives, invasives can arrive in other forms of landscaping. Hay, straw, mulch, and topsoil you use in your lawn or garden are common culprits. Invasive weed seeds can hide in these products, and when you spread them around, you give those seeds the perfect opportunity to grow. To reduce this problem, buy "weed-free" versions of landscaping materials whenever possible.

Finally, you may have bare patches of soil in your backyard on occasion, that bit of planting you just haven't gotten around to yet. These exposed areas are perfect for invasives, which often have evolved to do well at colonizing areas where other plants are absent.

Putting exposed soil in your landscaping is tantamount to asking invasive plants to take it over. Consider covering the bare patch with a native ground cover or a tarp until you're ready to plant. Photo credit: Lance Cheung, USDA NRCS

You can fight this challenge by keeping bare patches of dirt on your property to a minimum. If you can't put a native ground cover down, consider covering the area with a dark-colored tarp. The tarp will prevent light from reaching the ground and discourage weeds from sprouting.

Project 61. Prevent: Clean Clothes, Gear, and Equipment after Going in the Woods

Many invasive plants have rough, burry coatings on their seeds that stick to animal fur. Wild animals walk around, pick up the seeds accidentally, and later lose them as they walk through another area.

That's how these invasive plants spread in the wild, but these same coatings can also attach to clothes, shoes, tents, and most of the other gear we take outside. Often what looks like insignificant dirt or plant shreds on your backpack are really seeds from an invasive species.

Suppose you go hiking in a nearby state park. The next day, you walk around your land. Just like that, you can introduce invasive plant seeds from the park to your property.

You can limit this spread by being careful to wipe any clothing and gear you take in the woods clean before you leave for the day. If you have a dog, check them too. It's easy for invasive plant seeds to get lodged in their fur.

Shoes and boots are perhaps the most problematic of your gear, because they can get mud and plant parts wedged between their treads. A cheap, easy tool for removing that debris is a boot brush. A boot brush is a U-shaped block with long, coarse bristles inside it. After a walk, you drag each shoe through the boot brush, and the bristles pull off the dirt stuck to your shoes.

Cleanliness matters for equipment too. Bikes, ATVs, and logging

Boot brushes like this one cost less than $30. They're cheap, easy ways to remove mud and invasive plant parts from shoes.

equipment can all get plant parts wedged in mud in their tires. Clean the tires of your bike or ATV at the end of each trip. If possible, bag the dirt that comes off and throw it in the trash. Otherwise, you could end up with invasives growing wherever you clean the tires.

Logging vehicles can be a particular concern because loggers often move equipment directly from one timber harvest to another. While you can't know what was growing on the property before yours, it's safe to assume there are some invasive plants that may have hitched a ride. When planning a timber harvest, consider requiring in your contract that all equipment be cleaned and any mud or plant parts removed before that equipment may come on your land.

Project 62. Locate: Learn to Identify Common Invasive Plants

Even if you do everything right for preventing invasive plants, sooner or later they will arrive. They may spread by wind, a stream, or a bird flying overhead. Odds are you already have at least a few on your property. If your land is near a developed area like a city, you may have even more.

Wild parsnip is a good invasive to know, and not just because it can take over pastures and old fields from coast to coast (top). The plant can be dangerous, secreting a sap that burns your skin. Identify wild parsnip by looking for a plant about four feet tall with small, yellow flowers in a characteristic umbrella-like pattern (middle). The saw-toothed leaves and yellow-green stem with vertical grooves (bottom) are also indicators.

But invasive species don't go immediately from arriving on your land to taking over. More often there's a lag—a period of months or years where the invasive grows and builds its numbers. Left unchecked, those low levels will eventually explode. Once that happens, control becomes much more difficult.

That's why it's valuable to find invasive species shortly after they arrive on your land. If you can spot them while their numbers are low, you can remove them more easily.

To locate invasive plants, you first have to know how to identify them. Unfortunately, with hundreds of invasives in North America, you can't expect to know them all.

But that's okay. A more practical approach is to learn which invasives are the greatest threats in your county and then focus on learning to identify, say, the top ten.

To help you in this tailored learning, I've provided two links in Beyond the Book. The first is a database that lists the most common invasives for each US county. Once you know what to look for, you can use the *Invasive Plants* book I've provided the link to (or an Internet search) to learn how to identify those species.

Project 63. Locate: Monitor Your Property

Learning invasive plants won't do you any good unless you apply that knowledge on your land. Regular monitoring of your property is essential for spotting infestations while they're small.

You don't have to walk every inch of your property to look for invasives, though you can if you want to. Invasive plants tend to show up in certain areas first, so checking those spots can help you spot early infestations. Pay closest attention to these high-risk areas:

- Sunny areas with exposed soil
- Near structures (such as your house, cabin, stone walls, etc.)
- Along trails and roadsides
- Along streams
- In recently disturbed areas, such as those affected by fire, storm damage, or a timber harvest

Plants that have leaves when everything else is bare are red flags to check as possible invasives. I took this photo of an autumn olive shrub in November. While the rest of this oak woodland was bare, many of the autumn olive's leaves were still green.

While you can look for invasive plants throughout the year, early spring and late fall are the best times to search. One way many invasives outcompete native plants is by either sprouting their leaves first in the spring or keeping those leaves late in the fall. If you see plants with leaves when most everything else is bare, give those plants a closer look. They may be invasives hiding in plain sight.

If you can, check your property for invasive plants twice each year, once in spring and once in the fall. If you can only do one check a year, that's fine, but two checks will help you spot infestations faster.

When you find an invasive plant, write down the species and how severe the infestation is. I recommend four categories of severity: single plant, low, moderate, and heavy. If you have a property map, mark the location on it as well.

By recording what you find, you'll gain a sense of which invasive species are more or less common on your property. You'll also learn which areas are safe, at risk, or beyond help. That information will be crucial in the next phase of dealing with invasive species, where we fight back against these would-be conquerors.

Monitoring is useful not only for finding new infestations, but also for seeing whether your control work is effective. Visit the sites of invasive control projects annually to check for regrowth, and remove those plants if possible.

Project 64. Control: Decide What to Treat

Once you've located invasive plants, it's time to decide how you'll control them. Treating invasives can be a pricey, multi-year effort, so a good first step is to choose which areas you want to tackle.

Often landowners will pick the most infested spots and treat them first. The idea makes sense. After all, if the goal is to beat back invasives where they interfere with native plants, then the worst areas are the ones to treat, right? In a sense, yes, but I don't recommend starting with the disaster zones. This has nothing to do with biology and everything to do with psychology.

In the Catskill Mountains where I work, my employer funds a cost-share program to help landowners perform certain wildlife-improving practices. One of those practices is invasive plant control. Early on in our program, we received many applications from landowners who wanted to control acres upon acres of invasives. Do you know how many of those projects succeeded? Almost none. The landowner would start the project, be stunned by how difficult it was, and then give up.

After those early failures, we switched to a different model. When we get a hefty invasive application, we trim it down. If the landowner requests funding to treat ten acres, we might fund them for one. "Start small," we tell them, "to understand what you're in for."

Changing that model has made a big difference. More of the projects succeed, and more of those landowners come back to us to do larger projects.

The lesson here hearkens back to the planning chapter: start small. If you aim for your biggest invasive problem first, you'll set yourself up for failure. That failure will discourage you, and you may give up on dealing with any invasive plants. If instead you tackle a small project, you can gain knowledge, experience, and a sense of accomplishment. Those positive emotions will motivate you to move on to larger projects.

Focusing on small, scattered, and isolated infestations is not only easier, but it also can have a greater benefit to your property. By dealing with those infestations while they're small, you can keep them from growing into a full-blown invasion.

Aside from density, there are other factors that might influence where you focus your invasive control work. If you're going to harvest timber, for instance, controlling invasives in that area before loggers arrive will reduce the invasive spread in your sunnier post-harvest woods. Areas along trails are also priorities, because roads and trails often act as corridors for invasives to spread.

Project 65. Control: Use Mechanical Removal

Now that you know which invasives you have and which ones you want to control, the next question is: how will you do it? There are lots of methods for dealing with invasives, and different tools work better or worse for different plants.

As with invasive identification, I can't go through every control method for every invasive in one chapter. In the *Invasive Plants* book I mention in Beyond the Book, you can look up species-specific recommendations.

Since I can't go into detail on specific plants, what I'll do instead is give you an overview of the major techniques you'll see when you do look up a particular species. Broadly, control techniques fall into three categories: mechanical, chemical, and biological.

Mechanical control is the most straightforward. Gardeners in the audience will be well-versed in its techniques: hand-pulling, manual cutting with pruners or loppers, and motorized cutting with tools like brush hogs and chainsaws.

When it comes to mechanical removal, getting the roots is critical. If even a scrap of root remains, it can sprout up a new infestation.

For shrubs, there are special tools designed to give you the leverage you need to yank out root balls. I've included a link to one, the Pullerbear, in Beyond the Book as an example. The easiest time to do this work is in spring when the soil is moist.

Once you've pulled up the invasive plant, you'll need to dispose of it. If you just lay it on the ground, it may grow roots and come back to life. Bag up all the parts and throw them out.

For smaller invasive plants that would be tedious to remove by hand, an alternate method is to cover them with a thick tarp held down with rocks. The tarp blocks light and prevents the invasives from producing the food they need. This method only works in small areas, and it demands a tarp that can hold up to sunlight (it can take two years for the invasives to die). This method will also kill any native plants in the area, so be prepared to plant a native cover crop as soon as you remove the tarp.

When I talk with landowners about their options for invasive plant control, mechanical methods like these consistently rise to the top as favored choices (at least at first). It's no surprise why: you aren't applying anything unnatural in the form of chemicals or new species to the landscape.

When it comes to mechanical removal, it's important to get not just the above-ground part of the plant, but the roots as well. Devices like the weed wrench seen here can come in handy, especially for woody shrubs. In this photo, a man uses a weed wrench to remove the invasive shrub jetbead. Photo credit: Ryan Hagerty, USFWS

But as popular as mechanical techniques are, they have two major limitations. First, most mechanical methods are only suitable for the smallest infestations. Second, mechanical control by itself rarely gets rid of an invasive plant over the long term. Unless you pull up and destroy every last root and branch, the plant will come back endlessly. If you mow down an invasive shrub with a brush hog, for instance, it's not all that different from an animal eating the plant. Plants are prepared for that, and many invasives sprout back quickly after being mowed.

If mechanical methods will work for your invasive problem, by all means go for them. They have the least potential for unintended negative effects, and the tools are easily purchased and familiar. Recognize, though, that there is a tradeoff for limiting yourself to mechanical methods. Larger infestations will be out of reach, and even for smaller projects, you'll likely spend every growing season keeping the invader from regrowing.

Project 66. Control: Use Herbicides (Carefully!)

I can already hear many of you saying, "No! No chemicals! No '–icides' on my land!" I understand your concern. Pesticides from arsenic to DDT to Agent Orange have caused more than their fair share of environmental and human health problems. Used inappropriately, any herbicide treatment on your land has the potential for negative impacts.

But if you think about it, that statement could apply to any tool you use or action you take on your land. A chainsaw, used inappropriately, can have disastrous consequences for your woods and your health. So can pruning shears, though it might take you a while to get there. Recreational activities like mountain biking, horseback riding, and ATVing can all leave scars if not performed responsibly.

I'm not trying to excuse herbicides or claim they're harmless. They have the potential to cause great harm, and they take knowledge to use correctly. That said, herbicides aren't something to be feared or avoided just because they're chemicals. They're tools, like chainsaws and pruners.

Like any tool, herbicides need to be treated with care and respect. Just as you should use proper protective gear when using a chainsaw, do the same when using herbicides. Wear rubber gloves, long pants, and long sleeves to avoid skin contact with the chemical. Keep water and detergent handy for washing skin that does get herbicide on it. Stand upwind of whatever you're spraying to reduce the chance that herbicide blows back on you. And most important, always read the label and apply the herbicide only in the method and dosage it prescribes.

It's actually illegal to do otherwise. In the US, it's the law that when using pesticides, you must follow the label's instructions.[2]

But as long as you follow those directions, research shows that you can use herbicides without harm to your land's wildlife. A review of sixty studies assessing the common herbicide glyphosate—better known by one of its brand names, Round-Up—concluded it had minimal if any impact on the number and diversity of songbirds, small mammals, invertebrates, and even larger animals like deer. And because glyphosate helped control invasive plants and create room for native plants, the number and variety of plants either stayed the same or increased after use, depending on the study.[3]

A lot of people have a negative view of herbicides, but when used carefully, they can be a big help in dealing with invasive plants. In this photo, a volunteer with the National Park Service's Exotic Plant Management Team uses the cut stump method to spray herbicide on a freshly cut eucalyptus tree. The invasive eucalyptus vigorously resprouts after being cut, so the herbicide is important for long-term control. Photo credit: National Park Service

I say all this because as negative a view of chemical treatments as many of us understandably have, when it comes to invasive plants, herbicides can be an acceptable option. Often they're the only option. That's why I discouraged you from using them to maintain your young woods but am all right with using them for invasive plants. For maintaining young woods, there are other options like mowing, brush hogging, and prescribed burns. But as we saw in the last project, these mechanical methods often lead to an endless cycle of treating and retreating invasive plants. Herbicides can provide a longer-lasting solution.

Realize too that when I talk about herbicides, I'm not talking about chemicals dumped from the sky. I'm talking about small amounts of herbicide delivered directly to the invasive plants you're trying to control.

One such approach is the "cut stump" method. This is the herbicide technique recommended for many woody invasives like Tree of Heaven and oriental bittersweet. In cut stump, you first cut off the plant low to the ground using a chainsaw or other mechanical tool. You then immediately follow up that cutting by using a spray bottle to put herbicide on the stump you just created. By applying herbicide right away, before the stump's cells have time to close up from the injury, you allow the herbicide to travel into the plant's roots and kill them.

With the cut-stump method, there's no willy-nilly spraying of chemicals. You don't need to coat every leaf. With surprisingly little chemical, you can achieve what would be impossible through cutting alone.

There are other variations on this cut stump theme. For larger woody invasives like trees, "hack and squirt" is an option. In this case you don't even cut down the tree. Instead you make cuts into it with a hatchet, then spray the herbicide into those cuts.

In cases where there isn't an obvious woody stem or when that stem isn't accessible—think the thorn-infested tangle of the multiflora rose—spraying herbicide on the leaves of the plant can be effective. These types of treatments have more potential for drift onto other plants than cut stump methods, but if applied by hand using a backpack sprayer in low-wind conditions, the amount of unintentional damage can be reduced. The best time to spray is in the summer, after the invasive has grown its leaves but before the leaves change color in the fall.

There are important limitations to herbicides that don't make them a cure-all for invasive plants. Perhaps the most important is to restrict any herbicide use near water bodies. Most herbicides break down naturally in a short period of time, but in a wetland, certain chemicals can linger in the water and cause problems. There are some herbicides designed for wetland use, but I encourage extreme caution with them. Because of wetlands' sensitivity, consider other alternatives before resorting to herbicide in them.

You should also under no circumstances use a home remedy as an herbicide substitute. I was talking with a forester one day, and he told me this story about a logger he'd once met. The pair of them had gotten on the subject of controlling invasives, and the logger said his favorite method was "petro." When he had a weed on his land that he needed to get rid of, he "just sprayed a little petro, and that took care of it."

Exercise extreme caution before applying herbicide in wetlands, and consider it only as a last resort. In this case on the Edwin B. Forsythe National Wildlife Refuge in New Jersey, herbicide was the only practical method to deal with a heavy infestation of phragmites, an invasive grass. Left alone, phragmites forms dense thickets unsuitable for wildlife and displaces native wetland plants. Photo credit: Chelsi Hornbaker, USFWS

At first the forester was confused. Petro? Is it a brand name for some herbicide? Was it a new herbicide he'd never heard of? It took him several minutes before he realized what the logger meant: gasoline.

I've never run into a situation that bad, but I've had landowners tell me plenty of other home remedies. The most common one I hear is vinegar, but the one I find most curious comes from a landowner trying to get rid of Tree of Heaven. He would cut the tree, then put a deer salt lick on the stump. He figured the salt would go into the stump and kill the roots to prevent them from resprouting.

When I ask landowners why they use these home remedies over commercial herbicides, the answer is usually something like, "I don't want all those chemicals on my land." Sorry to break it to you (and them), but vinegar is a chemical (acetic acid). So is salt (sodium chloride, and it's actually more toxic than glyphosate[4]).

I can understand if chemical herbicides give you pause, but you should never resort to home remedies for dealing with invasive plants. Unlike a commercial herbicide, you don't get a detailed label and application instructions for that home-brewed concoction you read about in an online forum. You don't get the benefit of extensive testing and tight control on proper dosing either.

The reality is that in the best case, the home remedy will be ineffective. If it worked, don't you think Monsanto or some other corporation would have turned it into a product? In the worst case—think "petro"—you'll do more harm than you would using a commercial herbicide.

Project 67. Control: Remove Vines

Often a combination of mechanical and herbicide control is more effective than using either one by itself. An example of this dual control technique is when you want to deal with woody, tree-climbing vines like oriental bittersweet.

Both invasive and native vines can damage trees. As the vines grow, they put pressure on tree branches and restrict those branches' growth. Over time the vines get heavier and heavier. Eventually the weight becomes too much for the tree to support, and limbs break off. In severe cases, vine-covered trees can become so top-heavy that the whole tree can fall down.

To deal with vines, start by cutting them off near the ground. That will kill the vine in the tree and gradually allow the tree to recover. Smaller vines may be cut with pruners or loppers, but larger, woody vines may need a saw.

When making the cut, cut first around chest height, and then make a second cut at ground level. This two-cut approach will reduce the chance that resprouting vines could reattach to and restore the cut vine. Take care to avoid damaging the tree's bark when cutting.

It might sound crazy that a vine could damage a tree, but vines get surprisingly heavy. The invasive vine oriental bittersweet (left) can grow over six inches across, and a single tree can have dozens of vines climbing it (right).

Cut vines only during times of the year when leaves aren't on the tree. Otherwise the sudden increase in light can scorch tree leaves.

For native vines like poison ivy, Virginia creeper, and grapevines, cutting them is all you need to do. The remaining root structure will send up new growth, but it will be a while before that growth is large enough to threaten your trees again.

When it comes to invasive vines, in particular oriental bittersweet, long-term control requires more than cutting them. Bittersweet grows as a shrub on the ground before climbing a tree, and it has an extensive root system that allows it to spread across the woods to find more trees to scale. Those extensive roots mean that pulling these shrubs rarely works. It's simply too hard to get every last bit of root.

For that reason, using herbicide is the only practical way to gain lasting control of bittersweet. The simplest method is the "cut stump" approach from the last project.

This paired cutting and spraying works well for many other invasives too. The cutting provides immediate control of the existing plant, and the targeted herbicide provides longer-lasting control. By doing the initial cutting and removal mechanically, you reduce the amount of chemical you have to use. And by applying small amounts of herbicide, you save yourself countless hours of hard labor.

Even so, vine removal isn't as straightforward as attacking every vine you see. Although removing vines can protect trees and control an invasive plant, it can also harm wildlife if done too zealously. That's because native vines provide food for wildlife. Grapevines, for instance, produce small grapes favored by many animals. Even poison ivy berries are edible for some birds. If you wipe out these vines in your woods, you'll remove an important food source as well.

While native vines can be troublesome (especially the fuzzy poison ivy pictured on the left), they have wildlife value. Poison ivy produces white berries (right) that often persist through the winter. Over sixty bird species are known to eat these berries, and they provide a valuable winter food for birds that don't migrate. Photo credits: National Park Service

For this reason, exercise discretion when cutting native vines. There's usually no need to remove them unless they've taken over more than 25 percent of a tree's canopy. Before that, they'll be small enough that the tree should be fine supporting the extra weight. Beyond that level, the tree is at risk of broken limbs or toppling.

Oriental bittersweet is another matter. As a Chinese native, its foliage provides little wildlife value, and its rapid growth and heavy weight make it especially damaging to trees. Have no worries about cutting it.

Project 68. Control: Bring in the Goat Cavalry

I've mentioned several times how most plant-eaters feed on just one or a few kinds of plants.

But not all plant-eaters are so picky. Some will eat just about anything. A handful of these general eaters are domesticated, which makes them ideal for biological control, the last method of dealing with invasives that we'll discuss.

In biological control, you rely on some other living thing to deal with your invasive situation. When it comes to invasive plants, one animal has risen above the rest: goats.

Goats offer several advantages for dealing with invasives. First, they're small. That means they're less likely to churn up the soil and cause erosion problems or damage tree roots the way larger livestock like cattle would. Second, they don't require you to

With their voracious appetites and willingness to eat many kinds of plants, domestic goats can be a cost-effective solution to areas of your land overrun by invasive plants. Photo credit: Pixabay

spray chemicals. Third, they have no fears about eating invasive plants—even those covered in thorns.

And finally, they can eat. Oh, they can eat. A herd of two dozen goats set loose in an invasive-dominated area can clean out an otherwise impossible-to-treat spot in days.

Goats have proven so effective at dealing with invasive plants that they've been used to clean up the Congressional Cemetery in Washington, DC.[5] When the area around the cemetery gets overgrown, the nonprofit that manages the cemetery rents goats from a local farmer to deal with the situation. The cost is about $5,000, not a small investment. Still, the nonprofit estimates that the price works out to about $1 per goat per hour, which is cheap compared with hiring a professional to come in and remove the weeds.

That said, goats do have a major drawback. Because they will eat just about anything, they won't consume only the invasive plants. They'll eat most native plants too. Goats aren't a good choice for controlling an invasive plant here or there. Rather, they're best suited to major jobs, areas of your property overrun by invasive plants.

If you want to control invasive plants with goats, it probably isn't worth you becoming a goat farmer. Instead, look into goal rental companies. Yes, they exist. These farmers transport their goats from place to place, using portable fencing to block goats in the invasive-infested area. They make money through rental fees as well as selling goat milk, cheese, and meat. The best way to find one in your area is with an Internet search for "goat rental [your state]."

When you hire a goat farmer, the process works something like this. The farmer first sets up temporary fencing around the area you want treated. Then they bring the goats to your land and let them have at it. Once the invasives are knocked back, the farmer packs up the goats and fencing and leaves.

Sound crazy? Maybe. But as a way to deal with the toughest invasive problems in difficult terrain without resorting to herbicides, goats are hard to beat.

That said, keep in mind that goats are like some mechanical invasive treatments in that they only remove the above-ground part of the plant. Roots and seeds remain in the soil, ready to spring back to life. To fully control the invasive, you may need multiple goat visits. Alternately, you may be able to follow up the goats with spot mechanical or herbicide treatments to deal with the plants that resprout.

Project 69. Restore: Replant and Monitor

You've done all this work and knocked back invasive plants in a part of your land. A lot of people stop here, thinking the job is done. But it isn't. Remember, invasive plants thrive on disturbed land. That bare patch you just created is perfect for new invasive plants to take over. Before you can consider yourself victorious over invasives (for now), your last step is to ensure native plants come back in the area you just treated.

If you spot-treated your invasives, native restoration is easier. You'll already have native plants growing nearby that can provide a seed source. Even so, consider replanting the treated area with a native seed mix or native plants from a nursery. This replanting is more important in cases where you used a large-area treatment, such as goats.

If you can't get native plants in the ground right away—perhaps because it's the wrong season to plant them—do what you can to keep invasives from gaining a foothold. If the treated area is small, cover it with tarps to block light and prevent invasive seeds from sprouting.

This strategy won't work if you treated multiple acres. For those situations, time your control efforts so you can plant native species immediately after you finish knocking back the invasives.

Monitoring treated sites is also important. As the natives sprout, invasives may come back alongside them. They may be new plants from seeds left in the soil, or they could be sprouts from plants you controlled. When you see them, pull them while they're still small to keep them from getting large enough to stifle the regrowing natives.

Finally, be aware that replanting may not be enough to hold invasives at bay. As troublesome as invasive plants are, they're often merely a symptom of a bigger problem in your woods. Invasive plants usually take over because something else on your land is preventing native plants from growing. To truly restore native plants and keep invasives at bay for the long term, you need to figure out the root cause of these successful invasions and deal with that. At the very least, you need to reduce the effects of that cause within the area you're trying to restore to native plants.

But if invasive plants are a symptom of another problem, what is that problem? While there are several possibilities, the most likely culprit is the cute, brown, antlered one we'll talk about next.

10

OH, DEER!

"Nature has introduced great variety into the landscape,
but man has displayed a passion for simplifying it.
Thus he undoes the built-in checks and balances by
which nature holds the species within bounds."
—Rachel Carson

When landowners tell me they want to see more wildlife, often what they mean is they want to see more deer. And who can blame them? Whether you hunt or not, there's just something about deer. Maybe it's their size. Maybe it's the antlers. Maybe it's that classic Disney movie.

I'm no exception when it comes to excitement over deer. I get a rush whenever I see one. Even though I know the challenges deer can cause, I can't help but smile at the sight of one bounding between the trees.

Unfortunately, deer can also be a threat to other wildlife on your land. When deer become too numerous, they cause severe and lasting damage to native plants and even other animals. But deer aren't an invasive species. They're native. So how is it they can be a threat to your land?

In truth, it's not the deer's fault. It's ours. Since the European colonists set up shop in the New World, people have done a remarkable job of wiping out natural top predators like wolves and cougars. These are the species that once preyed on deer and kept their numbers in check. Other predators like black bears, bobcats, and coyotes will kill fawns, but attacks on adults are unusual.[1]

There's no arguing that deer are beautiful, majestic wildlife. But when they get too numerous in an area, they can do major damage to the woods and remove habitat for other animals. Photo credit: N. and M. J. Mishler, USFWS

When the wolves and cougars went away, so too went natural predator control on deer populations.

Thanks to the elimination of predators and the creation of tighter hunting laws, deer numbers soared through the twentieth century. By one estimate, we have more deer in the US today than were here before Columbus sailed.[2]

But isn't that what this book is about? Getting more wildlife? Yes, but the issue is that as deer numbers rose, their numbers increased beyond what the woods can support. In turn, that eliminated food and homes for many other creatures.

Deer need a lot of food to survive—about four to eight pounds of plant material every day. In the plentiful summer and fall, they meet that need with relative ease through fruits, nuts, new growth, and farm crops.

As the weather turns cold, those options go away. To make up the difference, deer turn to less nutritious sources like tree seedlings, twigs, and buds. Because these foods have fewer nutrients, deer eat more of them to make it through lean winter months. As deer numbers increase, woods can't keep up with that need. The low-growing plants start to disappear. With them go those ground and shrub layers that are so important for wildlife.

These effects can linger for decades, even after deer numbers return to normal. By eating tree seedlings, deer prevent new trees from growing. As older trees die, new ones aren't around to replace them. Even if deer numbers later go down, the woods can be missing decades' worth of trees.

That was the result of a series of long-term experiments in Pennsylvania. Even in areas with deer numbers lower than those occurring in many US woods, deer caused major declines in multiple tree species as well as the virtual elimination of shrubs.[3]

Often we don't see this damage on our own properties. It's only when we put a check on deer numbers that we realize the impact they're having. Consider Yellowstone National Park, which reintroduced wolves in the 1990s. Almost immediately, that action had a huge effect on the park. The wolves killed some of the deer, and they forced the remaining deer to stay on the move. As a result, areas that had been barren from overbrowsing resprouted. With that new growth came new habitat for birds, beavers, bears, otters, and a host of other species. These positive changes occurred because reintroducing wolves kept deer numbers at levels the landscape could support.[4]

It's unlikely we'll see the reintroduction of top predators like wolves and cougars in much of the US anytime soon. Our task, then, is to find ways to address deer that will let our woods and their wildlife flourish. We just can't rely on nature to do it. It's up to us.

Yellowstone National Park reintroduced wolves in the 1990s. The wolves provided a check on large plant-eaters like deer and elk. In turn, areas of the park that had been barren resprouted, creating new habitat for wildlife. Photo credit: National Park Service

Project 70. Assess Deer Impact with a Simple Visual Assessment

Plenty of landowning hunters have told me, "There's no way my property has too many deer. I hunt every year, and most days I don't even see one." At the risk of questioning those hunters' skills, seeing deer or not is a poor way to judge how many deer use your property or the impact they're having. A single deer will range over hundreds of acres, and their camouflage makes them easy to miss.

A more reliable approach to assess deer impacts is to look not for deer directly, but for indirect signs of their presence. In my previous book, *Backyard Woodland*, I described a method of counting deer pellet groups to estimate the size of your local deer herd. That method works, but it requires some complex field measurements and math. And while it can give you a number, it can't tell you the impact those numbers are having on your property. An area with a lot of deer food can support more deer than an area without much food.

For this book, I decided on a more straightforward deer assessment. It involves simply walking your woods and looking at the plants growing from the ground up to about eight feet in the air—the range deer can eat in.

Don't worry if plant identification isn't your strength. While I'll mention a few plant species, there are broader visual conditions that will reveal deer impacts. As long as you can separate conifers (trees with needles) and broad-leaved trees (trees with regular leaves), you can do this assessment. By the end of your walk, you'll have a sense of whether your land has a low, medium, or high deer impact.

What you're hoping to see, if deer aren't a problem on your land, is complexity in the undergrowth. You'll see a variety of shorter plants including herbs, shrubs, tree seedlings, and saplings.

By contrast, an area with too many deer will be simpler, with little undergrowth. What undergrowth you do see will be the few plant species deer don't like, often invasive shrubs or hay-scented fern.

Beyond these general conditions, there are more specific indicators that suggest how much deer impact your woods. Some of the best indicators are spring wildflowers like white trillium and wild lily-of-the-valley. These wildflowers are often the first plants to emerge in the spring. They take advantage of the bright light on the ground before the tree leaves come out and block the sun.

A woods with low deer impact will have diverse and abundant undergrowth (top). One where deer numbers are too high will be simpler, lack undergrowth (bottom), or be dominated by a few deer-resistant species, often invasive plants.

Just because your woods are green doesn't mean deer aren't a problem. Deer simplify the woods, leaving the plants they don't like to take over, like the hay-scented fern in this photo. Ground cover dominated by a single type of plant indicates high deer impact. It may look pretty, but it provides little for wildlife, and it offers few chances for new plants and trees to grow. Photo credit: National Park Service

Because of their early growth, spring wildflowers are particularly vulnerable to deer hungry from the winter. If you walk your woods in the spring and see wildflowers without having to look for them, that's a sign deer aren't an issue on your land. If you can only spot the occasional flower, that indicates at least low to medium deer impact.

Tree seedlings are another useful deer indicator. Deer will often turn to seedlings' succulent young branches for winter nutrition. As deer numbers increase, the tree seedlings can't keep up with all the hungry mouths. Sugar maple seedlings are especially telling, since deer like them and they grow well even in shaded woods. If sugar maple grows on your property, look for its seedlings in the undergrowth. If you can't spot them, or if the few around can't get above six feet tall, that indicates at least medium deer browse.

Spring wildflowers like this pink lady's slipper are some of the first plants to disappear when deer numbers grow too high for the woods to support.

Other good tree seedlings to look for are American beech and conifers. In these cases, seeing browse on them is a particularly concerning sign, because deer don't like beech or conifers. They'll eat other foods first and only turn to these species when they have no other choice. If you see deer browse on these species, then that indicates medium or high deer impact, because you've already lost many other native plants.

Species aside, the height of tree seedlings and stump sprouts from year to year is one of the most revealing ways of assessing deer impact. In a low deer impact situation, seedlings and stump sprouts will get taller each year. As deer pressure shifts into medium levels, those seedlings and sprouts stop getting taller and instead become shorter over time. Their new growth can't keep up with deer eating them. Look especially for cases of "witch's brooming," where

When deer impacts reach a medium level, shrubs and tree seedlings will often take on a bushy "witch's broom" appearance, shown here in the shrub on the right. Photo credit: Manfred Mielke, USDA Forest Service, Bugwood.org

seedlings take on a bushy appearance. This shape indicates deer pressure is enough to prevent these plants from growing taller.

As deer pressure shifts from medium to high, looking for native species becomes unproductive. They will all have been eaten. If invasive shrubs like Japanese barberry dominate your land, that's a symptom of high deer pressure. Invasives have a much easier time gaining a foothold when deer have cleared out the natives first. When deer are browsing these invasives, that's an even clearer sign that deer numbers are out of control on your land.

Structural conditions in your woods can also give a clue as to levels of deer impacts. One of the most telling is to seek out areas on your property where deer can't reach, such as the top of a large boulder. If you see plant growth in these deer-free areas but not in the woods around them where deer can reach, that is a clear indicator of high deer browse.

Perhaps the most extreme sign of high deer impact is a browse line—a clear, horizontal line through the woods below which nothing grows. In this case, deer are so numerous they have literally eaten everything within reach. For these situations, it's no longer a question of whether your property has too many deer. The issue instead is that the deer stand to die of starvation from exhausting all the available food.

I've thrown a bunch of indicators at you, and not all will apply to your property. Use the ones that make sense for your landscape. To help you out, here's a simple list including not just the indicators above, but a few others you can look for:

Low Deer Impact Signs
- Abundant undergrowth in a variety of species and forms.
- Short wildflowers plentiful and blooming in early spring.
- Tree seedlings, saplings, and stump sprouts grow taller each year.
- Sugar maple seedlings are abundant (if they grow in your area), and at least some are able to grow above the reach of deer.
- Young conifers have branches close to the ground.

Medium Deer Impact Signs
- Broad-leaf seedlings, saplings, and stump sprouts stay the same height or get shorter from year to year.
- Small trees and shrubs take on a bushy "witch's broom" appearance.
- Conifer seedlings like pines, spruces, and hemlocks show signs of deer browse.

High Deer Impact Signs
- Undergrowth is bare, sparse, or dominated by a few species, usually invasive plants or hay-scented fern.
- American beech leaves, stems, and twigs show signs of browse.
- Conifer saplings take on a "lollipop" appearance, with no branches or needles below six feet.
- A clear difference in plant growth exists between areas of your property where deer can and can't reach.
- Invasive plants like Japanese barberry show signs of deer browse.
- Open areas of your property that would naturally transition to shrublands or woods (such as old fields you no longer maintain by mowing or brush hogging) remain open for more than a decade.

Depending on the results of your visual assessment, your next steps will vary. If you only have a low level of deer impact, you can just keep doing what you're doing. Deer numbers aren't consistent from place to place. Your property may be one of the lucky ones that isn't dealing with overabundant deer. It's also possible that you're already doing some of the practices we'll talk about that help keep deer numbers in balance with what the woods provides.

If your survey reveals medium deer impact, then deer are harming your property, but not yet in a catastrophic way. You should start doing the projects in the rest of this chapter to address deer, but you should also keep up your visual monitoring over time. Also consider doing the pellet count method I described in *Backyard Woodland*. It can give you a more precise estimate over time of whether your local deer herd is increasing or decreasing. If it's going down, your property likely won't have deer issues in coming years. But if it's going up, you're headed for problems unless you take action.

If you find signs of high deer impact, then your property is being significantly harmed. Native plant and wildlife numbers are lower and less diverse than they could be, especially in the areas near the ground. Invasive species will have an easy time taking over if they haven't done so already. In the event of a disturbance like logging, fire, or an insect outbreak, your wooded areas will have a difficult if not impossible time renewing themselves with young trees to replace older ones that die. For all these reasons, you should take immediate steps to start addressing the size of the deer herd using your property. The rest of this chapter discusses projects to do that.

Project 71. Stop Feeding Deer Corn

To see more deer, some people put out food for them, usually corn. Often people feed deer in winter believing that, as with feeding birds, they're helping deer get through lean months.

Unfortunately, feeding deer isn't like feeding birds. It's bad for the deer, bad for other wildlife, and bad for your property.

Let's start with the most surprising: feeding deer harms them.[5] How's that possible? First, it's well-established that deer will congregate around feeders in densities unheard of in the wild. Those high densities raise the risk of disease.

One of the worst mistakes you can make trying to help wildlife is to feed mammals like deer. It teaches them to lose their fear of humans, a situation that often ends badly for both the animal and people. Photo credit: Pixabay

Specifically, chronic wasting disease—the deer equivalent of Mad Cow—is easily spread between deer gathering at feeders.

Even if disease doesn't spread, deer face harm in other ways from feeders. Unlike birds, mammals fed at feeders become dependent on human-provided food. They lose their fear of humans and become tame, at least until someone doesn't offer them food. These situations often end badly, occasionally with people injured and the animal needing to be put down.

Finally, although deer will eat corn from feeders, corn isn't good for them. Often deer can't even digest it. As a result, deer lose more calories traveling to and from feeders than they gain by eating corn. In still other situations, the bacteria in the deer's gut can react with the corn to produce an acid strong

Some people feed deer because they think they're helping deer survive the winter. Unfortunately, these well-meaning people are harming, not helping, both the deer and the land. Photo credit: Pixabay

enough to eat through the lining of the deer's stomach. That damage can lead to diarrhea, dehydration, and death.[6]

As for the harm to your land and other wildlife, that damage comes from deer congregating on your property. By drawing in deer, you'll wind up with more deer eating more of the undergrowth in your woods. As those plants disappear, with them will go understory birds like the ovenbird. You'll also harm pollinators by losing spring wildflowers, and you'll leave your property more vulnerable to invasive plants.

Because of all these dangers, state wildlife agencies across the country advise people not to feed deer or other mammals (the same problems exist for bears, raccoons, moose, etc.). In several states, including my home state of New York, feeding deer is illegal.

If you currently feed deer out of the sense that you're helping these poor creatures, know that you're hurting them instead. To really benefit deer, ditch the corn and focus on providing quality habitat through apple tree pruning, food plots, and increasing undergrowth in your woods. These natural foods are far better for deer than corn, and they offer the extra benefit of helping other wildlife too.

Project 72. Take Care with Hinge Cutting

Another way to provide natural food for deer is a specialized type of tree cutting called "hinge cutting." In hinge cutting, you fell small broad-leaf trees, usually those of sapling size (trunks less than six inches wide). But instead of cutting all the way through the tree as you would in traditional felling, hinge cutting leaves a narrow strip of uncut wood on one side. Because the tree is small, you can then push it over by hand or, for added safety, with a long pole.

A correctly hinge-cut tree won't die. Instead it will keep growing, because water and nutrients can still flow through the small section of uncut trunk. In addition, most hardwoods will grow sprouts from a cut stump. Together, all this plant growth means more food for deer close enough to the ground for them to reach it.

Hinge cutting leaves a tree alive by partially cutting it so it falls without severing the stump from the tree. The tree then keeps growing, providing food for deer. For safety reasons, limit hinge cutting to small trees like the one shown here.

Hinge cutting works best where you have broad-leafed trees and little undergrowth. Avoid hinge-cutting conifers, as these trees provide little deer food and don't sprout from the stump the way many broad-leaf trees do. Also, conifers are more useful for deer as winter cover. That said, if you have an area of broad-leaf trees next to a dense area of conifers, hinge cutting some of those broad-leaf trees will make for good deer habitat.

The trick to successful hinge cutting is to open up the canopy enough for the cut trees to get sunlight. If they're lying on shaded ground, they won't be able to keep on growing. Be prepared to cut as many as a third of the trees in an area to open it up enough for hinge cutting to work.

Although hinge cutting can provide more deer food, it does have limitations. First, it's not a project for the novice chainsaw user. Tree felling by itself is dangerous; logging is the deadliest job in America according to the US Department of Labor.[7] But hinge cutting is more dangerous than traditional logging, because it violates some of the safety techniques that loggers use. Topping that list is that since you have to stand beside the tree to push it over, you're at risk of being hit by the falling tree. Hinge cutting also puts the tree at a high risk for what's known in logging as a "barber chair," in which the trunk splits midway through the cut. This dangerous situation sends the trunk flying up toward your face, and then the top of the tree crashes down on top of you.

Because of these safety risks, it's paramount that you stick to small trees when hinge cutting. You should also have solid knowledge and experience felling trees before you attempt a hinge cut.

Beyond safety, hinge cutting's other limitation is that it's a short-term solution to a long-term problem. Adding food to your undergrowth will help, but if you have too many deer, those hinge-cut trees won't reduce their numbers. Eventually you'll be right back where you were with few plants in the undergrowth and little habitat for other wildlife. So while hinge cutting can be part of your strategy to deal with deer, it shouldn't be the only step you take.

Project 73. Keep Deer Out with Tree Tubes

As any gardener who has struggled with deer eating their plants can tell you, it's hard to keep deer out of a place they want to get into. If you want to keep deer off your undergrowth, prepare for some considerable expense and effort.

One common way gardeners try to keep deer off their plants is with commercial or homemade repellents. There are plenty of these out there, from soap to egg-water to human hair. Despite the stories, the reality is that these repellents typically don't work. At best they'll last a few days, and then you need to reapply them. That's a lot of work. Adding to the frustration, deer will become used to scents or repellents that you put out in the same place over and over. At that point, the repellent becomes worthless.

You'll need something longer-lasting than a repellent to protect young trees from hungry deer. For individual plants, tree tubes can work well. These tubes are plastic cylinders about five feet high that surround seedlings to protect them from deer. They're held in place by zip ties wrapped around a wooden stake or piece of rebar. Here in upstate New York, we've had success using tubes to keep deer off trees we plant along streams for water quality protection.

Tree tubes work well for protecting a few seedlings, like in this reverting field edge in Connecticut. Photo credit: Paul Fusco, USDA NRCS

Tree tubes aren't a one-and-done project. Each year in early spring, remove the tree tube and clean out any debris that's built up inside it, especially mouse nests. You can also prune smaller branches coming off lower on the tree seedling to speed its vertical growth. Once you've finished this work, put the tree tube back on the tree.

Tree tubes should remain on seedlings until they're a foot or so taller than the tube itself. At that point you should remove the tube so it doesn't prevent the seedling from getting wider.

Seedlings may still be vulnerable to deer at this point, though not because of chewing. Instead, bucks may use your seedlings to scrape the velvet off their antlers, an act that strips the bark off young trees.

Bucks scrape off the velvet on their antlers by rubbing them against trees. This scraping can peel the bark off young trees and kill them (left). To protect your young trees from buck rub, install a plastic mesh bark protector (right) after you remove the tree tube. Photo credits: USDA Forest Service–North Central Research Station, USDA Forest Service, Bugwood.org (left); author photo (right)

You can limit this damage by installing a plastic mesh bark protector around the base of each seedling. Leave the bark protector on until the tree trunk is four to six inches across. I've included links to sample tree tubes and bark protectors in Beyond the Book.

Project 74. Keep Deer Out with Deer Fencing

Tree tubes work best in small situations where you only have a few young trees you want to protect. Once you get beyond a few dozen seedlings, tubes become impractical. For situations with more trees, such as a shelterwood or small clearcut, a better option is to install a deer fence around the area.

Deer fences are temporary fences. They're installed in places where you want to grow native plants, especially trees, but where local deer numbers won't allow those plants to survive.

Historically, deer fences' main use was around timber harvests designed to get young trees growing, such as shelterwoods. They're useful in lots of other situations, though, like invasive plant control sites, blowdowns, and insect infestations. They remain in place for about ten years, and then they're removed once new plants inside the fence grow beyond the reach of deer. They come in a variety of materials, from cheap plastic mesh to more expensive metal boxwire.

In general, the tradeoff for cheaper fence materials is that they need more maintenance. Falling limbs and trees can flatten weaker fence materials and allow deer to enter the fenced area.

That said, the cost of installing a high-end metal fence adds up quickly. About ten years ago we installed a

This metal boxwire fence protects a white pine planting in southeastern New York. You can attach the fence to existing trees if they're available. If they aren't, you can install metal, cedar, or pressure-treated posts (cedar was used here). Note the cross-bracing to give the fence extra support.

Temporary fencing is expensive, but it keeps out deer and allows seedlings to grow. In this picture, young trees have come up inside the fence (left), while hay-scented fern, which deer and most other animals don't eat, dominates the area outside it (right).

high-end metal fence around a nine-acre shelterwood harvest at a demonstration woodlot here in the Catskills. It cost almost $20,000.

The reason deer fences are so expensive is that they need to be robust. Deer are amazing jumpers, so fences need to be at least seven feet tall. The fence also needs to be tight against the ground. Otherwise deer could crawl underneath it and get inside the protected area.

The payoff of a well-installed fence, though, is tremendous. Beyond keeping out deer and helping native plants grow, fencing also helps counter invasives. In the northern Lake States, University of Wisconsin researchers found invasive plants were twice as numerous outside deer fences as they were inside them.[8]

There's even evidence that some invasive plants aren't all that invasive—as long as deer are kept away. That's what UC-Berkeley researchers discovered in Pennsylvania and New Jersey hemlock forests. Across ten sites, tree seedlings inside deer fences grew faster and outcompeted Japanese stiltgrass and barberry. Outside the fences, those invasive plants dominated the woods.[9] The research's conclusion was simple. Reduce deer pressure on native plants, and those natives may well outgrow the invasives.

For all their benefits, both fencing and tree tubes have a serious drawback: they're a spot solution. The areas outside them will remain vulnerable, and once the tubes or fence come down, the area they protected will again get munched. The new trees may have grown tall enough to avoid hungry deer, but the spring wildflowers and shrubs won't be so lucky.

There's no getting around it. The only long-term way to get and keep the diverse undergrowth plants that will provide food and cover for the greatest variety of wildlife is to reduce the number of deer. Doing that requires a willingness to take an emotional step: increasing hunting on your land.

Project 75. Hunt (Or Allow Hunting)

The experiences of Yellowstone National Park reintroducing wolves illustrate the importance some form of deer population control has for benefiting other wildlife species. Yet in most parts of the country, we don't have and won't likely have top predators anytime soon. As a result, we face a tough ethics situation in the woods. If we want to protect wildlife in all its variety, we have to be willing to shoot deer.

This isn't about shooting trophy bucks either. Buck hunting does nothing to control deer populations, because one buck can impregnate many females. To reduce deer pressure on your land, doe hunting is essential.

But is there really no alternative to hunting? Unfortunately, there isn't. Deer biologists agree that there is no effective non-lethal method to lower deer numbers. Capturing and relocating animals is expensive, impractical, and usually leads to the moved animals dying anyway because of stress. Darting and sterilizing does is similarly infeasible due to costs and the difficulty of catching enough deer to make a dent in the population.[10] In one study from Cornell University, catching and performing a tubal ligation on a single adult doe cost $1,000.[11]

If you're a hunter, and you find your land has medium or high deer impacts based on your visual assessment, I encourage you to try to fill at least one doe tag on your land annually. The effect won't be instant, but over time, deer surveys suggest that concerted efforts to fill doe tags result in more stable deer populations, better woodland regrowth, and better trophy bucks.[12] Why? Because with less pressure for food sources, deer are healthier, put on more weight, and can grow larger antlers.

If you aren't a hunter, that's ok. I know lots of people who are uncomfortable with the idea of shooting an animal. Even so, if deer impact is high on your land, consider letting someone you trust, perhaps a neighbor or family member, hunt your property. Request that that person fill a doe tag before they shoot a buck. You'll help your woods recover, promote a greater abundance of wildlife, and ultimately support a stable, healthy deer population.

Hunting, especially doe hunting, is important for keeping deer numbers on your property in balance with the food the land can provide. Photo credit: Steve Maslowski, USFWS

Project 76. Donate Venison

Even when hunters recognize that deer overpopulation is an issue, many are reluctant to take the extra step of shooting more deer. Aside from the time and effort involved, there's a sense that it's wasteful to shoot more deer than a person needs to fill the freezer with venison.

Yet hunting remains the most effective tool you have for lowering deer impacts on your property. If you want to address deer problems without feeling like you're being wasteful, consider a venison donation program for the additional deer you hunt.

States across the country have donation programs. Program details vary, but they generally work like this. You bring the deer you want to donate to a state-approved butcher. The butcher handles the meat processing and supplies it for free to participating local food banks. The food banks then distribute the meat to families in need. Often, state hunting license fees compensate butchers for their work so the hunter donating the venison doesn't have to pay anything out of pocket.

Venison donation can make a big difference for those in need. The meat from just one donated deer can provide up to 200 meals.[13] In 2010, a national study on venison donation found that hunters donated almost 2.8 million pounds of venison to food shelters through these programs. That's enough to supply eleven million meals.[14]

If you want to find a venison donation program near you, the National Rifle Association has a map of butchers and food banks that take part in its Hunters for the Hungry initiative. I've included a link to the map in Beyond the Book.

Project 77. Accept Predators

Before we leave this chapter, there's one concept beyond deer impacts that I hope the past few pages have made clear: predators aren't evil. For centuries, that's how we've regarded them. Wolves in particular have long been the villains of our fairy tales. For many years it was commonplace for states to offer bounties to hunters who killed them. The same is true for cougars and grizzly bears. The results were predictable: all these species were nearly exterminated.

The days of bounties may have ended, but hostility toward predators hasn't gone away. In his 2013 book *Wildlife & Woodlot Management*, author Monte

Burch discusses predators in the same section as poachers. He begins his predator chapter with the sentence, "Predators and pests are common problems with land managed for wildlife; you can't have one without the other."[15]

This prejudice exists in state game laws too. In my home state of New York, the rifle season for deer is about three weeks long from sunrise to sunset. A regular hunting license will only let you take one buck; you need a special license if you want to take a doe.[16] By contrast, the season for coyotes lasts nearly six months, and hunters are free to shoot as many as they want at any hour of the day or night.[17]

Targeting predators this way can be catastrophic for your land and the wildlife that use it. Wildlife biologists describe top predators as having a "cascade effect" on plants and other animals. Remove the predators, and prey species become unnaturally abundant. In turn those prey species eat more, decimating plant variety and inviting invasive species to take over.

This isn't to say you should set up birdfeeders to expose birds to hawks or remove predator guards from your wood duck boxes. Yes, when you do those projects, it makes sense to protect the creature you're trying to help. But as for actively going out and trying to remove predators from your land, don't do it. They're a critical part of the woods. If the prey species on your land can't survive in the face of predators, that isn't the predators' fault. It usually means your land isn't providing enough of what those prey animals need to thrive: a diverse structure of native plants. Focus your efforts not on getting rid of predators, but on helping your woods develop more cavity trees, mast-bearing shrubs, healthy streams, and the many other habitat pieces we've discussed in this book.

Predators like the coyote pictured here are often considered pests. But predators play an essential role in keeping plant-eater numbers in check. If predators are an issue on your land, focus on improving the quality of your land for wildlife rather than trying to get rid of predators. Photo credit: National Park Service

11

KEEPING OPEN
SPACE OPEN

*"I think having land and not ruining it is the most beautiful art
that anybody could ever want to own."*

—Andy Warhol

While invasive species and deer can harm your woods and the wildlife that rely on them, at least these threats leave your land open for animals to use. That's why as serious as these threats are, neither is the biggest threat wildlife face. The greatest danger to North American wildlife today is that the space they depend on is slowly vanishing beneath a sea of asphalt and concrete.

Development threatens wildlife with a host of dangers. Fences and buildings restrict animals' movements, especially larger creatures with big ranges. Developed areas have far fewer standing or fallen dead trees compared to woods, contributing to low bird numbers.[1] The arrival of more people also means the arrival of pets, including outdoor cats, which devastate wild animals.[2]

Beyond these direct impacts, development leads to other problems for wildlife. Breaking up the woods with homes, lawns, and driveways removes interior woods habitat by creating openings. That makes woodland birds susceptible to predators like raccoons and parasites like the brown-headed cowbird. More homes and people also raise the chance of wildfire happening. Every six hundred homes built near lands prone to wildfire add on average another fire

One of the most important things you can do to protect wildlife on your land is to ensure that land remains open and undeveloped.

per square mile per year.[3] Finally, all that paved surface speeds up runoff and adds pollutants to water supplies, leading to poorer water quality, more severe floods, and lower stream levels during dry summer months.[4]

What makes these problems especially severe is their permanence. It's conceivable that a woods with too many deer or with an invasive plant problem could be restored through diligent effort. Once land is built on, though, it

The loss of open land to development happens gradually, so it can be hard to imagine that your land might someday be paved over. But when viewed over a longer time, the changes are striking. These two aerial photos are of the woods around Alsea Bay in Oregon. The one on the left is from 1954; the one on the right is from 2000. The lighter colors in the 2000 image show development, much of which replaced forest cover. Photo credits: US Geological Survey

almost never becomes undeveloped. That's why one of the most important steps you can take to help wildlife is to keep your land as intact, undivided, and free of construction as possible.

That doesn't mean you can't or shouldn't have a home or cabin on your land, but you should take steps to limit how much development occurs. Minimize the amount of road or driveway you put in. Reduce lawn space. Locate your home closer to the road, in an already open area, rather than creating a new gap in the woods.

It's also helpful to take steps to make it less likely that your land will be developed in the future. Most landowners want to see their land continue as open space. Without planning, that desire can be lost due to unforeseen circumstances and ownership changes.

That's why, for this chapter, we're shifting gears. We won't talk about deer fences, nest boxes, or native plants. Instead, we'll look at some of the social and economic factors that drive landowners to give up on land ownership—factors that lead to houses growing where fields and trees once did.

Let me be clear up front that these topics are complex, more complex than a single chapter can handle. My purpose in writing this chapter is to make you aware of both potential threats and options to address them. If after reading this chapter you want to discover more about these options, I recommend picking up my first book, *Backyard Woodland*. In it I devote a chapter to each of the three projects I discuss in this chapter, so you'll get more information and ideas for next steps.

Project 78. Enroll in Your State's Property Tax Reduction Program

Of the threats your land faces, taxes—especially property taxes—may be the biggest. That's because the leading cause of landowners selling their land isn't great offers from construction companies. It's financial pressure, with taxes and health-care costs recognized as the two most common problems that push landowners into selling.[5] There isn't much I can tell you about reducing health-care costs. When it comes to taxes, though, there are ways to lower your tax burden.

Every US state has some form of property tax incentive for landowners. The requirements and tax reduction amounts vary, but they're all geared toward making taxation on open land more in line with what the land can produce.

The reason these programs exist is that traditional property taxes base your land's assessment on how much it's worth for development. That's typically a much higher number than what it's worth as open land—at least from a financial perspective. But because the public gets value from your land just by you keeping it undeveloped (wildlife habitat, cleaner water, and scenic views to name three), states have a motivation to keep property taxes low on undeveloped land.

That doesn't mean these programs are free money. A few states offer breaks to all open space, but in most cases these are voluntary programs. Often you must meet certain requirements like agreeing not to develop your land for a set period of time. Other requirements may include following a management plan, limiting subdivisions, and in a few cases allowing public recreation access.

Even though these programs lower landowners' tax burdens, a shocking number of landowners have no idea the programs exist. A national US Forest

Financial pressure, especially property taxes, is the leading driver of landowners' selling their properties. Though not for everyone, state property tax reduction programs for woodlands may help you hold on to your land rather than chunking it up for house lots.

Service survey found two-thirds of landowners had never heard of their state's program, even though many programs offer property tax breaks of 50 percent or more.[6]

The program in your state may or may not be for you, but if you don't know it exists, you won't be able to make that decision. Take some time, do some research, and find out what your state offers. I've included links in the State Resources appendix to information about these programs to get you started.

Project 79. Get a Conservation Easement

Even if expenses like property taxes and health-care costs are no problem for you, there's still an unfortunate reality we all have to face: we don't live forever.

About 40 percent of woodland owners today are over sixty-five. That's double the figure for the general population.[7] You can protect wildlife on your land while you're around, but to benefit wildlife for the long term, you have to think beyond your own lifespan.

The strongest commitment you can make to keeping your land open for wildlife while retaining that land in private ownership is to donate a conservation easement. Easements are voluntary, permanent contracts between you and a nonprofit group (commonly called a land trust) to keep your land undeveloped forever.

To explain easements, think about all the rights you have as a landowner. You can build a cabin. You can farm. You can hang a bird-feeder. You can simply enjoy the view. Key to easements is that you can also give away or sell these indi-

The US Forest Service estimated in 2012 that the country's developed area will increase by 41 to 77 percent by 2060, resulting in the loss of up to thirty-four million acres of forested land.[8] A conservation easement can ensure your land never becomes a subdivision like the one pictured here. Photo credit: Lynn Betts, USDA NRCS

vidual rights exclusive of one another. Some landowners, for instance, sell hunting leases to sportsmen. They aren't selling the land, just the right to hunt on it.

Easements work the same way. You donate the right to develop your land to a land trust, who then agrees in a contract not to exercise that right. You still own the land. Depending on the easement's terms, you can still enjoy the property for hiking, hunting, timber harvesting, and other uses. It's just the ability to develop it that goes away.

Easements are almost always "in perpetuity," which means they carry beyond your ownership to every future owner. The easement becomes part of the property's deed and can not be revoked. As far as wildlife protection goes, there's nothing stronger than the permanence an easement provides.

Aside from the wildlife benefits, easements come with a few financial benefits to make up for your inability to develop the property. Often there's a big tax refund associated with easements, because the donated development value is a charitable donation. Some states will also let you take an income tax credit if you have land in a conservation easement. Depending on your situation, lower property and estate taxes are possible too.

All that said, easements aren't for everyone. First, many land trusts will only accept easements from larger properties, often those with more than one hundred acres. Second, because easements stay with the property, they can be an issue if your heirs want to do something different with the land. Before you get an easement, talk with your family and decide together if it's something you want to pursue.

If you decide to obtain an easement, the first step is to contact your local land trust. Most of these groups are small and focused on specific areas, so they're usually approachable. The Land Trust Alliance certifies land trusts across the US, and I recommend working with one of these organizations if possible. I've included Land Trust Alliance's list of accredited land trusts as a link in Beyond the Book.

Once you pick a land trust, the process works a lot like selling a house. There will be meetings to talk about what both you and the land trust want out of the easement. An appraiser will estimate the easement's value. Contract negotiations will shift that value as well as define the easement's terms.

The whole process can take a long time. In the Catskill Mountains where I work, a typical easement takes two years from initial contact to closing. That might sound like a long time, but it gives you many chances to think through your decision and make sure it's the right one.

Project 80. Plan Your Legacy

Even if you decide an easement isn't for you, part of the easement process is useful for every landowner: talking with your family about your land's future. That discussion takes a lot of forms, from the practical to the emotional. On the practical side, who will the next owner or owners of your land be? Will it pass down to one of your children? Will it be shared among several heirs? Will it go up for sale?

Then there are the emotional challenges. Are your children as committed to your land as you are? Do they even have an interest in the property, or will it be a burden for them?

These are all difficult questions to answer. It's hard to sit down with your children and talk about what will happen when you're gone. But as challenging as these discussions are, they're of vital importance. Decisions will get made even if you do nothing, and those decisions often aren't what you or your heirs would prefer. If you die without a plan in place, a judge will choose what happens to your assets, including your land. They use state rules called intestacy laws that divide your assets in the manner the government thinks is best. The only way to avoid that is to have a plan.

Lawyers refer to this plan as an "estate plan," but I prefer the term "legacy plan." Legacy planning includes the practical documents of an estate plan like a will and power of attorney, but it also addresses the emotional questions. It involves passing not just your land but your passion and vision for it to the next generation. No matter how much land you own, legacy planning is a critical process for ensuring your land and the wildlife it supports will be around even when you aren't.

A good place to start your legacy planning is to write down your wishes for your land. In a perfect world, what would you see your land looking like twenty, fifty, even a hundred years from now? If you have a spouse, each of you can write these wishes separately and then share them.

Once you have your broad wishes, bring in your heirs and talk to them. I know family meetings can be stressful, but open, honest conversation is key to limiting conflict. Have a face-to-face get-together, avoiding the emotional holidays if possible. Consider having each heir write down what they value in the land and what they see as their vision for it. Share these wishes as a group. You may find there's more agreement than you thought there was.

There aren't "right" or "wrong" answers for legacy planning. The best decision is the one that's best for your family. From a wildlife perspective, though, some outcomes are better than others. For example, passing land undivided is better than splitting it up into smaller parcels. As I hope you

If a formal meeting about your land's future is too emotional, a lower-key approach can be to get the family together for a walk around the land. On the walk, memories and stories will naturally come out. You may also find it easier to start a conversation about what you all want to see happen to the land when you're no longer able to take care of it. Photo credit: National Park Service/ Paula Alexander

saw with both grasslands and interior woods, bigger is better when it comes to land. Your heirs will have more options both for wildlife projects and for income (say, from timber harvesting) if the property is kept whole.

Don't be afraid to think outside the box when it comes to legacy planning. There are a lot of options for passing land intact, from trusts to LLCs to conservation easements. Some of these options can take years to enact even after you decide as a family what to do. That's why no matter what you end up deciding, the sooner you start the conversation about it, the better.

PART FOUR

MAKING IT LAST

12

FINDING FUNDING

*"Plans to protect air and water, wilderness and
wildlife are in fact plans to protect man."*
–Stewart Udall

What I hope the last chapter made clear is that attracting and protecting wildlife aren't one-and-done efforts. If your goal is to help wildlife, it's not good enough to help them for six months or a year or even ten years. You need to think long term. For the final chapters of this book, I'd like to build on that idea and talk about ways you can make helping wildlife into a lifelong (and then some) pursuit.

For many landowners, money limits their ability to take on certain projects. Some wildlife projects are cheap, but others can turn expensive in a hurry. If you have gobs of money lying around, cost may not be an issue for you. Most landowners I know, though, could use a helping hand now and then.

Major wildlife projects like stream restoration can be expensive and challenging. State and federal cost-share programs provide funding and advice to help you get the result you want. Guidance from the US Fish and Wildlife Service helped restore this stream so it could support brook trout again. Photo credit: Ryan Hagerty, USFWS

Fortunately, there are numerous local, state, and federal programs that can help you finance wildlife projects. They aren't free money. They usually require you to do and maintain certain practices on your land for a length of time. But if you already have a project in mind, some of these programs might align with what you want to do and could help you achieve it.

Most of these programs are cost-share programs. They're designed to offset some but not all project costs. No one is going to pay you to improve your own land, but they might fund some of the expense.

Before we dive into these programs, be aware that they all suffer from chronic underfunding. Competition is high. Although you probably won't see it written on official websites, bigger properties have a better chance of getting funded. The agencies who run these programs get more conservation bang for the taxpayer's buck by working with larger projects.

That said, don't despair if your application gets denied. These programs often fund projects in rounds, and there's usually more funding coming down the road. Tweak your application based on any feedback and try again next year.

Working in your favor with these programs is that most landowners have no idea they exist. Nationally, 67 percent of landowners know nothing about these programs, and just 8 percent have ever participated in them.[1] Simply by reading this chapter, you're gaining a big advantage in getting funds.

There are more programs out there than I can describe in one chapter. Many are state or local initiatives, so listing them all would be a waste for you anyway. What I'll cover here are some of the major national programs that lots of land-owners are eligible for. For more ideas, contact your state's woodland owner association. I have links to each of these groups in the State Resources appendix.

Let me stress up front that all the programs described in this chapter are voluntary. You are under zero obligation to use them. If the idea of working with a government program bothers you, feel free to skip this chapter.

Regardless of your politics though, I encourage you to at least consider these programs. Having worked with many of them in my career, I can say as an outsider that they and the people who run them do, in most cases, want the best for you, your land, and wildlife. For all these programs, you aren't giving up any land rights by participating. There may be some term contracts, but none of the programs below force you to sell your land, give it to the government, get an easement, or allow public access.

Project 81. Get a Management Plan: The Forest Stewardship Program

For decades, conventional forestry wisdom was that the first step in caring for your woods was to have a professional forester write a forest management plan for you. These plans identify the different types of trees on your property according to species, size, and how tightly together they're growing. The forester then uses that information to recommend certain practices to steward your woods over time.

This planning process can be expensive. Foresters' costs for time, travel, and field measurements all add up. A typical management plan can cost more than $1,000 even on a small property.

To help landowners with that cost, the US Forest Service oversees the Forest Stewardship Program. The program provides grants to state governments, which in turn hire foresters to develop free or low-cost management plans for landowners. In some states, these plans are called stewardship plans.

Exactly what goes into a management plan varies. While there are federal rules saying what the plans need to include, those rules are broad. My first job out of college was reviewing management plans, and they differed wildly depending on who wrote them. Some were short and boilerplate. Others were as thick as this book. They all met the program's guidelines, but some foresters did a better job than others.

To this day, management plans are touted by most forestry professionals. In recent years, though, this traditional paradigm has been questioned—including by myself. Traditional management plans tend to focus on timber harvesting, so I find they're less useful for landowners interested in wildlife, privacy, and aesthetics.

Most plans I've read are also more technical than a typical landowner needs. I've had many landowners tell me that they got a plan, but they never used it.

They tried to read it, got overwhelmed, and gave up. They put the plan on a shelf, and a year later couldn't find it.

In general, I think the traditional management plan with its detailed measurements is unnecessary for most landowners. It's expensive, time-consuming, and ultimately no more useful than cheaper options like reading books or paying a forester to spend a day walking with you on your land.[2] You can develop your own plan using some basic

Unless you have a strong interest in timber production, a traditional forest management plan will probably be overkill for your property. It can still be valuable to have one though, because it's often a requirement for other funding programs.

knowledge of plant identification, a walk in the woods, and the ideas I laid out in Chapter 3. The plan you create will be more useful than something technical by a consultant, and it will better reflect your values.

That said, you should still consider getting a traditional management plan for your land. Why? Because since it remains the paradigm, a management plan is often required before you can be eligible for cost-share programs. For instance, more than half of state programs to reduce woodland property taxes require that you have a management plan.[3] And while a few of these programs will accept a plan you write yourself, they're the exception. You will generally need a plan prepared by a professional to meet the standards of whatever program you're applying for.

To get started with a management plan, contact your state's Department of Natural Resources or similar agency. Although the Forest Stewardship Program is federally funded, it's carried out by the states. I've included links to these agencies in the State Resources appendix.

Another good starting point is your state's woodland owner association. They may be able to tell you who to contact at your state agency. And whether you participate in the Forest Stewardship Program or not, they may be able to recommend a forester or provide you with a list.

Project 82. Get Paid to Protect Your Streams: The Conservation Reserve Program (CRP)

I've tried in this book to avoid technical jargon and acronyms—especially acronyms. Conservation loves its acronyms. I work in this field, and even I get overwhelmed by the alphabet soup of agencies, organizations, and programs. So I apologize in advance for the deluge of acronyms coming in this chapter. But when it comes to specific government programs, there's just no avoiding them.

The Conservation Reserve Program (CRP), along with the related Conservation Reserve Enhancement Program (CREP, see what I mean about the acronyms?) is the oldest federal program for landowners in the United States. The program started in the 1950s under another name as a way to reduce soil erosion off farms. It's evolved through multiple Farm Bills into the program that exists today.

At its core, CRP is about protecting streams. It pays farmers annual rental payments in exchange for retiring streamside land from crop production for ten to fifteen years. This "reserved" land is then planted with native streamside plants. That buffer creates wildlife habitat, reduces soil erosion, and lowers the amount of farm pollutants like fertilizer that can reach the stream.[4]

Not only is CRP the oldest conservation program for private landowners, it's also among the largest. Nationwide, about twenty-three million acres on more than 350,000 farms are enrolled.[5]

If you aren't a farmer, then CRP isn't for you. The program requirements include that the set-aside area be or recently have been used for agriculture.

If you are a farmer, I urge you to look into CRP. It may take a few acres out of production, but the annual rental payments help make up

The US Department of Agriculture's Conservation Reserve Program pays an annual rental payment to this Minnesota farmer to leave a native grass filter strip (right side of photo) around a wetland rather than planting corn in that area. The filter strip protects water quality and provides food and cover for grassland wildlife. Photo credit: Lynn Betts, USDA NRCS

the lost revenue. Plus, you get the benefit of a healthier stream and streamside area that will support more wildlife.

To get started with CRP, a good first step is to visit your local Farm Service Agency (FSA) office. FSA is part of the US Department of Agriculture, and they have local offices across the country. I've included a link to an FSA office locator in Beyond the Book.

Your local FSA office is great for more than CRP. They usually also house local Natural Resource Conservation Service (NRCS) and Rural Development staff (both also part of the Department of Agriculture). All those agencies together make your local FSA office a one-stop shop for learning more about other conservation programs you may be eligible for. While you're meeting about CRP, talk about your land and situation. There may be opportunities the staff are aware of that you could benefit from. Even if you don't sign up for anything, at least you'll know what you're passing up.

Project 83. Get Help with On-the-Ground Projects: The Environmental Quality Incentives Program (EQIP)

CRP may only be for farmers, but the Environmental Quality Incentives Program (EQIP) is open to any landowner as long as you're either a farmer or engaged in "forest management." While I would argue over the definition, forest management under EQIP usually means that you harvest timber.

EQIP is a case where having a management plan comes in handy. A plan is your proof that you are managing your woods as opposed to wantonly logging them.

The agency that oversees EQIP, the NRCS (remember them?), has its own requirements for management plans. If you don't have a plan already, it can be helpful to talk to them first and make sure whatever you get will qualify you for their programs. If you already have a plan, meet with your local NRCS staff to see whether it qualifies, and if not, what changes you need to make.

EQIP funding helped the owners of this farm in Saco, Maine convert their inefficient sprinkler system (left) to a modern one (right). The change allows the farm to use less water on its crops. Photo credits: Wayne Munroe, USDA NRCS

Why would you go to all this work? Because in addition to its broader applicant pool, EQIP funds more practices than CRP does. EQIP funds can be used for projects as diverse as wildlife habitat improvement, renewable energy, and conversions from traditional to organic farming, among other things. Different states often have different eligible practices. Check with your local NRCS office to see what projects are going on in your area.

EQIP also differs from CRP in how you are paid. With CRP, farmers get annual rental payments for longer-term contracts. With EQIP, you get a one-time cost-share payment to do a certain project. The money helps offset costs like purchasing materials and hiring a contractor. In most cases the funds are a reimbursement, which means you'll only receive the funding after the job is finished. There are exceptions for certain groups like veterans and beginning farmers that will let you get some funding up front.

Don't forget that EQIP is a cost-share. For most projects, the money won't cover the full project cost.

The NRCS has a "Get Started with NRCS" page on its website that I've provided a link to in Beyond the Book. It gives an overview of the steps you should take to go from thinking about a project to getting funding to doing the work on the ground. If you're interested in EQIP, give that link a read, then head to your local FSA and NRCS office.

Project 84. Get Technical Advice and Funding for Habitat Restoration: Partners for Fish and Wildlife Program

CRP and EQIP are run out of the Department of Agriculture. By contrast, the Partners for Fish and Wildlife Program (hereafter referred to as "Partners") operates out of the US Department of the Interior. Specifically, it's run by the Fish and Wildlife Service. Where CRP and EQIP focus on lands in active production, Partners is open to any private landowner.

Partners focuses on wildlife, and it mainly funds restoration projects. Wetland and stream restorations are high priorities, especially where they benefit threatened and endangered species.

The US Fish and Wildlife Service oversees the Endangered Species Act, so it's no surprise that the agency's Partners for Fish and Wildlife Program looks to protect at-risk species. This Partners project funded the installation of a metal gate at the entrance to Trout Cave in Franklin, West Virginia. The gate prevents people from going inside the cave where they might disturb the endangered Indiana bat. Photo credit: Joe Milmoe, USFWS

Partners is like CRP in that it requires a longer-term commitment to maintain the funded practice. That commitment is typically at least ten years. More like EQIP, though, Partners pays a cost-share for expenses you incur during the restoration process. As with EQIP, you will need to complete the work first and then be reimbursed.

As nice as the cost-share is, the real benefit to Partners is the technical help the Fish and Wildlife Service provides. They'll help you design your project so it meets your and your land's needs.

If you want to explore the Partners program, a good first contact is your state's coordinator. I've included a link to a Fish and Wildlife Service contact information map in Beyond the Book.

Before you contact them, have some idea of what your habitat project might be. Also figure out what money, equipment, and labor you can contribute to the project. You don't need all the details, but having a general idea will help the coordinator figure out whether your project is a good fit. If it is, that person can help you start the funding process.

Project 85. Get Low-Cost Seed for Food Plots and Tree Planting: The Wild Turkey Federation's Conservation Seed Program

The federal government isn't the only group with programs for landowners. Both state and private groups offer myriad programs. Usually they're tailored around specific interests, like hunting.

If your interests align with a particular group's, these programs offer several advantages. First, there's the obvious: you're working with a smaller agency or nonprofit, not the federal government. Politics aside, that means you're in for less paperwork and bureaucracy.

These programs also offer greater flexibility. They're often willing to work with smaller acreages and projects than the big federal programs. Finally, competition for these programs can be lower, so you have a better chance of getting help or funding.

As I said before, there are too many programs for me to list them all. One larger example is the Conservation Seed Program run by the nonprofit

The owner of this Jackson County, Iowa farm made his property better for wildlife by adding this food plot that includes trees, shrubs, and grasses. The Wild Turkey Federation's Conservation Seed Program may be able to help you develop similar food plots on your land. Photo credit: Lynn Betts, USDA NRCS

National Wild Turkey Federation. This program provides low-cost and in some cases free conservation seed mixes. At times you can also get lower cost tree seeds, seedlings, and supplies to help create young woods habitat.

You need to be a Federation member to get the seed, and timing and availability will differ by which state and chapter you're in. I've included a link in Beyond the Book to more information about the Conservation Seed Program so you can see if it's for you.

Granted, National Wild Turkey Federation is a hunting organization. Part of the reason they want to protect turkeys is so there can be future turkey hunts. But don't let that be a turnoff. Hunting organizations are also some of America's most active conservation groups. If you're using their seed mixes to grow food plots and plant trees, the end result is still more wildlife habitat.

Project 86. Connect with Local Groups for More Opportunities: Urban and Community Forestry

If you only own a suburban backyard or a couple acres in the country, your chance of getting funding from the big federal programs is essentially nonexistent. You're better off saving your time rather than plowing into their lengthy applications. But another group of programs may have options for you. They're called urban and community forestry programs, and they're a growing area in conservation.

Urban and community forestry efforts are smaller and run at a state or local level. What they're called, how they work, and what projects they fund vary, so there's no one easy definition I can give to describe them. Depending on your area, these programs might give away tree planting supplies, help neighbors

Tree planting support is a popular urban and community forestry program. This planting was done in a streamside area in the developed community of Yorktown Heights, New York.

coordinate projects across property lines, or offer native plant gardening advice. There are many other possibilities too.

Because of the prevalence of lawn in developed areas, tree planting is an especially popular activity for urban and community programs. Maryland's Backyard Buffers program is a great example. Maryland has a lot of smaller landownerships, and a big issue for them is that mowed lawns often extend to the banks of streams. As we discussed in the streams chapter, that practice leads to water pollution from fertilizer, chemicals, and sediment. Planting native trees and shrubs along the streams can help, but each individual landowner doesn't own much stream length.

A massive program like CRP or Partners is a poor fit for this broken-up landscape. Backyard Buffers scales those stream restoration efforts down to a level that makes sense. Homeowners with streams can contact their county forester to sign up. Instead of a cost-share, Backyard Buffers sends them twenty-five free native tree and shrub seedlings all suitable for planting near water. The homeowner also gets instructions on how to plant and care for the seedlings.

Granted, each project in Backyard Buffers doesn't do much for water quality and wildlife habitat. But taken together, those projects add up to a lot more native trees and better water quality in streams.

Backyard Buffers is a statewide effort in Maryland, but many urban and community projects are funded by towns, cities, or nonprofit groups. Advertising budgets are usually small, so groups rely on word of mouth. The best way to discover these local options is to connect with a conservation group in your area. Conservation District offices and county extensions are always good starting points, but don't be afraid to seek out local nonprofits like chapters of the Audubon Society. I've included a link to an Audubon chapter map with contact information in Beyond the Book.

Even if there's no formal program available, connecting with these groups can help you find others who are interested in wildlife. And who knows? Aside from getting project ideas, you might find volunteers to help you get those projects done.

13

MONITORING YOUR WORK

"Watching ourselves and watching the world are not in opposition;
by observing the forest, I have come to see myself more clearly."
—David George Haskell

You've done the hard work. You planted some trees, installed some nest boxes, maybe even restored a section of stream. That's great! But how do you know those efforts paid off? How can you tell if all the time, money, and effort you've put into helping wildlife is making a difference?

Monitoring your projects is a critical—but often overlooked—part of supporting wildlife on your property. Granted, it's not as satisfying as completing an on-the-ground project. It's an ongoing effort with no "finish" to celebrate, and in the beginning it can feel like droll, useless sciency stuff.

But if you can work past that initial reluctance, monitoring can be the most fun part of the process. It's your chance to get out there and enjoy the fruits of your labor, to see and hear the wildlife you worked so hard to help. I urge you not to view monitoring as a tedious task but as a pleasant reward.

In that spirit, the monitoring projects in this chapter might not find their way into official scientific recommendations. They're not about taking measurements. They're about simply becoming more observant of your property and what's going on with it.

You've worked hard to improve wildlife habitat. Now comes the reward: getting out there and seeing the results of your work. Photo credit: Pixabay

Project 87. Keep a Nature Journal

The most important part of monitoring is writing down what you observe. It's easy to walk your property and see what you come across. But how do you compare those sights with a walk at the same time next year, or five years from now? Many wildlife projects take years to reach their full potential. That's a long time to remember the details of every walk. If you write down what you saw, you can look back to those notes months or years later.

That's what nature journaling is: a running record of what you see and experience on your land. It can take a variety of forms, but it usually combines writing, drawing, and photographing nature.

I understand if that sounds intimidating. The first time someone introduced me to nature journaling, I thought, "There's no way I can do this." It didn't help that my teacher was a fantastic artist and naturalist. Her decades of journals were filled with detailed, lifelike renderings of plants and animals I'd never heard of. She made it even harder by stressing that the point of a nature journal was to record things exactly as they happened, without embellishment. For the kid told by every teacher I ever had that "he can't draw," nature journaling as this artist described it was beyond anything I could hope to do.

That was in 2014. A year later, I met another woman who nature journaled, and she changed my view on it forever. She showed me pages from her nature journal. They were stick-figure sketches of her dog playing amid ferns and rocks as he chased a chipmunk. She talked about how she always knew when the chipmunks were active because of the way her dog behaved. Her journal wasn't technical. It wasn't great art. It was simply a way for this young woman to capture an outdoor moment in whatever way she could.

And that is the true essence of nature journaling. Don't sweat it if you "can't write" or "can't draw." Nobody has to see your nature journal. Forget any worries about "doing it right." The point isn't perfect accuracy, but to record what you see and experience outdoors.

You can do that in any number of ways. When I nature journal, I use a combination of field notes and photographs. I start with the easy stuff. What's today's date? What time is it? Where am I? What's the weather like? What temperature is it? These questions may seem basic, but by writing them down, I accomplish three things. First, I get over the "blank page" fear. I'm already writing before I even realize it. Second, answering them puts me in the observation mindset. I make a conscious effort to notice the humidity or what the clouds are doing. And third, so much in nature revolves around season, time of day, location, and weather. Recording this information now will help you later connect your observations with what's going on in the world around you.

Encourage the kids and grandkids in your life to nature journal too. It's something anyone can do, no matter how much or little talent they have with writing, drawing, or identifying animals or plants. Photo credit: Brett Billings, USFWS

With the basics jotted down, the question is always, *what should I observe?* The answer is simple: whatever captures your attention! Again, nature journaling isn't about covering every detail. It's about recording what you noticed so that months and years later, you can look back and remember.

A more technical nature journal would avoid reflection and only discuss what's actually happening. I personally don't like that approach. I encourage you to let your emotions and reflections find their way into your nature journal. Recording your mental state, as well as what you observe, will help with recall later. As a bonus, you'll get the well-documented mental health benefits that come with journaling.

When you start nature journaling, you may find it easier to focus on things that don't move, like flowers. That will give you more time to sketch and write. When you progress to journaling about animals, it's often easier to start with a sketch or photo. Animals won't stand still while you write about them. Nab a quick drawing—however terrible-looking—while you have a chance.

This approach is especially useful for birds. Noting general shape and discerning features like colors or tufts will help with identification if the bird flies away.

Your nature journal doesn't have to be all observations. It can also pose questions. The simplest may be, "What did I just see?" Write this next to your sketch of the plant or animal you couldn't identify. When you go back inside, you can use a field guide or online key to figure out what it was. Identification in the field is overrated. Focus instead on getting the best description you can, and worry about identification later.

Other questions could be broader. Seeing a beaver lodge might start you wondering about how the lodge works, or how many beavers use it, or whether it might actually be a muskrat nest. These questions can prompt further research.

You don't even have to venture outside or off your back porch to nature journal, though obviously I recommend doing so. You can nature journal about what you see in your backyard through a window. Which birds are visiting the feeder, and at what times? Try recording major weather events like storms and snowfalls. How many inches of snow did your land get this winter? When did the first snow of the season fall? How does that compare to previous years?

Nature journaling can be fun, but it becomes useful for monitoring if you do it regularly and over months or years. You could journal about what's going on at your new pond, or the site of a stream restoration, or a timber harvest. Looking back through those journal entries years later will give you a picture of how your actions have influenced the life on your property.

Project 88. Do an Egg Carton Observation

Perhaps nature journaling's greatest benefit is that it improves your observational skills. One way to develop these skills further is to do special journal entries called "egg carton observations."

In an egg carton observation, you choose something tiny to journal about. The only rule is that your subject has to be small enough to fit inside one of the divots in an egg carton. An insect, flower, leaf, or a fungus on a scrap of

Individual flowers make good subjects for egg carton observations. They're small, intricate, and won't run away from you.

bark are all good examples. Start with a sketch, focusing on the details. Next, write about the object and its role in the broader woods. Where did you find it? What is it part of? What does it do? Write down the species if you know it, but don't worry if you can't identify your subject.

The more egg carton observations you do, the better tuned your senses will become to details in nature. Eventually, things you would have blown past will start jumping out at you (figuratively), and you'll want to stop and notice them.

Once you learn to spot the little things in nature, you'll find that no two walks outdoors are ever the same. You will always see something odd, something different, something you've never seen before. It's a constant joy.

Project 89. Use Photo Points and Time Lapse Photos

Even at its best, nature journaling is subjective. You're choosing what to write or draw on any given day. A more objective way to track changes is to use photo points. Photo points are places where you take a picture from the same location time and time again. As the months and years pass, you can see things that happen more slowly than the eye can observe: plants growing, species changing, and streams shifting, to name some.

Key to photo points is taking them from the same spot every time. When deciding where to site a photo point, choose a location that will be easy to remember and where growing plants won't obstruct the camera's view. The ideal situation is to place your camera on a long-lasting feature of the area. That way the camera is guaranteed to be in the same position every time you return. Fenceposts are ideal for this purpose, and large boulders can also work well. If you don't have something like that, consider getting a tripod. Write down exactly where and how you set it up so that next year, you can do the same thing again. If you have a compass, write down the direction the camera was facing so you make sure you get the same field of view next time.

Also important is to take the photo in the same way, at least to the extent possible. Use the same camera and camera settings. Again, write this information down so you remember it from year to year. Do your best to go out at similar times of day and in similar weather.

When you bring your photo back to the house, make sure it has the date recorded. Create a single folder for all the pictures taken from the same photo point, and label it based on what you're recording. For example, you might have a folder for "logging job on the side-hill" or "lawn feathering in the backyard."

The payoff for this diligent recording comes when you stitch your photos together into a single time lapse sequence. As you look back over months and years of images of the same spot, you can see your property respond to a change or recover from a disturbance. I often encourage landowners to use photo points in areas that have experienced a fire, insect outbreak, wind storm, or timber harvest. Often these changes look horrible when they first appear, but over time, nature shows its resilience. Plants fill in the space. Wildlife comes

Photo points are great for seeing how your land recovers after a distur-
bance like logging. Lassen Volcanic National Park in California planned
to thin some of its woods to reduce fire hazards. The top photo was taken in
2007 before the harvest, while the bottom one was taken in the same spot
in 2013 after cutting finished. The park's photo points showed how logging
removed the smaller trees that could have spread flames into the crowns of
larger pines. Photo credits: National Park Service

back. These changes occur over years, so it's easy to miss them and focus on the negative. By using photo points, you can track your land's recovery and see how it bounces back often stronger than before.

You can also use photo points to observe changes on a smaller scale. A recently-dead tree is a good example. If you come across one in the woods, take a photo of it. Keep photographing it once a season or so. Over time, you'll see the decay process at work. Cavities may form. Mushrooms may grow. In the upper branches, a hawk or eagle nest might appear.

When the tree falls, your photos will shift to the ground. Now you might observe salamanders or a fox den. Through your photos, you'll discover how death in the woods cycles around to new life.

Project 90. Learn Bird Calls

One of the most frustrating aspects of monitoring wildlife projects is that it can be hard to see the animals you're trying to help. Most wildlife fear humans. They'll run, hide, or fly away at the first sign of your approach. In addition, animals often have better senses than we do, so they usually notice you before you notice them. Combine those two traits, and it can seem like your property is devoid of life, regardless of the work you do.

One way to get around this challenge is to learn not just to identify wildlife, but the signs of their presence. Bird calls are a superb example. Many woodland birds, for instance, keep a low profile. While a few like the summer tanager sport brilliant colors, still more are drab and unremarkable.

Consider one of the more common songbirds in North American woods: the warbling vireo. During the summer breeding season, warbling vireos can be found in woodlands from coast to coast, from Mexico to northern Canada, and from sea level to more than ten thousand feet.

As common as warbling vireos are, good luck spotting one. They hang out in the treetops where they forage for caterpillars among the leaves. More problematic, their olive-gray belly and brown wings and back blend in with the woods' dappled browns and greens.

But though you may never see a warbling vireo, you stand a good chance of hearing the male's lively, rollicking song. During the breeding season, male warbling vireos sing their lengthy tunes as they defend their territories and attract mates.

You may not see the many drab woodland birds like this warbling vireo, but by learning their calls, you can get a better sense of which species are using your land. Photo credit: Dave Menke, USFWS

By learning bird calls like the warbling vireo's, you can get a feel for which birds are using your property. You can even get a sense of which areas different birds prefer, based on where you hear them singing. If you have an open, shrubby area, stand in it on an early spring morning. Which birds do you hear? Now move into the deeper woods. What calls reach your ears now? I'd bet you'll hear some in one place that you didn't hear in the other.

There are loads of bird call learning aids available. The two I've found most useful for novices are the Peterson Guide's *Birding by Ear* CD sets and Larkwire, an online bird call game. Both are helpful because aside from playing the bird calls, they provide useful mnemonics to aid recall. They also group similar-sounding birds together to help you learn the differences between them. I've used both products and enjoyed them both. I've provided links to them in Beyond the Book.

Project 91. Learn Other Wildlife Signs

Bird calls aren't the only wildlife signs you can learn. For mammals, you may hear the occasional call, but in general, tracks and scat are more reliable signs. And yes, by scat, I mean poo.

It sounds gross, but every animal does it. More valuable for you, every animal does it in a different way based on its size, diet, and digestive system. If you can stomach the learning process, scat can tell you not just what animal left it, but how long ago and even whether that critter is in good health.

In the same way, an animal's tracks can tell you more than just what left it. Veteran deer hunters know that does have wider hips than bucks, so while a buck's rear tracks fall slightly inside its front tracks, doe tracks will be the opposite. And by looking at the size of a set of tracks and how far apart they are, a skilled tracker can estimate both the size of an animal and how fast it's moving.

Many wildlife species have distinct droppings you can use to identify which animals visit your land. Deer leave behind clusters of small, round balls like these. Just don't mistake them for breakfast cereal.

The moisture present in a track can give you a sense of how recently an animal passed through an area. The black bear that made this fresh track likely isn't too far away.

If your property gets snow, winter is an ideal time to see animal tracks. My favorite time to look for tracks is the day after a small snowfall, the kind where you get two to three inches. Those conditions are ideal for animals to leave tracks, and you'll likely surprise yourself with how many you spot.

Winter is a good time to see tracks. These tiny, hopping tracks are from a mouse. The line in the middle is from the mouse's tail dragging behind it.

There's way more to bird calls, scat, and tracks than I could hope to teach you in two projects. In Beyond the Book, I've included links to resources for getting started with these various wildlife signs.

Project 92. Take Apart an Owl Pellet

In addition to calls, tracks, and scat, some wildlife have unique signs that can reveal their presence. Bears will mark their territory by standing on their back legs and scratching tree trunks with their front claws. Bucks achieve the same task by rubbing their antlers against young trees.

One well-known wildlife sign is the owl pellet. Owls and other raptors don't have teeth, so they swallow their food whole. The parts they can't digest, like fur, feathers, and bones, get coughed up in sausage-shaped wads. If you aren't afraid to get your hands dirty, you can use these pellets not only to learn that you have an owl or other raptor on your property, but also what that bird is eating.

Great horned owls are found year-round throughout North America, but they're tough to spot because they're active at night. If you can find one of their pellets, though, you'll know an owl is nearby. They eat an impressive variety of prey from insects to mice to ducks. They're also one of the few animals that will prey on skunks. The owl's poor sense of smell renders the skunk's famous stench-based defense useless. Photo credit: National Park Service

Perhaps the trickiest part of taking apart owl pellets is finding some in the first place. Owls tend to have favorite trees, so most of their pellets will appear at the base of one tree. If you know an owl on your land likes to hang out in a certain spot, you can usually find plenty of owl pellets by looking on the ground in that area.

Another tricky part of owl pellets is sanitation. These are the coughed up remains of eaten prey, after all. When taking apart an owl pellet, take some safety precautions. Cover the surface you're working on; one of those foam trays that meat comes on works well because it has sides. Wear disposable gloves, work in an area away from food, and never put the pellet or the gloves in your mouth. Finally, when you're all done, toss the gloves and wash your hands with antibacterial soap.

To take your pellet apart, you'll need some tools: a pair of tweezers and a few toothpicks will usually suffice. I prefer the sharp, pointed tweezers over the standard blunter ones because of their greater precision.

You can dissect dry pellets, but I recommend soaking them in water first. Let your pellet sit in a bowl of water for about half an hour or until it sinks. You can add some disinfectant to the water to help with bacteria. After the pellet finishes soaking, remove it from the water and blot it dry with a paper towel.

With the pellet prepped and tools in hand, you're ready to dissect. Use your tweezers and toothpicks to separate the bones from the fur or feathers that make up the bulk of the pellet. Lay the fur or feathers aside for now, and keep the bones in a separate area of your tray.

Gentleness and patience are the watchwords when taking apart owl pellets. Owls eat small prey: mice, voles, frogs, and birds are all common in pellets. These small prey have even smaller bones. If you aren't careful, you can break or miss those bones.

Be especially cautious with any skulls or jawbones you find. They're your best tool for identifying what the owl ate, and frankly, they're the coolest part of the dissection. You don't want to ruin them.

Once you've gone through and pulled out as many bones as you can, take the discarded bits of fur and feather and rub them gently between your fingers. Often you'll find tiny bones or teeth that you didn't spot during your first go-around.

With all the bones pulled out, you can use a bone key (I've linked to one in Beyond the Book) to figure out what animals were in your pellet. It's common to find the bones of several different species in a single pellet.

If you're lucky and have done a thorough dissection, you might have enough bones to reconstruct the prey animal's skeleton. Even if you can't do that, you'll still have gained insight into the eating habits of a beautiful bird of prey.

Project 93. Install Trail Cameras

While all these indirect wildlife signs are useful, I know some of you are saying, "Come on, Josh! I want to *see* wildlife! Do better!"

If you want to see actual animals, particularly large mammals, there's no option more reliable than trail cameras. Also called game cameras, these

Game or trail cameras can help you capture photos of wildlife you would rarely see otherwise, like this fisher photographed at Saint-Gaudens National Historic Site in New Hampshire. Photo credit: National Park Service

motion-triggered beauties will help you see wildlife you would have almost zero chance of spotting live.

A lot of game cameras are marketed toward hunters, hence the term *game* camera. They are admittedly great tools for keeping an eye on that trophy buck. But you don't have to be a hunter to appreciate game cameras. Wildlife will get their pictures taken regardless of whether you go out later with a gun.

Game cameras offer several advantages over other wildlife monitoring techniques. First and most important, they can take photos without disturbing animals. You get to see wildlife doing what they do uninterrupted by human presence. In addition, game cameras can get pictures in conditions that are

Trail cameras are a surprisingly inexpensive way to get great images of wildlife on your land. Photo credit: NPS Domain

difficult to photograph in, such as the dead of night. Finally, depending on the model you buy, you can capture not just photos but videos of wildlife action.

Cameras are also cheaper than you might think. An assortment of brands and models are available for under $100, and several high-quality cameras have price tags below $200. Just one or two of these cameras on your land can reveal some stunning images. If you can commit a little more money, for $1,000 you could get five to ten of these cameras and set them up across your property to get a detailed view of the action.

Even though cameras have gotten cheaper, you still want a good one. To narrow your list, consider the following six features. We'll tackle each of them in order:

- Night image type
- Detection zone
- Trigger and recovery time

- Battery life
- Cellular capability
- Megapixels

Night Image Type

Night image type is based on whether the camera uses infrared or a traditional light flash to take photos after dark. Infrared gives black-and-white images, but it has the advantage of not emitting a bright flash. Flash models will give you color, but the flash can startle animals.

I prefer infrared models for two reasons. First, I'd rather not scare animals if I can avoid it. Second, the quality of a flash photo at night is usually poor. Yes, it's in color, but those colors are often disrupted by harsh shadows and weird contrasts. The black-and-white infrared photos are much crisper.

The infrared models are also useful if you're concerned about trespassers. A traditional flash photo will reveal to a trespasser 1) that they've been photographed and 2) where the camera is so they can break it.

If trespassers are an issue on your land, look for "no-glow" infrared trail cameras. They emit no visible light when taking photos and work best for security purposes. If trespassers aren't an issue, then consider "red-glow" infrared. These cameras emit a slight red glow when they take a photo, but it isn't enough to spook wildlife. Red-glow cameras will give brighter, clearer images than no-glow models.

Detection Zone

Detection zone is the area that, once an animal enters it, the camera will take a picture. In product descriptions, detection zone is often represented as a detection angle and a detection range. Detection angle refers to how wide a view the camera has, and detection range is how far away an animal can be and still trigger the camera. In general, look for wider angles and longer ranges to get the best chance of taking a photo.

Trigger and Recovery Time

Trigger and recovery time deal with how quickly the camera takes photos. Trigger time is how long the camera needs to take a photo after an animal enters the detection zone. By contrast, recovery time is how long after that first photo the camera will wait before it takes another shot. Shorter times for both mean you'll get more pictures of the same animal, and also more chances for a crisp, close-up image.

You might think the shorter these times are, the better. But there's a tradeoff. If the recovery time in particular is too short, you can wind up with an overload of images of the same animal in slightly different positions. That will wear down your camera's battery and fill up its memory, which in turn means you'll either need to visit your camera more or miss photographing other animals. Weigh carefully your desire to get that perfect shot against your hope of seeing as much wildlife as possible.

Battery Life

Trail cameras work because animals don't think there are people around. If you have to go out every day and swap out the rechargeable battery, your smell will be all around the camera, and animals may avoid it. When camera shopping, look for long battery life. You'll see more wildlife, and you'll save time and effort visiting your camera less often.

Cellular Capability

In addition to battery charging, the other time you'll need to check your camera is when you want to take photos off it. As with batteries, going out all the time to retrieve photos will make the area smell more like human and deter animals. The less often you check your camera, the better.

One way to reduce the number of times you head out to the camera is to give it a memory card with a lot of space. That way it can take more images before getting full.

If you're willing to spend extra money, you can eliminate the need to retrieve photos by getting a cellular-capable trail camera. These cameras use cellphone networks to send images wirelessly from the camera to another device, like a computer or smartphone.

Cellular-capable trail cameras work well if you want to see in the moment what wildlife are using your property and where—a feature that makes these cameras popular with hunters. They're also helpful for catching trespassers, because you can see right away that someone is on your property.

For general purpose wildlife viewing, though, I have a hard time justifying the extra cost of these cameras. If you have oodles of money to throw around, consider them. Otherwise, the non-cellular versions work just fine.

Megapixels

In digital cameras, the number of megapixels describes the size of the final image. A "pixel" is one tiny square that can be different colors, and one megapixel has one million pixels. All the pixels together add up to a digital photo.

Camera manufacturers love to tout the number of megapixels. And it seems like an obvious selling point: more megapixels means a bigger, sharper image, right? Well, not quite. The reality is that with modern cameras, there's little practical difference between megapixel sizes. Most trail cameras these days have plenty of megapixels to create large images in both camera and video modes.

Moreover, higher megapixels doesn't mean sharper photos. Sharpness comes from the quality of the camera's lens and sensor, not the megapixel count.

My advice here is simple. Pay little attention to megapixel numbers. Use the features above to narrow down your choice, and then look up sample photos from the models that meet your needs. Look for sharp, distinct colors and clear, unblurred images.

Also, don't settle under the notion that "it's just a trail camera; you can't expect too much." The days of grainy trail camera photos are over. There's no reason you can't get a trail camera that delivers crisp images every bit as good as if you were out there pushing the shutter yourself.

The days of grainy trail camera photos are over. You can get quality images even from moderately-priced cameras. The above photo was taken with a moderately-priced trail camera. Photo credit: National Park Service

I Have My Camera. Now What?

Buying a sweet trail camera doesn't do you any good if you don't place it well. To get the best shots and videos, placing cameras where wildlife are likely to visit is essential. Spend some time scouting your property for likely locations.

Food and water sources are perfect camera spots, because animals will linger in those locations to eat or drink. If you've added a food plot, for instance, a camera focused on it can show you how well your project is working.

Trails are another good option for locating cameras. Wildlife don't tend to linger on trails, but like you, they will use them as easy ways to get around. Locating cameras along trails also makes swapping batteries and memory cards easier.

You also have to account for the camera's workings when placing it so that when it takes a shot, it's a good one. Trail cameras use heat sensors as well as motion detectors to spot wildlife, so pick a location with decent shade that doesn't face the rising or setting sun. Otherwise the direct heat of the sun could trigger the camera.

When positioning a camera near water, take care that the water itself is outside the camera's detection range. The water's motion could set off the camera.

Once you've chosen a location for your camera, mount it in a way that will keep it secure. Most likely you'll attach it to a tree, so pick one with a trunk at least ten inches wide. Smaller trees may sway in the wind and trigger the sensor.

Most animals are shorter than people, so install your camera low on the tree. Three feet off the ground works well for a variety of mammals, including deer.

As a final test of your camera, photograph yourself. Walk in front of the camera a few times at different hours, speeds, and distances and then review the photos. It might sound silly, but this dry run will give you an idea of the pictures you can expect from a particular location.

14

THE NEXT GENERATION

"It's a good thing to learn more about nature in order to share this knowledge with children; it's even better if the adult and child learn about nature together. And it's a lot more fun."
—Richard Louv

I mentioned in an earlier chapter how important it is to think about your land's future beyond your lifetime. The next generation will someday own the land you own now. When that happens, will they be as passionate about it as you are?

Unfortunately, passion for nature is at risk in younger generations. As our society becomes more digital, today's children are losing connections with the outdoors. According to the US Fish and Wildlife Service, participation in hunting and fishing by children aged six to fifteen has dropped 22 percent since the 1990s. The number engaged in wildlife-viewing has fallen by even more: 27 percent.[1]

Bestselling author Richard Louv writes about this loss in his book, *Last Child in the Woods*. In it Louv chronicles the harm a loss of natural connections has for kids, such as higher rates of obesity, ADHD, and depression. But this same loss hurts nature too, because in the not too distant future, those screen-addicted kids will be the caretakers of our country's private lands.

Youth participation in outdoor activities like fishing, hunting, and wildlife watching has dropped more than 20 percent since the 1990s. Perhaps the most important thing you can do to ensure wildlife have a future on your property is to encourage a love of nature in your kids and grandkids. Photo credit: Steve Hillebrand, USFWS

That's why I decided to end this book not with more ways to attract wildlife to your property, but with ways to attract kids to wildlife. More than anything I've talked about in this book, I believe getting your children, grandchildren, nieces, nephews, and other youngsters involved with nature is the most important step you can take to ensuring wildlife have a home in the future.

Project 94. Turn over Fallen Logs

I mentioned in the chapter on older woods that dead, fallen logs have a lot of wildlife value. Turns out, they also have a lot of value for connecting kids with that wildlife.

You and a child can start investigating logs by simply looking at them. Even from the outside, you may find signs that animals use the log. Nutshells may reveal that a squirrel has been using the log as a dining room table. Holes bored into the log may be from woodpeckers searching for insects.

Inside the log you can find more. If the log still has some bark on it, peel that back and see what's underneath it. Odds are you'll spot some insects like beetles and other invertebrates like millipedes.

Hollow logs often become nests for smaller animals like chipmunks and snakes. Don't put your arm in, but you can use a stick to see if there are nesting materials inside.

Finally, flip the log over. In this moist, sheltered environment, you may find salamanders as well as snake or lizard eggs.

This mix of animals and animal sign create a lot of opportunities to talk to a child about nature. What did you find, and what was it doing there? The lizard that laid eggs was hoping for shelter for her young. Other animals were there seeking food, whether from the log itself or the insects feeding on it.

Millipedes (left) and red-backed salamanders (right) are two animals commonly found living in or under rotting logs. They provide a good chance for your child to see wildlife up close.

Once you've finished with the log, don't leave it turned over. Return it to its original position so it can go on providing a home for the animals you discovered.

Project 95. Look and Listen for Spring Frogs

Plants and animals change as they grow and develop. One way to teach your kids about this cycle of change is to look at frogs as they transform from tadpoles into adults.

To find tadpoles and frogs, you'll need a wet area like a pond, bog, or vernal pool. Frogs lay their eggs in water, and young tadpoles spend the first part of their lives there.

The best time to look for frogs and tadpoles is in the spring. As the weather warms in March and April, listen on your walks for the calls of spring peepers. They're some of the first (and loudest) frogs to call.

Spring peepers are widespread in eastern North America. They're active at night and rarely seen, but it's easy to hear their loud calls in early spring. Photo credit: Ryan Hagerty, USFWS

Odds are you'll hear frogs long before you see them. Just visiting a pond in the spring is usually enough to hear a chorus of them.

If you and your kids want to actually spot frogs, you'll need to be quiet. If you're noisy, you'll scare the frogs, and they'll jump into the water to escape. Fortunately, a few quiet moments standing still are usually enough to make the frogs comfortable enough to come back.

Much like with birds, frogs have distinct calls. Before wandering in search of them, take some time to learn the calls of the major frogs in your area. Spring peepers and American bullfrogs are good species to start with.

If you continue visiting the pond or pool throughout the spring and into early summer, you and your child can see the young frogs grow up. At first, jelly-like egg clumps will appear in the water. Later, you'll see tadpoles. As the tadpoles grow, they'll develop legs and lose their tails. Eventually they'll be adult frogs.

Project 96. Screen a Nighttime Bug Movie

Something that endeared me to nature was that it was an excuse to relax the rules of bedtime. Whether camping or telling stories around a fire, the outdoors are a place where it can be all right to spend some time after dark.

One more way to relax those bedtime rules is by looking for insects at night. This might sound impossible, but it's easy. Here's what you do. First, you'll need a length of clothesline that you can hang outside, say between two trees. Hang it so the line is about five or six feet in the air. Next, pin a white pillowcase or small sheet to the clothesline so it hangs down to child head height. This will be the screen for your bug movie.

With your screen set up, now you need a light. A pole lamp with a wide, sturdy base and the shade removed works well, though you may need an extension cord to get power to it in the backyard. If that isn't an option for you, you can use a lantern.

Turn on the lamp or lantern and position it in front of the pillowcase. The light should shine on the case, illuminating it in white. If you have other outside lights, turn them off so the pillowcase is the only thing lit up. Now the show is ready to begin.

Insects will be drawn to the lit pillowcase. It may take a few minutes, but over time you and your child will see more and more critters come and land.

If you know what kinds of insects they are, you can tell your child about them, but don't feel pressured with identification. You can do other activities, like counting how many of each type of insect arrive or drawing pictures of them.

Don't stress too much about bugs in the hair or other unpleasant interactions. The insects drawn to the light will generally ignore you and your child. That said, consider wearing a little mosquito repellent if you're concerned about bug bites.

Project 97. Go on an Owl Prowl

Another way for you and your kids or grandkids to experience nighttime animals is on an Owl Prowl. Owls sleep during the day, so it's hard to notice them on day walks. But at night they come alive, calling to each other with a complex mix of sounds including screeches, sighs, and snorts as well as the more familiar hoots.

Before you and your kids head out on an Owl Prowl, devote some time to learning the calls for common owls in your area. Since it will be after dark, you won't be able to consult a field guide to check your identification. Instead you'll have to go by hearing.

Fortunately, owl sounds are distinct from species to species, and they're easy to learn. Good ones to start with are the great horned owl, barred owl, and screech owl. All these owls are common in many places in the US.

To have the best chances of a successful Owl Prowl, go out between December and February. Owls breed in the winter, and it's during this breeding season that they're most active in calling. Their hoots and other sounds are ways to signal their presence to other owls as they attract mates and guard territory.

"Who cooks for you? Who cooks for you all?" The barred owl's distinct series of nine hoots is easy for kids and parents alike to learn. Photo credit: Mark Musselman/National Audubon Society, USFWS

As for what time to go out, your Owl Prowl doesn't need to be late at night. Many owls are most active at dusk and dawn, so aim for the hour just after sunset or just before sunrise.

You don't have to be in the middle of nowhere to do an Owl Prowl. Owl Prowls are annual events in many city parks, even in New York City! If you don't own enough land to do an Owl Prowl on your own property, search online for

Not all owls hoot. The diminutive eastern screech owl calls out a long, mournful sigh. Photo credit: National Park Service

one hosted by a local park or nature group. They're a fun introduction to wildlife and to other people who care about wildlife.

If you want to actually see the owls and not just hear them, pick a clear night with a full moon. The moon will provide extra light and make it easier to spot an owl once you hear its call.

Finally, here are a few tips on getting the best experience out of your Owl Prowl. First and most importantly, keep quiet. If you're noisy, the owl may consider you a threat and fly away. Second, keep your distance. Remember that these birds are nesting, and they're protective parents with sharp talons. Third, don't use flashlights, flash photography, or audio recordings. The light from a flashlight or camera can disrupt an owl's night vision and make it panic, and recordings of prey or of other owls confuse the birds, distracting them from their nesting or hunting duties. If you absolutely must have a flashlight to follow a trail, then you can bring one. If you do, keep it pointed at ground level and never up into the trees.

Project 98. Call a Turkey

You might get lucky and spot an owl on your Owl Prowl, but odds are you'll only hear them. A more reliable way to see some large birds on your land is to call in some wild turkeys.

Turkey calling has its roots in hunting. Hunters typically hunt turkeys using bows or shotguns, which have short ranges. To compensate, hunters draw in male turkeys by convincing them another turkey is nearby. The hunter uses a device that mimics the sound of either a female (that the male would want to mate with) or a male (that the male would want to fight). Tom turkey comes to investigate, and when he gets within range, the hunter shoots.

But you don't have to hunt turkeys to call them to you. My coworker calls birds with his seven-year-old son, no weapon required. I enjoy going and shooting birds with a camera rather than a gun.

If you have the patience for it, calling turkeys holds an undeniable thrill. When you call and a turkey answers back, it sends shivers through you. It dawns on you that you're having a conversation with a bird. As the turkey gets closer and closer, you get an amazing view of an even more amazing creature.

Calling turkeys takes some equipment. First of all, turkeys have superb eyesight, so head-to-toe camouflage is important. You'll be spending a good bit of time on the ground outside, so a comfortable seat pad is worth the money.

Calling in wild turkeys takes patience, but it can connect you and your child or grandchild with nature by having a conversation with a bird. Photo credit: Pixabay

Finally, you may or may not want to use a decoy. Some hunters swear by them, while others think they just get in the way. For your first calling, I suggest skipping the decoy and seeing how it goes.

Your most important gear is the turkey call itself. There are a bunch of kinds, from simple push-button calls to hollow wooden boxes to diaphragms you put in your mouth. For beginners, I recommend the box call. Push-buttons are easier

Even though it needs two hands to operate, the box call is ideal for beginners calling turkeys. It's cheap, easy to learn, and can make a variety of sounds.

to use, but they have the disadvantage of only being able to make one sound. Turkeys are social birds, and they like to have conversations. If someone just said, "Hello" to you over and over again, you'd get annoyed and leave. Turkeys do the same thing. The box call is easy to learn, and it offers a range of sounds. It does take two hands to operate, but since you aren't hunting, that won't be an issue.

Along with equipment, turkey calling takes practice and especially patience. Calling turkeys isn't a mobile activity. The idea is to stay as still as possible and let the turkey come to you. Remember, you're trying to convince the bird that you're another turkey. If they see you, they'll know you're a big faker and won't approach.

To fool them, you and anyone coming with you need to be in position before dawn. As the turkeys wake and come down from their roosts in the trees, they'll start calling to each other. That's when you can join in. Keep still and quiet, except for your call.

The best time to call turkeys is in the spring, when they're mating. Males and females are calling to each other then, and the males are more apt to check out an unfamiliar call.

The drawback to this seasonal nature of turkey calling is that it also aligns with most states' turkey hunting seasons. That can create dangerous situations, because you're pretending to be a turkey while dressed in full camo. If a hunter comes along, it's easy for that person to mistake your call for a turkey.

To avoid this situation, practice turkey hunting safety even if you aren't carrying a gun. Never wear anything red, white, or blue while turkey calling, as turkeys sport these colors. When you call, sit on the ground with a large tree at your back. Don't wave or make other large movements that could be misinterpreted as a turkey.

As an extra precaution, you can tie an orange vest around a tree near your calling location. It isn't required, but it will help hunters in the area know there's a person there.

I recommend following these safety tips at all times, even if you're calling on your own land. Property boundaries aren't always well marked, and unfortunately not all hunters pay attention to them even if they are. The old adage applies: it's better to be safe than sorry.

Project 99. Do a Backyard Scavenger Hunt

Turkey calling can be a thrill, but younger kids may not have the patience to sit still without speaking for hours on end. For these kids, a better way to get them interested in nature is to get out exploring in it. Give them a chance not just to see your land, but to interact with it. One way to encourage that interaction is with a scavenger hunt.

Scavenger hunts do more than let children experience nature firsthand. They also build children's creativity and observation skills. Kids will often need to look beyond the obvious to find something that fits the list. Also, because scavenger hunt lists can change from game to game, kids get a new experience every time they play.

If the idea of coming up with a scavenger hunt list seems intimidating, don't worry. While you can create your own, there are many free nature scavenger hunt lists on the Internet that you can use or adapt for your backyard or land. I've included a link in Beyond the Book that has several lists to choose from, including one with drawings for younger explorers.

You can also get away from the traditional lists with a little creativity. For kids learning their letters, challenge them to find something that begins with each letter of the alphabet. Because letters like Q, X, and Z can be challenging, consider making it easier by giving them more common letters.

Another scavenger hunt I enjoy is the Paint Chip Scavenger Hunt. In this hunt, you first go to a hardware store and pick up a handful of those free paint chip squares. With those in hand, your family's task is to find something in nature that matches the color on each square. Don't limit yourself to typical browns and greens. Throw in some yellows, pinks, and oranges for an extra challenge.

As your child grows and becomes more comfortable in the outdoors, you can raise the difficulty of the scavenger hunt items. Instead of looking for any leaf or acorn, perhaps you'll now look for particular species: a basswood leaf and a red oak acorn. You can also have them look for signs of wildlife, say a set of squirrel tracks. Don't be afraid to challenge your child or grandchild a bit. If they do get stuck, be ready with some ideas to help them out.

Project 100. Encourage Free Play

I grew up on a dairy farm. I remember spending whole days in the surrounding fields and woods, just exploring and inventing games with the few neighbor kids. Those experiences taught me to be curious, creative, and to work well on a team. They also gave me confidence and independence, not to mention an interest in nature. For all these reasons, I've come to believe there are few better things for kids than to let them free play outside.

This kind of unstructured play isn't risk-free. I had a fair number of scrapes along the way. It's important to know your children or grandchildren and what's appropriate for them. Your presence might be required at first, but "helicoptering" will keep them from getting creative and coming up with their own ideas.

Instead of hovering, set clear expectations. Teach your kids to identify hazardous plants like poison ivy and what to do if they encounter potentially dangerous wildlife. Establish rules like how far kids may roam and when they should be back inside.

You don't need endless acreage to give kids room to roam. When you visit a public park, for instance, let your children decide which trails to take. In your backyard, leave space for kids to run. Provide areas where they can dig and explore tall grass. Remember those projects from Chapter 4 on decreasing

Letting kids explore and play in nature has documented benefits on creativity, attention span, and problem-solving skills. It's also a fantastic way to kindle a lifelong love of the outdoors. Photo credit: National Park Service

lawn? Those same wilder areas can provide places for kids to explore (just be sure to check them for ticks afterward). The plants in them may be shorter than you are, but to a child, they can seem like an endless jungle waiting to be investigated.

Along these lines, it's okay to let children touch nature. Let them pick up leaves, turn over rocks, and get muddy. Scott Sampson, author of *How to Raise a Wild Child: The Art and Science of Falling in Love with Nature*, argues that nature connection is a contact sport. Scrapes should be expected. "Clothes can be washed, and cuts heal," Sampson writes.[2] Let them fall down and learn to pick themselves up when they do.

If you aren't comfortable letting children roam unsupervised, that doesn't mean they can't enjoy free play outside. If you have to be out with your child, keep them in sight while giving them freedom by doing your own outdoor projects at the same time. Better still, free play alongside them. Make up games. Let your child decide what to do and go along with it (within limits, of course). You might just rediscover that childlike sense of wonder and creativity you used to have.

Project 101. Involve and Inspire

Independent free play is important for kids, but time with you matters too. It sounds obvious, but recent research in the journal *Pediatrics* has confirmed that the activity levels between parents and children are linked. More active parents have more active kids, while parents who sit around tend to have kids that do the same.[3]

This intuitive result applies to nature too. If you want your kids to value the outdoors, you need to show them that you value the outdoors. Free play can help, but you can go deeper than that. Involve the kids in your life with as many of the outdoor projects and activities you do as possible. Like to hike? Bring them along. Fishing? Do that too. Birdwatching? Grab some child-size binoculars.

Time together can also show your kids or grandkids the impact they can have on nature and wildlife. Many of the projects in this book are suitable for kids to do either on their own or with your help. The various nesting box activities in particular are ideal for this purpose. They're hands-on, easy to do, and your child gets to see the results right away when they spot a bluebird flit out of a birdhouse.

Does all this outdoor interaction really make a difference? I can say with certainty that it does. In my career, I've lost track of how many stories I've heard from landowners,

If you want your kids and grandkids to inherit your passion for wildlife, share that passion with them. Birding is a great pastime to do together. Photo credit: Steve Hillebrand, USFWS

naturalists, foresters, and others involved in the outdoors. When the subject of how these people became so passionate about nature comes up, they always share an experience from their childhood. Someone in their lives also loved nature and took the time to share that love. Maybe it was a grandfather who led family walks in the park. Maybe it was a mother who gardened with her daughter. Maybe it was a dad who took his son camping in the Appalachians of central Pennsylvania and cooked s'mores with him over a fire next to a brisk mountain stream.

That last one's me, by the way. From the bottom of my heart, Dad, thank you.

Beyond the Book

Chapter 1: Private Landowners and Wildlife: A Vital Connection

- **tinyurl.com/Backyard-Woodland**—This book focuses on wildlife. If you want a broader overview of woodland stewardship topics, please consider my previous book, *Backyard Woodland: How to Maintain and Sustain Your Trees, Water, and Wildlife*. It includes some information about wildlife, but it also has insights into topics like recreation, trespassing, taxes, timber harvesting, and passing land to the next generation.

Chapter 2: What Do Wildlife Need, Anyway?

- **nwf.org/garden-for-wildlife/certify.aspx**—Wildlife need food, water, cover, and nesting spots to survive. If you've provided all these in your yard, consider getting your property designated as a Certified Wildlife Habitat by the National Wildlife Federation. It's a great way of showing how the work you do benefits wildlife. You can use this link to find out more about the Certified Wildlife Habitat Program, including how to sign up.

Chapter 3: Getting Started

- **google.com/earth/resources**—Google Earth is free software that lets you view and print aerial photos. To print photos, you'll need to download the program. Click "Download" under "Earth Pro on Desktop" to get started.
- **earthpoint.us/TopoMap.aspx**—You can view more than aerial photos on Google Earth. Once it's installed, visit this Earth Point website to download a free US topographic map viewer for Google Earth.

Topographic maps show elevation, so you'll be able to see not just a birds-eye view of your land, but also how steep or flat various areas are.

- **yardmap.org**—This free website from the Nature Conservancy and the Cornell Lab of Ornithology is an excellent way to map your property, plan projects, and keep track of your work.

Chapter 4: Backyards

- **audubon.org/native-plants**—The Audubon Society put together this free, searchable database of native plants. Enter your zip code, and the site suggests native plants for your area. You can narrow the search by the type of plant you want and even by the types of birds or other critters you hope to help.
- **wildflower.org/suppliers**—The Lady Bird Johnson Wildflower Center provides this national database of native plant nurseries. You can search by company name or by city, state, or zip code.
- **tinyurl.com/Building-Bat-Houses**—The Wisconsin Department of Natural Resources put together this free *Building a Bat House* guide. It includes bat box plans and installation tips.
- **batconservation.org/product-category/bat-houses**—If you want to buy a bat box, the Organization for Bat Conservation has several models available.

Chapter 5: Grasslands, Shrublands, and Young Woods

- **tinyurl.com/Food-Plot-Video**—This video by Wisconsin landowner Nate Francois is the first in a series of three. Together the videos show how to build and maintain a food plot.
- **nacdnet.org/general-resources/conservation-district-directory**— This map from the National Association of Conservation Districts helps you find contact information for your local Soil and Water Conservation District's office.
- **npic.orst.edu/pest/countyext.htm**—I realize this map is on a website about pesticides, but it's a great resource that provides phone numbers and web addresses for every US county's Cooperative Extension office.

- **nysbs.org/handouts/ThePetersonBox.pdf**—If you want to build your own bluebird box, consider using these free plans from the New York State Bluebird Society.
- **tinyurl.com/Bluebird-Houses**—If you'd rather buy a bluebird box, here's a link to some options from Duncraft, a wild bird supply store.
- **nestwatch.org/learn/all-about-birdhouses/right-bird-right-house**—The Cornell Lab of Ornithology developed this interactive website within its NestWatch program. Choose your region and habitat type, and the site recommends birds to install bird boxes for. You can then download free birdhouse plans for the species you want to attract.
- **tinyurl.com/Apple-Tree-Pruning**—This website is from the land-owner outreach website MyWoodlot and provides resources on how to prune apple trees. It includes a pocket reference, a how-to video, and a magazine article that shows example pruned trees.

Chapter 6: Old and Interior Woods

- **tinyurl.com/Tree-Planting-Video**—This National Gardening Association video shows you how to plant a tree. It's geared toward yard trees, but the techniques apply to most tree-planting situations.
- **tinyurl.com/Brush-Piles**—This page from the Humane Society offers tips on building brush piles. It includes a video demonstration of a woman building one in her backyard.
- **tinyurl.com/Tree-Girdling**—In this video from the University of Kentucky, a man girdles a tree with a chainsaw and explains his technique. Check it out before creating snags on your property.
- **nac.unl.edu/practices/silvopasture.htm**—This website from the USDA National Agroforestry Center has resources for those interested in silvopasture.

Chapter 7: Streams

- **tinyurl.com/Macroinvertebrate-Key**—This easy key will help you identify macroinvertebrates. You can also use it to figure out your stream's water quality based on the kinds of critters you find. In the key, the letters represent how tolerant to pollution a species is: S for "sensitive," F for "fairly tolerant," and T for "tolerant."

- **stateforesters.org/state-forestry-BMPs-map**—Every state has different BMPs and ways of enforcing them. The National Association of State Foresters created this interactive map that helps you access your state's BMP guidelines.

Chapter 8: Wetlands

- **tinyurl.com/Duck-Box-Plans**—These free wood duck box nesting plans from Ducks Unlimited show you how to build the box and give tips on locating and installing it.

Chapter 9: Invasive Plants

- **tinyurl.com/Native-Alternatives-Book**—The book *Native Alternatives to Invasive Plants* is a great idea generator for similar-looking native plants that can replace invasives in your landscaping.
- **tinyurl.com/Invasive-Plants-Book**—The book *Invasive Plants: Guide to Identification and the Impacts and Control of Common North American Species* provides identification and control options of invasive plants. It covers two hundred species.
- **eddmaps.org/tools/recordsbysubject.cfm**—Run by the University of Georgia, the Early Detection and Distribution Mapping System allows people to report invasive plant locations to a central database. This link lets you search that database by state and county. The result is a list of invasive plants found in your state or county sorted from most to least common. You can use these lists to figure out which invasive plants you should be on the lookout for on your land.
- **pullerbear.com**—When removing invasive plants mechanically, it's important to get the roots too. There are several tools available to help with that job, especially for shrubs. The Pullerbear is an example of one of these tools.

Chapter 10: Oh, Deer!

- **tinyurl.com/Tree-Tubes**—If you need tree tubes, here's an example of a place where you can buy them.

- **tinyurl.com/Bark-Protectors**—Once the tree tubes come off, bark protectors help keep deer from damaging your young trees. Here's an example of one kind of bark protector.
- **hfth.nra.org/get-involved**—This website hosted by the National Rifle Association includes a searchable map of venison donation facilities nationwide. Type in your town or zip code to find participating butchers and food banks near you.

Chapter 11: Keeping Open Space Open

- **landtrustaccreditation.org/land-trust-locator**—While there are more than 1,700 land trusts across the US, only about four hundred have earned accreditation by the Land Trust Alliance. When deciding whether to pursue an easement, start with this list of established groups.
- **tinyurl.com/Easement-Interviews**—Before getting an easement, meet other landowners who have easements and learn from their experiences. This MyWoodlot page has video interviews with landowners so you can hear why they chose easements to protect their properties.
- **tinyurl.com/land-legacy**—*Your Land, Your Legacy* is a legacy planning primer from the University of Massachusetts. It's written with a Massachusetts landowner in mind, but its step-by-step approach and many case studies will be helpful no matter where your land is.

Chapter 12: Finding Funding

- **tinyurl.com/FSA-Office-Locator**—Your local Farm Service Agency is a good one-stop shop for learning more about funding options. This map lets you find your local office by clicking on your state, then your county.
- **nrcs.usda.gov/GetStarted**—Natural Resources Conservation Service programs can be confusing. This site from the NRCS breaks down their program process into five steps.
- **fws.gov/partners/contactus.html**—Similar to the Farm Service Agency map, this map from the US Fish and Wildlife Service helps you find regional and state contact information for Partners for Fish and Wildlife coordinators. Click on your state to find its coordinator.

- **nwtf.org/conservation/category/seed-program**—This Wild Turkey Federation webpage has information about the various seed programs they fund.
- **audubon.org/audubon-near-you**—The Audubon Society has state and local chapters across the US. This link shows a map of all their locations. Click on one near you for contact information and a link to the chapter's website.

Chapter 13: Monitoring Your Work

- **tinyurl.com/Birding-by-Ear-Eastern**—The *Birding by Ear* CDs are the tool I used when I was starting to learn bird calls. This link is for the eastern half of North America.
- **tinyurl.com/Birding-by-Ear-Western**—If you live in a western state, here's the *Birding by Ear* link for western North America.
- **larkwire.com**—Larkwire is an online bird call learning tool. Set up as a game, Larkwire adapts which birds it shows you and quizzes you based on previous answers. Give its free trial a whirl before committing to buying the full product.
- **tinyurl.com/Animal-Tracks-ID**—This illustrated guide to animal tracks isn't comprehensive, but it covers several common tracks like rabbits, weasels, and foxes.
- **www.earthskills.com/pdfs/Howlearntracking.pdf**—Once you can identify tracks, what do they mean? This article from Jim Lowery, author of *The Tracker's Field Guide*, provides an introduction on interpreting wildlife tracks.
- **icwdm.org/inspection/scat1.aspx**—I know it's gross, but you can tell a lot about wildlife visiting your property from the droppings they leave behind. This key will help you identify scat from various woodland wildlife.
- **tinyurl.com/Owl-Pellet-Bone-Chart**—When taking apart owl pellets, you can use this bone chart to help you identify the bones you find.
- **trailcampro.com/pages/trail-camera-selection-guide**—This click-by-click trail camera buyer's guide is excellent for finding the right camera to suit your needs. Answer a few basic questions about which features you want, and in two minutes you have potential options narrowed down.

Chapter 14: The Next Generation

- **tinyurl.com/NWF-Family-Fun**—I only had space to talk about a few kid-friendly outdoor ideas. This website from the National Wildlife Federation provides a searchable database of more than six hundred nature-related activities for families. You can search based on the age of your kids, the topic you'd like to explore, and even by season.

- **tinyurl.com/Outdoor-Scavenger-Hunt**—Looking for inspiration for your backyard scavenger hunt? This MyWoodlot webpage has four different lists for children of various ages and knowledge of the woods.

- **tinyurl.com/Frog-Call-List**—Which frogs and toads might you hear while exploring your property? The US Geological Survey put together this list of frog calls. Choose a species to hear its call. You can also choose your state to see a list of frogs that live there. The site will be most useful if you live east of the Rocky Mountains.

- **tinyurl.com/Turkey-Call-Overview**—The box calls I mention are far from the only turkey calls available. This buyer's guide walks you through the different types of calls as well as the pros and cons of each.

State Resources

National Resources
Landowner Organization: National Woodland Owners Association (woodlandowners.org)
Forestry Agency: US Forest Service – State and Private Forestry (www.fs.fed.us/spf)
Wildlife Agency: US Fish and Wildlife Service (fws.gov)

Alabama
Property Tax Program: Current Use (tinyurl.com/Alabama-current-use)
Natural Heritage Program: Natural Heritage Program (alnhp.org)
Landowner Organization: Alabama Forest Owners Association (www.afoa.org)
State Forestry Agency: Forestry Commission (forestry.alabama.gov)
State Wildlife Agency: Department of Conservation and Natural Resources (outdooralabama.com)

Alaska
Property Tax Program: Automatic exemption for forestland
Natural Heritage Program: Natural Heritage Program (accs.uaa.alaska.edu/alaska-natural-heritage-program)
Landowner Organization: Alaska Forest Association (akforest.org)
State Forestry Agency: Division of Forestry (forestry.alaska.gov)
State Wildlife Agency: Department of Fish and Game (adfg.alaska.gov)

Arizona
Property Tax Program: Automatic reduction for forestland
Natural Heritage Program: Heritage Data Management System (azgfd.gov/w_c/edits/hdms_abstracts.shtml)
Landowner Organization: None, use National Woodland Owners Association

State Forestry Agency: Department of Forestry and Fire Management (dffm.az.gov)
State Wildlife Agency: Game and Fish (www.azgfd.com)

Arkansas
Property Tax Program: Automatic reduction for forestland
Natural Heritage Program: Natural Heritage Commission (naturalheritage.com)
Landowner Organization: Arkansas Forestry Association (arkforests.org)
State Forestry Agency: Forestry Commission (forestry.arkansas.gov)
State Wildlife Agency: Game and Fish Commission (www.agfc.com)

California
Property Tax Program: California Land Conservation Act/Williamson Act (www.conservation.ca.gov/dlrp/lca)
Natural Heritage Program: Natural Diversity Database (wildlife.ca.gov/ data/cnddb/about)
Landowner Organization: Forest Landowners of California (forestlandowners.org)
State Forestry Agency: Board of Forestry and Fire Protection (bof.fire.ca.gov)
State Wildlife Agency: Department of Fish and Wildlife (wildlife.ca.gov)

Colorado
Property Tax Program: Forest Ag Program (csfs.colostate.edu/forest-ag-program)
Natural Heritage Program: Natural Heritage Program (cnhp.colostate.edu)
Landowner Organization: Colorado Forestry Association (coloradoforestry .org) and Colorado Tree Farmers (treefarmer.com)
State Forestry Agency: State Forest Service (csfs.colostate.edu)
State Wildlife Agency: Parks and Wildlife (cpw.state.co.us)

Connecticut
Property Tax Program: Public Act 490 (tinyurl.com/Connecticut-490)
Natural Heritage Program: Recreation and Natural Heritage Trust Program (tinyurl.com/Connecticut-natural-heritage)

Landowner Organization: Connecticut Forest & Park Association (ctwoodlands .org) and Eastern Connecticut Forest Landowners Association (ecfla.org)

State Forestry Agency: Department of Energy & Environmental Protection– Forestry (tinyurl.com/Connecticut-DEEP-forestry)

State Wildlife Agency: Department of Energy & Environmental Protection– Wildlife (tinyurl.com/Connecticut-DEEP-wildlife)

Delaware

Property Tax Program: Commercial Forest Plantation Act (dda.delaware .gov/forestry/conser.shtml; scroll down to "Property Tax Exemptions")

Natural Heritage Program: Wildlife Species Conservation & Research Program (dnrec.delaware.gov/fw/nhesp)

Landowner Organization: Delaware Forestry Association (delawareforest.com)

State Forestry Agency: Forest Service (dda.delaware.gov/forestry/conser .shtml)

State Wildlife Agency: Division of Fish and Wildlife (dnrec.delaware.gov/fw)

Florida

Property Tax Program: Greenbelt Law (tinyurl.com/Florida-Greenbelt-1; see also tinyurl.com/Florida-Greenbelt-2)

Natural Heritage Program: Natural Areas Inventory (fnai.org)

Landowner Organization: Florida Forestry Association (floridaforest.org)

State Forestry Agency: Forest Service (freshfromflorida.com/Divisions-Offices/ Florida-Forest-Service)

State Wildlife Agency: Fish and Wildlife Conservation Commission (myfwc.com)

Georgia

Property Tax Program: Conservation Use Assessment (dor.georgia.gov/ conservation-use-assessment-information)

Natural Heritage Program: Rare Species and Natural Community Data (georgiawildlife.com/node/1370)

Landowner Organization: Georgia Forestry Association (gfagrow.org)

State Forestry Agency: Forestry Commission (www.gfc.state.ga.us)

State Wildlife Agency: Wildlife Resources Division (georgiawildlife.org)

Hawaii

Property Tax Program: Each county has its own. Visit tinyurl.com/ Hawaii-forest-incentives, then scroll down to "Reduce your property taxes" and click on your county for more information about its program.

Natural Heritage Program: Biodiversity and Mapping Program (hbmpweb2 .pbrc.hawaii.edu/ccrt/hbmp)

Landowner Organization: Hawaii Forest Institute (hawaiiforestinstitute.org)

State Forestry Agency: Division of Forestry and Wildlife (dlnr.hawaii.gov/ forestry)

State Wildlife Agency: Division of Forestry and Wildlife (dlnr.hawaii.gov/ wildlife)

Idaho

Property Tax Program: Productivity Tax or Bare Land and Yield Tax (tinyurl .com/Idaho-timber-tax; scroll down and click on "Forestland Taxation Law" for more information)

Natural Heritage Program: Natural Heritage Program (tinyurl.com/ Idaho-natural-heritage)

Landowner Organization: Idaho Forest Owners Association (idahoforestowners.org)

State Forestry Agency: Department of Lands (www.idl.idaho.gov/forestry/ service)

State Wildlife Agency: Fish and Game (idfg.idaho.gov)

Illinois

Property Tax Program: Conservation Stewardship Program (www.dnr.illinois .gov/conservation/CSP)

Natural Heritage Program: Natural Heritage Database (tinyurl.com/ Illinois-natural-heritage)

Landowner Organization: Illinois Forestry Association (ilforestry.org); see also Northwest Illinois Forestry Association (www.nifatrees.org)

State Forestry Agency: Division of Forestry Resources (www.dnr.illinois. gov/conservation/Forestry)

State Wildlife Agency: Department of Natural Resources (www.dnr.illinois.gov)

Indiana
Property Tax Program: Classified Forest & Wildlands (state.in.us/dnr/forestry/4801.htm)

Natural Heritage Program: Natural Heritage Data Center (in.gov/dnr/naturepreserve/4746.htm)

Landowner Organization: Indiana Forestry & Woodland Owners Association (ifwoa.org)

State Forestry Agency: Department of Natural Resources (in.gov/dnr/forestry)

State Wildlife Agency: Department of Natural Resources (in.gov/dnr/fishwild)

Iowa
Property Tax Program: Forest Reserve Law (tinyurl.com/Iowa-forest-reserve-law)

Natural Heritage Program: Natural Heritage Foundation (inhf.org)

Landowner Organization: Iowa Woodland Owners Association (iowawoodlandowners.org)

State Forestry Agency: Forestry Bureau (iowadnr.gov/Environment/Forestry.aspx)

State Wildlife Agency: Department of Natural Resources (iowadnr.gov)

Kansas
Property Tax Program: Automatic reduction for forestland

Natural Heritage Program: Natural Heritage Inventory (biosurvey.ku.edu/ksnhi)

Landowner Organization: Rural Forestry Program (kansasforests.org/rural_forestry)

State Forestry Agency: Forest Service (kansasforests.org)

State Wildlife Agency: Wildlife, Parks and Tourism (ksoutdoors.com)

Kentucky
Property Tax Program: Automatic reduction for forestland

Natural Heritage Program: Natural Heritage Database (naturepreserves.ky.gov/data)

Landowner Organization: Kentucky Woodland Owners Association (kwoa.net)
State Forestry Agency: Division of Forestry (forestry.ky.gov)
State Wildlife Agency: Department of Fish and Wildlife Resources (fw.ky.gov)

Louisiana

Property Tax Program: Automatic reduction for forestland
Natural Heritage Program: Natural Heritage Program (wlf.louisiana.gov/wildlife/louisiana-natural-heritage-program)
Landowner Organization: Louisiana Forestry Association (laforestry.com)
State Forestry Agency: Department of Agriculture and Forestry (www.ldaf.state.la.us/forestry)
State Wildlife Agency: Department of Wildlife and Fisheries (www.wlf.louisiana.gov)

Maine

Property Tax Program: Tree Growth Tax Law (tinyurl.com/Maine-tree-tax)
Natural Heritage Program: Natural Areas Program (maine.gov/dacf/mnap)
Landowner Organization: Small Woodland Owners Association of Maine (swoam.org)
State Forestry Agency: Forest Service (maine.gov/dacf/mfs)
State Wildlife Agency: Department of Inland Fisheries and Wildlife (maine.gov/ifw)

Maryland

Property Tax Program: Forest Conservation and Management Program (dnr.maryland.gov/forests/Pages/programapps/fcmp.aspx)
Natural Heritage Program: Natural Heritage Program (tinyurl.com/Maryland-NHP)
Landowner Organization: Maryland Forests Association (mdforests.org)
State Forestry Agency: Forest Service (dnr.maryland.gov/forests)
State Wildlife Agency: Department of Natural Resources (dnr.maryland.gov)

Massachusetts

Property Tax Program: Chapter 61 Current Use Tax Programs (tinyurl.com/Massachusetts-chapter-61)

Natural Heritage Program: Natural Heritage & Endangered Species Program (mass.gov/eea/agencies/dfg/dfw/natural-heritage)

Landowner Organization: Massachusetts Forest Alliance (massforestalliance .org)

State Forestry Agency: Bureau of Forestry (tinyurl.com/Massachusetts-forestry-bureau)

State Wildlife Agency: Division of Fisheries and Wildlife (mass.gov/eea/agencies/dfg/dfw)

Michigan

Property Tax Program: Qualified Forest Property Tax Program (tinyurl.com/Michigan-qualified-forest) and the Commercial Forest Program (tinyurl.com/Michigan-commercial-forest)

Natural Heritage Program: Natural Features Inventory (mnfi.anr.msu.edu)

Landowner Organization: Michigan Forest Association (michiganforests.org)

State Forestry Agency: Department of Natural Resources – Forestry (tinyurl .com/Michigan-DNR)

State Wildlife Agency: Department of Natural Resources (michigan.gov/dnr)

Minnesota

Property Tax Program: Sustainable Forest Incentive Act (tinyurl.com/Minnesota-sustainable-forest) and 2c Managed Forest Land (tinyurl.com/Minnesota-2c)

Natural Heritage Program: Natural Heritage and Nongame Research Program (dnr.state.mn.us/nhnrp)

Landowner Organization: Minnesota Forestry Association (minnesotaforestry.org)

State Forestry Agency: Division of Forestry (dnr.state.mn.us/forestry)

State Wildlife Agency: Fish and Wildlife (dnr.state.mn.us/fishwildlife)

Mississippi

Property Tax Program: Automatic reduction for forestland

Natural Heritage Program: Natural Heritage Program (mdwfp.com/museum/seek-study/heritage-program)

Landowner Organization: Mississippi Forestry Association (msforestry .net)
State Forestry Agency: Forestry Commission (mfc.ms.gov)
State Wildlife Agency: Wildlife, Fisheries and Parks (mdwfp.com)

Missouri
Property Tax Program: Forest Crop Land (tinyurl.com/Missouri-Forest-Croplands)
Natural Heritage Program: Natural Heritage Program (tinyurl.com/Missouri-natural-heritage)
Landowner Organization: Forest & Woodland Association of Missouri (forestandwoodland.org)
State Forestry Agency: Department of Conservation (mdc.mo.gov/your-property)
State Wildlife Agency: Department of Conservation (mdc.mo.gov)

Montana
Property Tax Program: Forest Lands Tax Act (tinyurl.com/Montana-forest-land)
Natural Heritage Program: Natural Heritage Program (mtnhp.org)
Landowner Organization: Montana Forest Owners Association (montanaforestowners.org)
State Forestry Agency: Forestry Division (dnrc.mt.gov/divisions/forestry)
State Wildlife Agency: Fish, Wildlife and Parks (fwp.mt.gov)

Nebraska
Property Tax Program: Automatic reduction for forestland
Natural Heritage Program: Natural Heritage Program (outdoornebraska .gov/naturalheritageprogram)
Landowner Organization: None–use National Woodland Owners Association or contact a state District Forester
State Forestry Agency: Forest Service (nfs.unl.edu)
State Wildlife Agency: Game and Parks (outdoornebraska.gov)

Nevada

Property Tax Program: Agricultural or Open Space Use (tinyurl.com/Nevada-ag-bulletins, then click on the most recent "Ag Bulletin" to find out more)
Natural Heritage Program: Natural Heritage Program (heritage.nv.gov)
Landowner Organization: None–use National Woodland Owners Association
State Forestry Agency: Division of Forestry (forestry.nv.gov)
State Wildlife Agency: Department of Wildlife (ndow.org)

New Hampshire

Property Tax Program: Current Use Taxation Program (nh.gov/btla/appeals/currentuse.htm)
Natural Heritage Program: Natural Heritage Bureau (tinyurl.com/New-Hampshire-natural-heritage)
Landowner Organization: New Hampshire Timberland Owners Association (nhtoa.org)
State Forestry Agency: Division of Forests and Lands (nhdfl.org)
State Wildlife Agency: Fish and Game (wildlife.state.nh.us)

New Jersey

Property Tax Program: Farmland Assessment (nj.gov/agriculture/home/farmers/farmlandassessment.html)
Natural Heritage Program: Natural Heritage Program (nj.gov/dep/parksandforests/natural/heritage)
Landowner Organization: New Jersey Forestry Association (njforestry.org)
State Forestry Agency: State Forestry Services (nj.gov/dep/parksandforests/forest)
State Wildlife Agency: Division of Fish and Wildlife (njfishandwildlife.com)

New Mexico

Property Tax Program: Automatic reduction for forestland
Natural Heritage Program: Natural Heritage New Mexico (nhnm.unm.edu)
Landowner Organization: The Forest Trust (www.theforesttrust.org)
State Forestry Agency: State Forestry Division (www.emnrd.state.nm.us/SFD)
State Wildlife Agency: Game and Fish (wildlife.state.nm.us)

New York

Property Tax Program: Forest Tax Law Program 480-a (www.dec.ny.gov/ lands/5236.html)

Natural Heritage Program: Natural Heritage Program (www.dec.ny.gov/ animals/29338.html)

Landowner Organization: New York Forest Owners Association (nyfoa .org); see also Catskill Forest Association (catskillforest.org) and Adirondack Landowners Association (adklandowners.org)

State Forestry Agency: Division of Lands and Forests (www.dec.ny.gov/ about/650.html)

State Wildlife Agency: Department of Environmental Conservation (www. dec.ny.gov)

North Carolina

Property Tax Program: Present-use Value Program (tinyurl.com/North-Carolina-present-use) and the Wildlife Conservation Land Program (tinyurl .com/North-Carolina-conservation)

Natural Heritage Program: Natural Heritage Program (www.ncnhp.org)

Landowner Organization: NCWoodlands (ncwoodlands.org); see also North Carolina Forestry Association (ncforestry.org)

State Forestry Agency: Forest Service (ncforestservice.gov)

State Wildlife Agency: Wildlife Resources Commission (ncwildlife.org)

North Dakota

Property Tax Program: Forest Stewardship Tax Law (tinyurl.com/ North-Dakota-forest-tax)

Natural Heritage Program: Natural Heritage (parkrec.nd.gov/nature/heritage .html)

Landowner Organization: North Dakota Urban & Community Forestry Association (nducfa.com)

State Forestry Agency: Forest Service (tinyurl.com/North-Dakota-forest-service)

State Wildlife Agency: Game and Fish Department (gf.nd.gov)

Ohio

Property Tax Program: Forest Tax Law (forestry.ohiodnr.gov/oftl)

Natural Heritage Program: Natural Heritage Database (tinyurl.com/Ohio-natural-heritage)

Landowner Organization: The Ohio Forestry Association (ohioforest.org)

State Forestry Agency: Division of Forestry (forestry.ohiodnr.gov)

State Wildlife Agency: Division of Wildlife (wildlife.ohiodnr.gov)

Oklahoma

Property Tax Program: Automatic reduction for forestland

Natural Heritage Program: Natural Heritage Inventory (oknaturalheritage.ou.edu)

Landowner Organization: Oklahoma Forestry Association (oklahomaforestry.org)

State Forestry Agency: Forestry Services (www.forestry.ok.gov)

State Wildlife Agency: Department of Wildlife Conservation (wildlifedepartment.com)

Oregon

Property Tax Program: Oregon has multiple tax reduction programs with varying requirements. Visit tinyurl.com/Oregon-Forestland-Tax to learn about them.

Natural Heritage Program: Biodiversity Information Center (inr.oregonstate.edu/orbic)

Landowner Organization: Oregon Small Woodlands Association (oswa.org)

State Forestry Agency: Department of Forestry (oregon.gov/ODF)

State Wildlife Agency: Department of Fish and Wildlife (dfw.state.or.us)

Pennsylvania

Property Tax Program: Clean and Green (conservationtools.org/guides/44-clean-and-green)

Natural Heritage Program: Natural Heritage Program (naturalheritage.state.pa.us)

Landowner Organization: Pennsylvania Woodland Owners Associations (tinyurl.com/Pennsylvania-woodland-assoc)

State Forestry Agency: Bureau of Forestry (tinyurl.com/PA-Bureau-of-Forestry)

State Wildlife Agency: Game Commission (pgc.pa.gov)

Rhode Island

Property Tax Program: Farm, Forest, and Open Space Act (tinyurl.com/Rhode-Island-open-space)

Natural Heritage Program: Natural History Survey (rinhs.org/biodiversity-data)

Landowner Organization: Rhode Island Forest Conservators Organization (rifco.org)

State Forestry Agency: Division of Forest Environment (dem.ri.gov/programs/forestry)

State Wildlife Agency: Division of Fish & Wildlife (dem.ri.gov/programs/fish-wildlife)

South Carolina

Property Tax Program: Agricultural Use Land (tinyurl.com/SC-Ag-Use-Land)

Natural Heritage Program: Heritage Trust Program (dnr.sc.gov/species/index.html)

Landowner Organization: South Carolina Forestry Association (scforestry.org)

State Forestry Agency: Forestry Commission (state.sc.us/forest)

State Wildlife Agency: Department of Natural Resources (dnr.sc.gov)

South Dakota

Property Tax Program: Automatic reduction for forestland

Natural Heritage Program: Wildlife Diversity Program (gfp.sd.gov/wildlife/management/diversity)

Landowner Organization: Black Hills Forest Resource Association (bhfra.org)

State Forestry Agency: Department of Agriculture – Conservation & Forestry (sdda.sd.gov/conservation-forestry)

State Wildlife Agency: Game, Fish and Parks (gfp.sd.gov)

Tennessee

Property Tax Program: Greenbelt (tinyurl.com/Tennessee-greenbelt)

Natural Heritage Program: Natural Heritage Inventory Program (tinyurl .com/Tennessee-natural-heritage)

Landowner Organization: Tennessee Forestry Association (tnforestry.com)

State Forestry Agency: Department of Agriculture (tn.gov/agriculture/ section/forests)

State Wildlife Agency: Wildlife Resources Agency (tn.gov/twra)

Texas

Property Tax Program: Agricultural, Timber Land and Wildlife Management Use Special Appraisal (tinyurl.com/Texas-Timberland-Tax)

Natural Heritage Program: Wildlife Diversity Program (tpwd.texas.gov/ huntwild/wild/wildlife_diversity)

Landowner Organization: Texas Forestry Association (texasforestry.org)

State Forestry Agency: Forest Service (txforestservice.tamu.edu)

State Wildlife Agency: Parks and Wildlife (tpwd.texas.gov)

Utah

Property Tax Program: Utah Farmland Assessment Act (tinyurl.com/ Utah-farmland-assessment)

Natural Heritage Program: Conservation Data Center (dwrcdc.nr.utah. gov/ucdc)

Landowner Organization: none available, use National Woodland Owners Association

State Forestry Agency: Division of Forestry, Fire, and State Lands (ffsl.utah.gov)

State Wildlife Agency: Division of Wildlife Resources (wildlife.utah.gov)

Vermont

Property Tax Program: Use Value Appraisal (tinyurl.com/Vermont-use-value)

Natural Heritage Program: Natural Resources Atlas (anr.vermont.gov/ maps/nr-atlas)

Landowner Organization: Vermont Woodlands Association (vermontwoodlands.org)

State Forestry Agency: Department of Forests, Parks, and Recreation (fpr .vermont.gov)

State Wildlife Agency: Fish and Wildlife Department (vtfishandwildlife.com)

Virginia

Property Tax Program: Use Value Assessment Program (usevalue.agecon. vt.edu)

Natural Heritage Program: Natural Heritage Program (dcr.virginia.gov/ natural_heritage)

Landowner Organization: Virginia Forestry Association (vaforestry.org)

State Forestry Agency: Department of Forestry (dof.virginia.gov)

State Wildlife Agency: Department of Game and Inland Fisheries (dgif .virginia.gov)

Washington

Property Tax Program: Designated Forest Land (tinyurl.com/Washington-designated-forest)

Natural Heritage Program: Natural Heritage Program (dnr.wa.gov/natural-heritage-program)

Landowner Organization: Washington Farm Forestry Association (wafarmforestry.com)

State Forestry Agency: Department of Natural Resources (dnr.wa.gov/ programs-and-services/forest-practices)

State Wildlife Agency: Department of Fish and Wildlife (wdfw.wa.gov)

West Virginia

Property Tax Program: Managed Timberland Program (tinyurl.com/West-Virginia-timberland)

Natural Heritage Program: Wildlife Diversity Program (wvdnr.gov/wildlife/ wdpintro.shtm)

Landowner Organization: WV Woodland Stewards (wvstewards.ning.com)

State Forestry Agency: Division of Forestry (wvforestry.com)

State Wildlife Agency: Division of Natural Resources (wvdnr.gov)

Wisconsin

Property Tax Program: Managed Forest Law (dnr.wi.gov/topic/ ForestLandowners/tax.html)

Natural Heritage Program: Natural Heritage Inventory (dnr.wi.gov/topic/ nhi)

Landowner Organization: Wisconsin Woodland Owners Association (wisconsinwoodlands.org)

State Forestry Agency: Department of Natural Resources (dnr.wi.gov/topic/ Forestlandowners)

State Wildlife Agency: Department of Natural Resources (dnr.wi.gov)

Wyoming

Property Tax Program: Automatic reduction for forestland

Natural Heritage Program: Natural Diversity Database (uwyo.edu/wyndd)

Landowner Organization: Wyoming Association of Conservation Districts (conservewy.com/FORESTRY.html)

State Forestry Agency: State Forestry Division (wsfd.wyo.gov)

State Wildlife Agency: Game and Fish Department (wgfd.wyo.gov)

PROPERTY CHECKLIST

Instructions

Print an aerial photo of your property using a program like Google Earth. Mark your boundaries on it as best you can. Use this map to complete the first table, Broad-Scale Features, based on the rough percentages of each type of land cover.

Next, take a walk through your land. If you can, take a couple walks, each during a different season. Based on what you observe, complete the second table, Specific Features. Check off "lots," "a few," or "none" for each habitat feature.

Once you have both tables filled out, compare your Broad-Scale Features against the third table, Recommended Percentages. That will give you an idea of how your property compares to what wildlife biologists consider preferred for the greatest diversity of animals.[1]

For the Specific Features, look at which items you checked "a few" and especially "none" for. These missing features could be limiting factors on your property. Increasing their number on your land could help attract more wildlife. Consider projects that add more of these features as priorities.

To go further with these charts, repeat the Broad-Scale Features chart using an aerial photo that shows not just your property, but the surrounding landscape, say an area of about 2,500 acres. Even if your land isn't in line with the Recommended Percentages, that's okay as long as the landscape around your property is.

Broad-Scale Features

Feature	Your Land	Around Your Land
	Approximate Percentage	
Conifers (trees with needles)		
Broad-leaf trees (everything else)		
Mixed woods (both conifers and broad-leaf trees)		
Meadows, old fields, shrublands, and other open areas not used for farming or lawn		
Lawn		
Cropland		
Livestock pasture		
Developed areas (ex. house, driveway, and roads)		
Wetlands (ex. marshes, swamps, and bogs)		
Water (ex. streams, ponds, and lakes)		

Specific Features

Feature	Lots	A Few	None
Areas of dense canopy with little sunlight reaching the ground			
Areas of partial canopy with moderate sunlight reaching the ground			
Open areas with full sunlight reaching the ground			
Treetop perches for hawks, owls, eagles, etc.			
Areas of mostly conifers that have a few broad-leaf trees mixed in			
Areas of mostly broad-leaf trees that have a few conifers mixed in			
Dead or dying trees with trunks wider than twenty inches			

Feature	Lots	A Few	None
Nut-producing trees (ex. oak)			
Berry-producing plants (ex. blackberry)			
Short trees interspersed with taller trees			
Shrubs interspersed with trees. NOTE: Do not count invasive shrubs like bush honeysuckle.			
Ground cover beneath trees (ex. spring wildflowers). NOTE: Do not count hay-scented fern, as it has minimal wildlife value.			
Fallen logs			

Recommended Percentages

Note: These are rough percentages based on research in New England. For this reason, these figures should not be treated as absolute. Rather, view them as a general guide. Slight deviations are fine. Where you see large differences between your property and these recommendations, that suggests land cover types to focus on creating or enhancing.

General Landscape Uses	Recommended Percentage
Natural landscape (ex. wooded, meadow, shrubland)	>70 percent
Human uses (ex. home, lawn, farming)	<30 percent
Water (including wetlands)	5 percent
Ages of Wooded Landscapes	**Recommended Percentage**
<25 years	5–15 percent
25 to 100 years	30–40 percent
>100 years	50–60 percent

ENDNOTES

Chapter 1: Private Landowners and Wildlife: A Vital Connection

1. Jacek Siry, Frederick Cubbage, and David Newman, "Global Forest Ownership: Implications for Forest Production, Management, and Protection," (Buenos Aires, Argentina: XIII World Forestry Congress, 2009), 10 p.

2. Ross Gorte and others, *Federal Land Ownership: Overview and Data*, Congressional Research Service Report for Congress, http://fas.org/sgp/crs/misc/R42346.pdf, Summary. See also Natural Resources Council of Maine, "Public Land Ownership by State," 2000, http://www.nrcm.org/documents/publiclandownership.pdf.

3. Brett Butler, "Forest Ownership" pp. 19-21 in W. Brad Smith, Patrick Miles, Charles Perry, and Scott Pugh, *Forest Resources of the United States, 2007*, (Washington, DC: US Forest Service, 2009), 19.

4. Delwin Benson, Ross Shelton, and Don Steinbach, *Wildlife Stewardship and Recreation on Private Lands*, (College Station, TX: Texas A&M University Press, 2005), 184 p.

5. Michael Bean and others, *The Private Lands Opportunity: The Case for Conservation Incentives*, (New York: Environmental Defense, 2003), 21 p., 1.

6. North American Bird Conservation Initiative, US Committee, 2013, *The State of the Birds 2013 Report on Private* Lands, US Department of Interior: Washington, DC, 48 p., 7.

7. Ibid., 20.

8. US Fish and Wildlife Service, "Our Endangered Species Program and How It Works with Landowners," July 2009, fws.gov/endangered/esa-library/pdf/landowners.pdf.

9. Susan Stein and others, *Threats to At-Risk Species in America's Private Forests: A Forests on the Edge Report*, (Newtown Square, PA: US Forest Service, 2010), 20 p., 2 and 5.

10. US Fish and Wildlife Service, "Red Hills Salamander," October 2010, http://www.fws.gov/daphne/Fact_Sheets/RHS percent20fact percent 20sheet_final.pdf.

11. Susan Stein and others, 4.

12. North American Bird Conservation Initiative, 18.

Chapter 2: What Do Wildlife Need, Anyway?

1. Douglas Tallamy, *Bringing Nature Home: How You Can Sustain Wildlife with Native Plants* (Portland, OR: Timber Press, 2009), 358 p., 52.

2. Ibid., 22-24.

3. US Environmental Protection Agency, "Assessed Waters of United States," January 12, 2016, http://ofmpub.epa.gov/waters10/attains_nation_cy.control#total_assessed_waters.

4. Richard DeGraaf and others, *A Landowner's Guide to Wildlife Habitat: Forest Management for the New England Region*, (Lebanon, NH: University Press of New England, 2005), 111 p., 28.

5. See, for example, "Habitat Loss," National Wildlife Federation, accessed November 15, 2016, http://www.nwf.org/wildlife/threats-to-wildlife/habitat-loss.aspx. See also "Impact of Habitat Loss on Species," World Wide Fund for Nature, accessed November 15, 2016, http://wwf.panda.org/about_our_earth/species/problems/habitat_loss_degradation.

Chapter 3: Getting Started

1. Douglas Tallamy, *Bringing Nature Home: How You Can Sustain Wildlife with Native Plants* (Portland, OR: Timber Press, 2009), 358 p., 171-172.

Chapter 4: Backyards

1. Matt Walker, "Mammal and Bird Pollinators Are Heading towards Extinction, a Study Finds," *BBC Earth*, March 6, 2015, http://www.bbc.com/earth/story/20150304-global-pollinators-in-decline.

2. David Mizejewski, "New Numbers Show Monarch Butterfly Populations Still in Trouble," National Wildlife Federation, February 15, 2017, blog.nwf.org/2017/02/new-numbers-show-monarch-butterfly-populations-still-in-trouble.

3. Kristi Sullivan and Margaret Brittingham, "Meadows and Prairies: Wildlife-Friendly Alternatives to Lawn," Penn State Extension, *Pennsylvania Wildlife* no. 5 (2013), http://extension.psu.edu/natural-resources/wildlife/landscaping-for-wildlife/pa-wildlife-5/extension_publication_file, 6 p., 1.

4. National Wildlife Federation, "Little Brown Bat," accessed November 15, 2016, https://www.nwf.org/Wildlife/Wildlife-Library/Mammals/Bats/Little-Brown-Bat.aspx.

5. Brian Mann, "Ten Years Later, White Nose Syndrome Still Ravaging Bat Populations," June 26, 2017, *North Country Public Radio*, https://www.northcountrypublicradio.org/news/story/34180/20170626/ten-years-later-white-nose-syndrome-still-ravaging-bat-populations. See also Dene Moore, "Bats Nearly Wiped Out by White-Nose Syndrome in Eastern Canada," October 27, 2014, *CBC News*, http://www.cbc.ca/news/technology/bats-nearly-wiped-out-by-white-nose-syndrome-in-eastern-canada-1.2814088.

6. David Mizejewski, *Attracting Birds, Butterflies, and Other Backyard Wildlife*, (Upper Saddle River, NJ: National Wildlife Federation/Creative Homeowner, 2004), 128 p., 88.

7. Gustave Axelson, "30 Years of Project FeederWatch Yield New Insights about Backyard Birds," *Living Bird Magazine*, (Winter 2017), https://www.allaboutbirds.org/30-years-of-project-feederwatch-yield-new-insights-about-backyard-birds.

8. Stephen Kress, *The Audubon Society Guide to Attracting Birds: Creating Natural Habitats for Properties Large and Small*, (Ithaca, NY: Cornell University Press, 2006), 466 p., 357.

9. Travis Wilcoxen and others, "Effects of Bird-Feeding Activities on the Health of Wild Birds," *Conservation Physiology* 3, no. 1 (2015): 1-13.

10. Joe Smith, "Winter Bird Feeding: Good or Bad for Birds?" The Nature Conservancy, January 5, 2015, http://blog.nature.org/science/2015/01/05/winter-bird-feeding-good-or-bad-for-birds.

11. The Cornell Lab of Ornithology, "Should I Stop Feeding Birds in Fall So They Can Start Their Migration?" April 1, 2009, https://www.allaboutbirds.org/should-i-stop-feeding-birds-in-fall-so-they-can-start-their-migration.

12. Scott Loss and others, "Bird-Building Collisions in the United States: Estimates of Annual Mortality and Species Vulnerability," *The Condor* 116, no. 1 (2014), 8-23, 8. See also Stephen Kress, 387.

13. Stephen Kress, 388.

14. Scott Loss and others, "The Impact of Free-Ranging Domestic Cats on Wildlife of the United States," *Nature Communications* 4 (2013), 1-7.

15. See, for example, Petco, "Safety Precautions for Outdoor & Indoor Cats," accessed March 4, 2016, http://www.petco.com/content/petco/PetcoStore/en_US/pet-services/resource-center/new-pet/safety-precautions-for-outdoor-and-indoor-cats.html. See also The Humane Society of the United States, "Home, Sweet Home: How to Bring an Outside Cat Indoors," accessed March 4, 2016, http://www.humanesociety.org/animals/cats/tips/bringing_outside_cat_indoors.html. See also Mobile Society for the Prevention of Cruelty to Animals, "Your Cat—Indoors or Out," accessed March 4, 2016, http://www.mobilespca.org/Portals/0/downloads/documents/Your percent20Cat percentE2 percent80 percent94Indoors percent20or percent20Out.pdf.

Chapter 5: Grasslands, Shrublands, and Young Woods

1. Matthew Wilson, Winsor Lowe, and Keith Nislow, "Family Richness and Biomass of Understory Invertebrates in Early and Late Successional Habitats of Northern New Hampshire," *Journal of Forestry* 112, no. 4 (2014), 337-345.

2. Audubon New York, *Wildlife and Forestry in New York Northern Hardwoods: A Guide for Forest Owners and Managers*, (Albany, NY: Audubon New York, 2002), 40 p.

3. Hoosier Heartland Resource Conservation and Development Council, "Edge Feathering for Native Habitat," accessed November 15, 2016, hhrcd.org/pdf/Edge percent20Feathering percent20Fact percent-20Sheet-final.pdf.

4. Stephen Kress, *The Audubon Society Guide to Attracting Birds: Creating Natural Habitats for Properties Large and Small*, (Ithaca, NY: Cornell University Press, 2006), 466 p., 68.

5. Scott Stoleson, "Condition Varies with Habitat Choice in Postbreeding Forest Birds," *The Auk* 130, no. 3 (2013), 417-428.

6. DeGraaf and others, *Landowner's Guide to Wildlife Habitat: Forest Management for the New England Region*, (Lebanon, NH: University Press of New England, 2005), 111 p., 82.

7. USDA Forest Service TEAMS Enterprise Unit, *New York City Watershed Forest Management Plan*, 2011, 283 p., 66, http://www.nyc.gov/html/dep/pdf/watershed_protection/dep_forest_management_plan_2011.pdf.

8. Stephen Kress, 69.

9. New Jersey Audubon, "Northern Bobwhite Restoration Initiative," January 27, 2016, http://www.njaudubon.org/SectionConservation/StewardshipInAction/NorthernBobwhiteRestorationInitiative.aspx.

10. Ibid.

11. Ibid.

12. Ibid.

13. University of Maine, "UMaine Research Cited in AP Article on Canada Lynx, Showshoe Hare," September 8, 2015, https://umaine.edu/news/blog/2015/09/08/umaine-research-cited-in-ap-article-on-canada-lynx-snowshoe-hare/. See also David Sharp, "Can Maine Landowners Save the Canada Lynx from Decline?" September 8, 2015, http://www.csmonitor.com/Science/2015/0908/Can-Maine-landowners-save-the-Canada-lynx-from-decline.

14. National Wildlife Federation, "Lynx in Maine," accessed April 29, 2016, https://www.nwf.org/~/media/PDFs/Wildlife/LynxInMaine.ashx.

15. Cornell Lab of Ornithology, "Eastern Bluebird: Life History," accessed March 6, 2016, https://www.allaboutbirds.org/guide/Eastern_Bluebird/lifehistory.

16. Stephen Kress, 317.

17. Bill Marchel, "How to build an artificial grouse drumming log," *The Star-Tribune*, February 6, 2015, http://www.startribune.com/how-to-build-an-artificial-grouse-drumming-log/290971191/.

18. Douglas Tallamy, *Bringing Nature Home: How You Can Sustain Wildlife with Native Plants* (Portland, OR: Timber Press, 2009), 358 p., 166.

Chapter 6: Old and Interior Woods

1. W. Brad Smith and others, *Forest Resources of the United States, 2007*, (Washington, DC: USDA Forest Service, 2009), 336 p., 221. See also Starre Vartan, "More Trees Than There Were 100 Years Ago? It's True!" *Mother Nature Network*, February 9, 2011, http://www.mnn.com/earth-matters/wilderness-resources/stories/more-trees-than-there-were-100-years-ago-its-true.

2. Stephen Kress, *The Audubon Society Guide to Attracting Birds: Creating Natural Habitats for Properties Large and Small*, (Ithaca, NY: Cornell University Press, 2006), 466 p., 50.

3. Ibid.

4. Michael Gaige, "A Place for Wolf Trees," *Northern Woodlands*, February 25, 2011, http://northernwoodlands.org/articles/article/a-place-for-wolf-trees.

5. Ibid.

6. Cornell Lab or Ornithology, "Wood Thrush," *All about Birds*, accessed January 19, 2016, https://www.allaboutbirds.org/guide/Wood_Thrush/lifehistory.

7. Virgil Scott and others, *Cavity-Nesting Birds of North American Forests*, (Washington, DC: USDA Forest Service, 1977), http://na.fs.fed.us/spfo/pubs/wildlife/nesting_birds/index.htm.

8. Holly May, *Managing Forests for Fish and Wildlife*, (Washington, DC: USDA Natural Resources Conservation Service Wildlife Habitat Management Institute, 2002), 44p., 13-14.

Chapter 7: Streams

1. Thomas Pauley and others, "Ecology and Management of Riparian Habitats for Amphibians and Reptiles," ch. 10 in Elon Verry, James Hornbeck, and C. Andrew Dolloff, eds., *Riparian Management in Forests of the Continental Eastern United States*, (New York: Lewis Publishers, 2000), 402 p., 169.

2. Bernard Sweeney and J. Dennis Newbold, "Streamside Forest Buffer Width Needed to Protect Stream Water Quality, Habitat, and Organisms: A Literature Review," *Journal of the American Water Resources Association*, 2014, 50 (no. 3): 560-584.

3. Bernard Sweeney and others, "Riparian Deforestation, Stream Narrowing, and Loss of Stream Ecosystem Services," *Proceedings of the National Academy of Sciences* 101, no. 39 (2004), 14132-14137.

4. See, for instance, Jeff Opperman and Adina Merenlender, "The Effectiveness of Riparian Restoration for Improving Instream Fish Habitat in Four Hardwood-Dominated California Streams," *North American Journal of Fisheries Management*, 2004, 24: 822-834.

5. US Environmental Protection Agency, "Polluted Runoff: Forestry," October 22, 2012, water.epa.gov/polwaste/nps/forestry.cfm.

6. C.E. Beeson and P.F. Doyle, "Comparison of Bank Erosion at Vegetated and Non-Vegetated Channel Bends," *Journal of the American Water Resources Association* 31, no. 6 (1995): 983-990.

7. E.R. Micheli and others, "Quantifying the Effect of Riparian Forest Versus Agricultural Vegetation on River Meander Migration Rates, Central Sacramento River, California, USA," *River Research and Applications* 20 (2004): 537-548.

8. H. Johannesson and G. Parker, "Linear Theory of River Meanders," in S. Ikeda and G. Parker (eds.), *River Meandering*, (Washington, DC: American Geophysical Union, 1989), 181-213. See also A. Jacob Odgaard, "Streambank Erosion along Two Rivers in Iowa," *Water Resources Research* 23, no. 7 (1987): 1225-1236.

9. Carl Richards and Bob Hollingsworth, "Managing Riparian Areas for Fish," ch. 11 in Elon Verry, James Hornbeck, and C. Andrew Dolloff, eds., *Riparian Management in Forests of the Continental Eastern United States*, (New York: Lewis Publishers, 2000), 402 p., 165.

10. Ibid.

11. Jeff Opperman and Adina Merenlender.

12. Douglas Tallamy, *Bringing Nature Home: How You Can Sustain Wildlife with Native Plants*, (Portland, OR: Timber Press, 2009), 358 p., 147.

13. Sweeney and Newbold, 2014.

Chapter 8: Wetlands

1. National Wildlife Federation, "Tiger Salamander," accessed January 22, 2016, https://www.nwf.org/Wildlife/Wildlife-Library/Amphibians-Reptiles-and-Fish/Tiger-Salamander.aspx.

2. William Healy and Mary Jo Casalena, "Spring Seep Management for Wild Turkeys and Other Wildlife," National Wild Turkey Federation, accessed January 22, 2016, Wildlife Bulletin No. 20, 8 p., 2, http://www.mainenwtf.com/news/spring percent20seep percent20management.pdf.

Chapter 9: Invasive Plants

1. Andrew Liebhold and others, "A Highly Aggregated Geographical Distribution of Forest Pest Invasions in the USA," *Diversity and Distributions* 19 (2013), 1208-1216.

2. National Pesticide Information Center, "Regulation of Pesticide Labels," Oregon State University, October 14, 2015, http://npic.orst.edu/reg/label.html.

3. T.P. Sullivan and D.S. Sullivan, "Vegetation Management and Ecosystem Disturbance: Impact of Glyphosate Herbicide on Plant and Animal Diversity in Terrestrial Systems," *Environmental Reviews*, 2003, 11 (no. 1): 37-59, 37.

4. David Jackson and James Finley, *Herbicides and Forest Vegetation Management: controlling Unwanted Trees, Brush, and Other Competing Forest Vegetation*, (University Park, PA: Penn State College of Agricultural Sciences, 2005), 31 p., 12.

5. Jennifer Calfas, "No Kidding: Goats Get the Weed-Whacking Done in D.C.'s Congressional Cemetery," *USA Today*, August 6, 2015, http://www.usatoday.com/story/news/nation/2015/08/06/goats-congressional-cemetery/31208815. See also Ben Terris, "Why There Are Currently Goats in the Congressional Cemetery," *The Atlantic*, August 8, 2013, http://www.theatlantic.com/national/archive/2013/08/why-there-are-currently-goats-in-the-congressional-cemetery/278485.

Chapter 10: Oh, Deer!

1. For those of you screaming at me that coyotes devastate deer numbers, a study from Penn State found the opposite, that coyote predation even at the highest reported levels was not significant enough to cause deer populations to decline. For more information, see Jeff Mulhollem, "Research Indicates Coyote Predation on Deer in East Manageable," May 9, 2014, *Penn State News*, http://news.psu.edu/story/315340/2014/05/09/research/research-indicates-coyote-predation-deer-east-manageable.

2. Kurt VerCauteren and Scott Hygnstrom, "Managing White-tailed Deer: Midwest North America," *Papers in Natural Resources*, digitalcommons.unl.edu/cgi/viewcontent.cgi?article=1384&context=natrespapers. See also David Von Drehle, "America's Pest Problem: It's Time to Cull the Herd," *Time*, December 9, 2013, time.com/709/americas-pest-problem-its-time-to-cull-the-herd.

3. Stephen Horsley, Susan Stout, and David DeCalesta, "White-tailed Deer Impact on the Vegetation Dynamics of a Northern Hardwood Forest," *Ecological Applications*, 2003, 13 (no. 1): 98-118, 98. See also Chandra Goetsch and others, "Chronic Over Browsing and Biodiversity Collapse in a Forest Understory in Pennsylvania: Results from a 60 Year-Old Deer Exclusion Plot," *Journal of the Torrey Botanical Society*, 2011, 138 (no. 2): 220-224, 220.

4. Brodie Farquhar, "Wolf Reintroduction Changes Ecosystem," *Yellowstone*, June 21, 2011, yellowstonepark.com/2011/06/wolf-reintroduction-changes-ecosystem.

5. For more information on the harm feeding deer corn can do, please see Al Cambronne, *Deerland: America's Hunt for Ecological Balance and the Essence of Wildness*, (Guilford, CT: Lyons Press, 2013), 263 p., 83-108.

6. Ibid., 91.

7. Max Ehrenfreund, "Charted: The 20 Deadliest Jobs in America," *Washington Post*, January 28, 2015, https://www.washingtonpost.com/news/wonk/wp/2015/01/28/charted-the-20-deadliest-jobs-in-america.

8. Katie Frerker and others, "Long-Term Regional Shifts in Plant Community Composition Are Largely Explained by Local Deer Impact

Experiments," *PLOS ONE* 9, no. 12, (2014), journals.plos.org/plosone/article?id=10.1371/journal.pone.0115843.

9. Anne Eschtruth and John Battles, "Acceleration of Exotic Plant Invasion in a Forested Ecosystem by a Generalist Herbivore," *Conservation Biology* 23, no. 2 (2008), 388-399.

10. Al Cambronne, 194-195.

11. Jason Boulanger and others, "Sterilization as an Alternative Deer Control Technique: A Review," *Human-Wildlife Interactions*, 2012, 6 (no. 2): 273-282, 273.

12. See, for instance, Jason Boulanger and others, "Use of 'Earn-a-Buck' Hunting to Manage Local Deer Overabundance," *Northeastern Naturalist* 19, (2012), 159-172.

13. National Shooting Sports Foundation, "NSSF Study: Hunters Donate 11 Million Venison Meals," November 14, 2011, http://www.nssf.org/newsroom/releases/show.cfm?PR=111411-huntersdonate.cfm&path=2011.

14. Ibid.

15. Monte Burch, *Wildlife and Woodlot Management: A Comprehensive Handbook for Food Plot and Habitat Development*, (New York: Skyhorse Publishing, 2013), 327 p., 315.

16. New York Department of Environmental Conservation, "Deer and Bear Hunting Seasons," accessed January 31, 2016, http://www.dec.ny.gov/outdoor/28605.html. See also New York Department of Environmental Conservation, "Deer and Bear Hunting Regulations," accessed January 31, 2016, http://www.dec.ny.gov/outdoor/8305.html.

17. New York Department of Environmental Conservation, "Coyote Hunting Seasons," accessed January 31, 2016, http://www.dec.ny.gov/outdoor/28945.html.

Chapter 11: Keep Open Space Open

1. Christina Blewett and John Marzluff, "Effects of Urban Sprawl on Snags and the Abundance and Productivity of Cavity-Nesting Birds," *The Condor* 107, (2005), 678-693, 678.

2. David Theobald, James Miller, and N. Thompson Hobbs, "Estimating the Cumulative Effects of Development on Wildlife Habitat," *Landscape and Urban Planning* 39, (1997), 25-36, 27.

3. Jason Johnston and Jonathan Klick, "Fire Suppression Policy, Weather, and Western Wildland Fire Trends," pp. 159-177 in Karen Bradshaw and Dean Lueck, ed., *Wildfire Policy: Law and Economics Perspective*, (New York: RFF Press, 2012), 164.

4. See, for instance, Chester Arnold and C. James Gibbons, "Impervious Surface Coverage: The Emergence of a Key Environmental Indicator," *Journal of the American Planning Association* 62, no. 2 (1996), 244. See also Corey Bradshaw and others, "Global Evidence that Deforestation Amplifies Flood Risk and Severity in the Developing World," *Global Change Biology* 13, no. 11 (2007), 2379-2395, 2379.

5. Catherine Mater, *The Forest Health-Human Health Initiative: Linking Landowners, Carbon Markets, and Health Care to Conserve and Sustainably Manage Family Forests*, (Washington, DC: The Pinchot Institute for Conservation, 2012), 33 p. See also Rebecca Stone and Mary Tyrrell, "Motivations for Family Forestland Parcelization in the Catskill/Delaware Watersheds of New York," *Journal of Forestry* 110, no. 5 (2012), 267-274.

6. Brett Butler and others, *USDA Forest Service National Woodland Owner Survey: National, Regional, and State Statistics for Family Forest and Woodland Ownerships with 10+ Acres, 2011-2013*, (Newtown Square, PA: US Forest Service, 2016), 48 p., 30.

7. Ibid., 42.

8. US Forest Service, *Future of America's Forests and Rangelands: Forest Service 2010 Resources Planning Act Assessment* (Washington, D.C., 2012), 198 p., xiii.

Chapter 12: Finding Funding

1. Brett Butler and others, *USDA Forest Service National Woodland Owner Survey: National, Regional, and State Statistics for Family Forest and Woodland Ownerships with 10+ Acres, 2011-2013*, (Newtown Square, PA: US Forest Service, 2016), 48 p., 28.

2. Brett Butler and others, "Effectiveness of Landowner Assistance Activities: An Examination of the USDA Forest Service's Forest Stewardship Program," *Journal of Forestry* 112, no. 2 (2014), 187-197. See also Joshua VanBrakle and others, "Do Forest Management Plans Increase Best Management Practices on Family Forests? A Formative Evaluation in the New York City Watershed," *Journal of Forestry* 111, no. 2 (2013), 108-114.

3. Brett Butler and others, *Effects of Federal, State, and Local Tax Policies on Family Forest Owners,* (Amherst, MA: Family Forest Research Center, 2010), 74 p., iv.

4. US Farm Service Agency, "Conservation Reserve Program," July 15, 2014, http://www.fsa.usda.gov/FSA/webapp?area=home&subject=copr&topic=crp.

5. US Farm Service Agency, "Conservation Reserve Program Status – End of October 2016," accessed January 3, 2017, https://www.fsa.usda.gov/Assets/USDA-FSA-Public/usdafiles/Conservation/PDF/oct2016onepager.pdf.

Chapter 14: The Next Generation

1. Ibid.

2. Scott Sampson, "Encouraging Nature Play," *PBS Parents*, June 26, 2015, http://www.pbs.org/parents/expert-tips-advice/2015/06/encouraging-outdoor-play.

3. Andrew Seaman, "Mother and child activity levels linked: study," *Reuters*, March 24, 2014, http://www.reuters.com/article/us-mother-child-activity-idUSBREA2N0M020140324.

Appendix: Property Checklist

1. I based the tables in this appendix on figures from DeGraaf and others, *Landowner's Guide to Wildlife Habitat: Forest Management for the New England Region*, (Lebanon, NH: University Press of New England, 2005), 111 p., 81-82.